GRANDMA'S ON THE CAMINO

GRANDMA'S ON THE CAMINO

REFLECTIONS ON A 48-DAY WALKING PILGRIMAGE TO SANTIAGO

To Julie — Come walk the Camino with me to Santiago de Compostela.

MARY O'HARA WYMAN

Mary O'Hara Wyman

authorHOUSE®

St. Gregory of Nyssa — Nov. 2013

AuthorHouse™
1663 Liberty Drive
Bloomington, IN 47403
www.authorhouse.com
Phone: 1-800-839-8640

Published by AuthorHouse 11/16/2012

ISBN: 978-1-4772-8923-5 (sc)
ISBN: 978-1-4772-8922-8 (hc)
ISBN: 978-1-4772-8921-1 (e)

Library of Congress Control Number: 2012921322

Cover design by P. G. Meier

This book is printed on acid-free paper.

For my Grand Daughter
Elena Varela

—

And with deepest appreciation for
The support and encouragement and love
shown me during the writing period by

Larry Wyman
Nathan Wyman
Amelia and Francisco Varela
Genevieve O'Hara
Ann & Bill Swofford
Nancy Sinton

—

Thanks, Thanks and ever Thanks
To the endless string of friends who listened to me read chapters aloud

And to the Centering Prayer group at Most Holy Redeemer Church

And to Abbot Joseph and the monks who invited me to talk about the Camino Pilgrimage at Snowmass Monastery

And to Jill Day and Sarah Dillane, supportive and generous Camino Pilgrims

And to John R. Crossan of Chicago, who helped sort out intellectual property issues

And to P. G. Meier who spent endless hours designing the cover and layout of

Grandma's on the Camino

CONTENTS

Introduction

Letter to My Grand Daughter

Instructions for living a life:
Pay Attention.
Be Astonished.
Tell about it.

—Mary Oliver, Red Bird Collection

October 13, 2012

My dear grand daughter Elena: I have prepared this little book of postcards I sent from Spain to you in San Francisco, plus my journal entries and personal reflections, to describe the time in 2010 when I walked the 500 mile pilgrimage trail called the Camino to the city of Santiago de Compostela. You were five years old at the time, and as my first and only grandchild (at least at this time), you were very much in my heart during the 48 days I walked the Camino trails alone across northern Spain. Therefore, it is my hope that over the years as you grow older, this book will help you remember our extraordinary relationship, help you see with your heart who I was in my 70th year, and also give you insight into one of the most extraordinary of all human adventures—the Camino Frances walking pilgrimage from St. Jean Pied de Port in France to Santiago de Compostela in Spain.

As you read this book, you will see that I have written about each of the 48 days I walked the Camino. Each chapter, or calendar day, has three parts. The first reproduces the image and word for word narrative I sent you that particular day by postcard. The second part of each chapter reproduces my personal journal entry for that day—both of these written religiously in a bar each early evening. While there may be a bit of repetition between the postcard sent to you and personal journal entry for the day, when read together they tell the day's story. Finally, to conclude each Chapter, I have prepared a Reflection on that Day written back home in San Francisco.

The Reflections written since I returned home have allowed me to review the experiences I had in managing the day to day rigors of walking the Camino alone—for example, finding my way through the myriad villages and cities, locating a dormitory bed each evening, feeding myself, encountering pilgrims and numerous animals on the trail, treating my foot injury and blisters, enduring falls on truly rough mountain trails and paths, plus rain and mud and unexpected cold weather.

And so my Reflections are partially about the rigors of the Camino—but Elena, as importantly, about the spirituality of the Camino as I experienced it. They will show you who I have been in life. I hope you will be amused and perhaps inspired by my adventures and all those little coping mechanisms that got me from the starting point of the walking trail in the village of St. Jean Pied de Port in southern France, across the Pyranees to Spain, south to Pamplona, then westward across northern Spain to the grand spiritual destination of Santiago de Compostela. These Reflections are my little present to you, wrapped not with ribbons, but with words. As Ralph Waldo Emerson said: "The only true gift is a portion of yourself."

I wouldn't have had the energy or the insight to write a Reflection each evening as I walked, nor did I find that upon return home to San Francisco, I could tackle the reflecting part right away. I took ten months, returning to my normal routine, until I was ready to begin writing this book for you. Life was very busy, but everyday, my mind drifted to the Camino, drawn there like a gentle breeze by some unexpected memory. I came to feel certain that as the physical aspects of the Camino walk subsided, the spiritual aspects presented with greater clarity. This quote from Teilhard de Chardin was my guiding message, "Above all, trust in the slow work of God."

Background To Walking the Camino in 2010: The relationship between me and the Camino began about 20 years ago in 1990 (I was fifty at the time) when I came across an article about the trail and its religious and historic significance. You will read some of the Camino's history in various parts of this book—the salient point here is to tell you, Elena, I knew as I read that first short article, this was to be my Camino. If possible, I would make this 500 mile walk.

I cannot say that either the religious or historical aspects enticed me, but for the next twenty years, the Camino became a spiritual notion—a siren-like call to me that never diminished, that was fed by my own research and from many unexpected and even somewhat mysterious resources that landed on my desk. The Camino would often appear full-blown in my dreams and imagination, probably fed by this quote from Rudyard Kipling pinned for years on my bulletin board at work:

"Something hidden. Go and find it.
Go and look behind the Ranges.
Something lost behind the Ranges;
Lost and waiting for you . . . Go!"

So walking a personal pilgrimage on the Camino was not a passing fancy, but a passion nurtured secretly during my professional career with the Department of Labor, Office of Job Corps in San Francisco. After retiring from government service in 2006, for the next 3 years I coordinated the northern California Centering Prayer meditation network called Contemplative Outreach, but the Camino dream became more insistent. In a single day in late 2009, I came across the following two wisdom quotes—one by St. Francis of Assisi: "The journey is essential to the dream", and the 2nd, a Kashmiri wisdom saying "If not now—when?" Reading these words pried open my heart. No more hesitation. And no more procrastination. It was time for my pilgrimage walk to Santiago de Compostela.

I approached your Grandfather Larry with my plan to go to Spain and asked if he would like to accompany me walking the Camino. He was surprised, declined thoughtfully, and I suspect that he really understood me better than I did myself. "Mary, this is apparently a longtime idea you have nurtured, and it sounds important to you. I encourage you to pursue this walking pilgrimage, but I don't want to be gone that long from home. Who among our friends could you ask to accompany you?" I fairly blurted out "absolutely no one but you—and thank you, thank you for your encouragement. I will walk the Camino alone." This exchange between us was vintage—your grandfather open to our personal freedom and growth, our marital ties secured with a strong but fluid tether. Somewhat as Kahil Gibran said: "Let there be spaces in your togetherness."

Over the next few days, a plan emerged for your grandfather Larry to accompany me to Spain for a vacation together before I started the Camino walk alone. This vacation together, Elena, would prove to be of enormous assistance to orienting me to Spain, the people, culture, money, food and in general ready me to be on my own. And in a way, I know that it gave your grandfather confidence that I would be o'k by myself for two months in a country where I did not speak any Spanish.

Your mother Amelia and your Uncle Nathan were less sanguine but curious, interested, concerned and polite about the plan for their 70 year old mother to walk alone. Close friends and extended family with whom I shared this proposed walking adventure were also curious—many highly supportive, others barely polite, pointing out every dire and extreme eventuality and suggesting that I could see just as much and go the 500 miles to Santiago by train or bus from the starting point of St. Jean Pied de Port. Or as an alternative, some sniffed, why not take a nice escorted pilgrim tour with other seniors?

I responded with some close version of Sr. Joan Chittister's wonderful quote from The Gift of Years—Growing Older Gracefully in which she suggests that "Old age is the time to be dangerous. Dangerously fun-loving, dangerously alive . . . This is the time to do every single thing we can possibly do with all the life we can bring to it. This is the time to live with an edge, with strength, with abandon. There is nothing for which to save our energy. Now it is simply time to spend time well."

Preparation began in earnest. I purchased a backpack and sturdy Keen walking shoes. I targeted "stuff" I thought I'd need to carry—clothes, extra shoes, cosmetics and toiletries, raingear, bedroll, medicines, books, journals, water bottles and mementoes from home. The weight hovered around 30 pounds and I ruthlessly jettisoned so-called essentials until I lightened the pack to 18 pounds. I would be walking from the last week of April, 2010 until about mid-June. It would be anyone's guess what the weather would be like or what clothes would be the best to take. I carefully selected two credit cards and informed the companies that I would be in Spain until mid June. My USA passport completed the list.

As for my physical training regimen, it was minimal at best. For one month I walked briskly for one hour and covered a single 3 mile stretch each day. Then one day, I just kept walking to a 5 mile marker . . . on another day a marathon for me of 10.5 miles. And that was it!!! I thought I was in shape to do the 500 mile trek.

I visited with a sports medicine doctor at Kaiser Permanente who taught me half a dozen exercises to limber up my arthritic knees. She strongly advised me to walk with a walking stick or better yet, two walking poles. I nodded yes to the poles, but was certain that I could never keep track of poles as well as the belly pack and the backpack. The hat and my guidebook. The water bottle. The passport, credit cards and airline ticket home. No, I definitely would not be able to keep track of walking poles as well, so dismissed that piece of advice.

And very quickly, your grandfather Larry and I were off to Spain in late March for a month long driving vacation that began with three days in Madrid. It tickled us that our hotel in Madrid was named the Palace Maria Elena, which reminded us everyday of you. Both of us loved the charming city of Madrid, but especially El Prado, where we experienced a day-long infusion of El Greco, Fra Angelico, Rafael, Caravaggio, Velasquez, Goya, Tiziano, Bruegal, Tintoretto, Rembrandt, Rubens, Murillo and Durer. Oh, the lovely, overwhelming richness of that day in the Madrid Museum. Despite jet-lag, daytime naps and great food brought us into the Spanish rhythm of life and we were soon ready for the driving trip.

The countryside of Spain between the big cities and smaller towns is beautiful beyond compare. Madrid, Toledo, Cordoba, Seville, Cadiz, Algeciras and Gibralter, Ronda, Granada, Almiria, Alicante, St. Carles de la Rapita and Barcelona. We drove through the magnificent grape-growing regions, the olive ranches and intoxicatingly scented orange growing areas, the mysterious white hilltop villages in the mountains, the farmlands, along the sunny coastlines of the Mediterranean—such an intensely beautiful country to visit.

We discovered each city to be steeped in incredible ancient history of racial and religious tolerance (and intolerance,) of cultural blendings evident everywhere in the architecture and the cuisine. We found as we studied guidebooks, visited major museums, mosques and cathedrals, palaces and old Jewish quarters, ate delicious and exotic foods, drank wonderful earthy wines, that the history of Spain unfolding for us was complex, alluring and downright seductive.

We soon fell into sightseeing and a driving routine according to Spanish time. Breakfast, mid-morning cafe con leches, lunch from 2:00 to 4:00pm, tapas and drinks about 7:00pm and dinner about 9:00pm. And of course all the wonderful variations that accompany a Spanish daily schedule. All these experiences of travelling in Spain for a month before beginning my walk by no means gave me a deep understanding of things Spanish, but instead a general familiarity which readied me to walk the Camino alone.

One evening, it pleased me greatly that your grandfather took me to an exciting flamenco show, a whirlwind of fabulous guitar and drums, torrid rhythms set by castanets and stylized handclapping, a cacophany of echoes exploding from steel tipped dancing shoes worn by some of the most beautiful men and women we had ever seen. The men, hair slicked back, so lean and sleek in their open to the navel shirts, tight black trousers, cummerbunds and knee high boots—their dark eyes smoldering straight at me. The women were spectacular in brilliantly colored and form-fitting traditional flamenco dresses. Seductive ruffles, lace, decolletage, hair combs, fans, mantillas blurred as the women twirled and stamped the beat with increasing passion—their eyes smoldering, yes, Elena, straight at your grandfather.

As we neared the end of our month-long driving trip together, the approaching Camino walk took on distinct and solemn shape for each of us. We traveled out to stay in the Benedictine monastery at Monserrat, making a three day retreat, attending the religious services in the monastery church, hearing the Monserrat Boys Choir sing multiple times per day, and walking extensively and meditatively in the massive hills of the Monserrat region.

We targeted Friday, April 23 as my Camino start date, which gave us time to drive to Bilbao for a visit to the Guggenheim Museum, that fluidly silvered and curved structure housing the world's great modern art and designed by architect Frank Gehry. We were thrilled to see the permanent exhibit of Richard Serra's Steel Walls, entitled "The Matter of Time." Your grandfather and I then enjoyed another not to be missed museum: the Museu de Bellas Artes, where we saw the work of a Spanish sculptor new to us: Chillida.

Time together dwindled . . . early the next morning, we drove from Bilbao north through Biarritz in sunshine and blue skies and then, with weather changing dramatically, crossed the border into France in fog and rain to my Camino starting point—St. Jean Pied de Port. For the last 30 miles, we were both very quiet, lost in our thoughts of what was to come and at least for me, sobered that soon I would be heading alone on my two feet into those ranges of the Pyranees that lay before us. I felt petrified as we pulled into St. Jean, fog covering the foothills. I was reminded of a Spanish proverb: "It is not the same to talk of bulls as to be in the bullring."

We easily located the entrance on Plaza de Gaulle to the medieval section of St. Jean Pied de Port, parked and booked a room at the Hotel Central looking down over the river and a waterfall. I walked alone to the Pilgrims' Office where I would register my start point and receive the blank credential allowing me to stay in special dormitories for Santiago pilgrims. What an experience to start the Camino! The office was in a lovely old building on the cobbled streets in the oldest part of town. Several pilgrims were lounging about, backpacks spread out, discussing maps, having snacks, resting, and here I entered wearing a seersucker suit, open-toed sandals, hair perfect, jewelry and full make-up. Two women clerks looked up, immediately curious: "May I help you, Madame?" one asked. "Yes, I'm here to walk the Camino and I need a Credential." With this, I inexplicably burst into tears.

Here's what I wrote in my journal that evening. "I wept as soon as I began talking to the women about the credential, and I'm sure that they thought I was a nutcase, or a basket case, and shouldn't be allowed to start anywhere unattended. But I rallied, and the women proceeded to register me as a Camino Pilgrim. When they heard that Larry was with me but would return soon to San Francisco, and that I also had two grown children living close by our home, they insisted on sending three scallop shells home with Larry, to be hung on the three front doors until I returned safely from Spain. At last I received my credential, had my picture taken while selecting a shell to attach to my backpack, and another picture having my credential stamped with the St. Jean Pied de Port insignia, proof of my departure point on the Camino."

As I was leaving, one woman drew me aside and said confidentially: "Madame, we had a woman come through here a few years ago who wanted a credential to stay in the dormitories, but she ended by booking in deluxe Parador hotels as she walked. I think you will need this," and she thrust into my hand a list of Paradors along the 500 miles of the Camino to Santiago. "Oh, thank you, but no, I won't be staying at any Paradors. I'm a real Pilgrim," and I hurriedly stepped into the cobbled street.

I left the Pilgrim office clutching my scallop shells and credential, realizing how strange I sounded and looked in that environment in my dressy clothing and make-up. As I walked some distance down the street, I heard my name called urgently, and the woman from the office was hurrying towards me. She took my arm insistently: "Madame. Do not start today in fog. It is too dangerous to get lost in the mountains. And rain is coming tomorrow. Start only when clear and sunny. Please listen to me about rain. And pray for me. God go with you." I was speechless. And she kissed me on both cheeks, turned and walked quickly away.

I meandered slowly back to the hotel, watching the mountains disappear in rain and fog, dark clouds overhead, and understood that due to the weather, I would not be starting in the morning as planned. Certainly I would not start until it was sunny. Your grandfather took this news in stride, and seemed far more interested in the scallop shells and credential that I received in the Pilgrim Office. He thought the shells were souvenirs of the Camino but I described to him the centuries' long tradition of scallop shells from Galicia being worn on pilgrims' hats and thereby becoming symbols of the Camino.

Supposedly, every contemporary pilgrim wending their way to Santiago would also attach a shell somewhere on their person. One of the women in the office, as she was polishing up my shells, told me that the deep scallop shell lines represented the various Caminos from all over Europe ending at a single point—the Tomb of St. James in the city of Santiago de Compostela. Reluctantly, your grandfather wrapped up and packed the fragile shells, agreeing to attach one on each door at home (kind of a spiritual insurance policy) until I returned safely to San Francisco.

We also looked carefully at the "Credential del Peregrino" I'd just received. It was about 4 by 7 inches, printed on a heavy card stock, and had many foldout pages where I would be expected to secure at least one stamp per day from a particular lodging or town along the Camino. I would carry this credential for two reasons: it would gain me admittance to the various accommodations set up for pilgrims along the trail, assuring me of a bed at a reasonable price in the dormitory of a refugio or an albergue, and secondly, the stamps and dates would cumulatively prove to officials of the Catholic Church in Santiago that I had walked the Camino, and therefore could be issued a Compostela, or diploma with my name inscribed in Latin. On the inside page of the Credential, I filled out my name, home address, nationality USA and my passport information. For the space asking for Date Pilgrimage Begins: I looked out at the uncertain weather, and shrugged as I wrote "Saturday, April 24, 2010."

When we awakened on Friday, April 23, it was sprinkling and fog shrouded the mountains. Indeed, I couldn't start today. Here is what I wrote in my journal: "This am I had expected to leave on the walk over the Pyranees, but I'm uncertain, nervous about even tomorrow's prospects. I told Larry I'll walk out alone, assess, try to understand what I should do. Weather seemed most uncertain. Dark clouds, thunder rolling. Woman at the front desk of the hotel cheerily called out: "No Camino today. Maybe tomorrow. Tomorrow's o'k." I could barely manage a smile in return. My stomach was in knots looking at the clouds, hearing thunder. "Good Lord, what am I in for?" In my naïve planning for the walk in April, I hadn't even considered the weather being a deterrent."

St. Jean Pied de Port was deserted at 8:00am. and I walked to the middle of the bridge crossing the river by our hotel. Three stalwart and noisy Germans came hiking by, and asked me to take their picture as they started up into the mountains. "You're leaving today?" I asked. "Oh yes, we have so few days to walk. We hope we don't get lost in the mountains and fall over a cliff." And they roared with laughter. "Are you a tourist?" they asked. "No, no. I'm a pilgrim, but I won't start until it's sunny." "Good," one responded. "Sunny is projected for tomorrow, so you have one more day to commit lots of sins. You know when you get to Santiago, all your sins before you walk on the Camino will be forgiven. Buen Camino." And off they went, in the pouring rain. I quickened my pace back to the hotel, puzzling whether I should share with Larry the German's admonition to sin before I started.

And that, dear Elena, takes me up to Day 1—Saturday, April 24, 2010, the day I actually left St. Jean Pied de Port in France and started walking alone across the Pyranees towards Spain. That sunny day, I found the Camino. Now the Camino has found me. Writing this book, Elena, has been a Camino in itself. I embarked on the walking path and I didn't know where it would take me. I thought at first, the destination was Santiago, but know for certain now that the destination was found in every single step along the way and every word in this book. Please read on and walk with me, sharing my pilgrimage adventures on the Camino.

With deepest love and affection,
Your Grandmama, Mary O'Hara Wyman

Thomas Merton's Prayer

My Lord God, I have no idea where I am going.
I do not see the road ahead of me.
I cannot know for certain where it will end.

Nor do I really know myself,
And the fact that I think that I am following your will
Does not mean that I am actually doing so.

But I believe that the desire to please you
Does in fact please you.

And I hope I have that desire in all I am doing.
I hope that I will never do anything
Apart from that desire.

And I know that if I do this
You will lead me by the right road
Though I may know nothing about it.

Therefore will I trust you always
Though I may seem to be lost
And in the shadow of death.

I will not fear, for you are ever with me,
And you will never leave me
To face my perils alone.

"The Road Ahead" from "The Love of Solitude" from THOUGHTS IN SOLITUDE by Thomas Merton

Camino—Day 1

Off I Go, Into the Wild Blue Yonder

Postcard # 1—April 24, 2010 sent from Roncesvalles, Espana

Dear Elena—Love from Grandma Mary. Hello to you, your mama & papa, Nathan (& Grandpa when he gets home from Spain). Today is clear and sunny, & I kissed Grandpa good-bye in St. Jean Pied de Port in France and walked off into the Pyranees—starting my Camino to Santiago de Compostela—for hours climbing gently through open pastures close to sheep & cows & horses . . . always seeing shepherds & hearing the bells tied to some of the animals. Always seeing farms high up on the Pyranee foothills. Trees are in bloom & Elena, I am hearing birdsong all the time. Climbing, climbing on paths leading across the Pyranee Mountains from France into Spain. Beautiful Griffon Vultures circle everywhere & once I encountered quite close by about 20 feeding on a dead sheep . . . Today I walked 24.8 km or 14.9 mi. I am very tired & sleeping tonight in the Roncesvalles Monastery dormitory with 120 Pilgrims—a stone bldg/all of us together in one large hall with great arched ceilings. Darling Elena, Grandma's on the Camino at last.

Journal—Day 1 (Saturday) April 24, 2010—written at Roncesvalles

Well, here is my plan for the trip—each day to write a postcard to be sent to 5 year old granddaughter Elena in San Francisco & to follow that up with my personal journal entry more detailed for the same day. So, having just finished Postcard # 1, I am writing about Day # 1 in this journal. This morning I started walking the Camino Frances, a 500+ mile series of ancient pathways & roads which start in St. Jean Pied de Port in southern France, cross the Pyranees into Spain, and continue westward to the city of Santiago de Compostela. Larry & I lingered at the Hotel Le Central in St. Jean Pied de Port, finalized packing, and he tied a scallop shell onto my backpack. Then he spoke to me—of what? love & friendship, wishes for safety, of caution, of any outcome—successful or unsuccessful, of courage, then walked me to Plaza Espana & the gate out of town . . . we looked at each other and I was off—the first day of the Camino a kind of dream—a hard but joyous day of continuing with no hope of stopping short of Roncesvalles. Crossed the border into Spain at Frontera. Other pilgrims on the trail . . . I walked with Germans Anne and Sylvia for a bit, and later with Finnish women Oiver and Gunn—hard going, steeper inclines up, up, up. Snow covered mountains in the distance. Flowers everywhere. Vultures overhead. Traumatic encounter as they fed on a dead sheep. Cows & horses, sheep—nonstop metallic clanging of bells around animal necks (mostly horses) huge cultivated fields, many beautiful farms on the lower levels of the Pyranees, not many people in view except sheepherders. Took 11 hours walking to get to Roncesvalles. Exhausted the last few steep up & down miles. Tripped on roots growing across a path and took a tumble. I thought of a saying I learned in Puerto Rico: "An oak is not felled at one blow." I was upright again, but badly shaken. Arrived into Roncesvalles Monastery at dusk with another woman. There were only two bunks left and I motioned for her to take the nearby lower bunk. I was led to the middle of the dorm, and felt sickened by the sight of an upper bunk, & the effort it would take to climb into it, but a spry young woman named Ann I'd met on the trail earlier today came right over & gave me her lower bunk, orchestrating the move. My first experience of a random act of kindness. A quick shower, then dinner & wine all happening too fast to be enjoyable at a next-door Pilgrims

Restaurant—meal consumed at fever pitch to beat dormitory lights out at 10:00pm! The lights are out now—complete quiet except for a few shadowy figures finally settling in for the night—reminds me of the vultures. Grateful not to be moving any part of my body except hand and pen across this page. I am sitting on a ledge, writing by dimmed lights in a stairwell leading down to the bathrooms. Really tired, but too jazzed to sleep. I already hear the night sounds and snorings of 119 other exhausted pilgrims echo in this enormous one-room stone dormitory.

Reflection on Day 1, written back home in San Francisco

"It is essential that we cast out fear and face the unknown".
Eleanor Roosevelt

I tell people, when asked about my Camino pilgrimage in 2010, that I was never afraid walking alone during my 48 days on the trail. But here's the truth—on Day 1, looking into the eyes of my husband Larry and telling him goodbye at St. Jean Pied de Port's gate leading to the Camino trail, I felt world class emotions of irrational fear and sudden loathing for the trek across the Pyranees to Spain.

Thoughts raced to an easy solution: "Mary, you don't have to start today. Put your backpack into the rental car and let Larry drive you across the Pyranees to Spain. Skip the mountain walk today. Have a nice dinner and hotel stay with him tonight in Pamplona, and start the Camino tomorrow from there." My False Self squared off with my True Self, and skirmished for several long and very silent moments. The winner was declared! The die was cast! I turned and started up the path, feeling the mental energy Larry was radiating towards me. We would not see each other again for eight weeks.

After about a half hour of steady walking in the gorgeous and sunny weather, I turned to catch my breath and look down at St. Jean Pied de Port, gauging the altitude I'd climbed. The village looked so tiny and far away. I realized with a little burst of joy that I was actually walking alone on the Camino towards Santiago de Compostela, doing what I'd dreamed about for years. Fear was gone. I relaxed. How hard could this be? I felt personally safe, free and thankful for the love and support given to me by my family to undertake this pilgrimage which they barely understood. I remembered a remark made by travel writer Paul Theroux: "If one is loved and feels free and has gotten to know the world somewhat, travel is simpler and happier."

Gratefulness permeated my thoughts. Curiosity. Enthusiasm. It was impossible not to be awed by the gorgeous scenery ahead, miles of foothills and beautiful valleys stretching before me into full mountain ranges. I had freely chosen to walk a series of paths that would lead me that very day to the French border with Spain and on to my first overnight stop—the Spanish Monastery Roncesvalles, which I'd remembered reading as being about ten miles away. I felt confident I could make it in six hours and would arrive to claim a dormitory lower-bunk mid-afternoon. I was about to learn my first serious lesson on the Camino. Calculate your mileage carefully.

And so, in a naive and dream-like state, I continued the walk. The shoes were comfortable, and I congratulated myself for having chosen a sturdy pair of Keen hiking shoes. I wore a waistpack where I secured my valuables—passport, cash, credit cards, my Brierley GuideBook, postcards, journal, pens, plastic water bottle, plus WetWipes for handwashing and kleenex for toilet stops—whether indoors or outdoors. I soon realized that the backpack, although not heavy at a pared down 18 pounds, did not sit well on my hips, and the shoulder straps slipped, needing adjustment constantly. I would ignore the problematic backpack, I reasoned, it's not that important.

During the first few hours of the walk alone across the Pyranees, I marveled at everything I saw: spring flowers covering the beautiful green hills; birdsong, and overhead, large Griffon Vultures gliding and playing on the thermal winds; the countryside filled with farms spread beautifully out across the hills, and at higher elevations, cultivated land giving way to enormous pastures, picturesque with herds of sheep, and many free-ranging cows and horses.

Few farmers or sheepherders were evident, and I could not help but think about the rural lives of the men and women who lived here ... how the mountains shaped their work and families, their relationship to the outside world. As I walked unafraid quite close to free range animals, I reminded myself that the animals were much more used to trespasser pilgrims than I was comfortable walking among animals grazing across the Camino paths. I delighted in the wooden bells on the horses. I knew the bells served for farmers to keep track of their animals, especially in the thick mountain fogs and winter snowstorms. The clacking sounds of the wooden neck-bells reminded me of a Zen Retreat and the calls to meditation. All created an idyllic, peaceful mountain scene.

Throughout that first day, as hour after hour passed, and the paths endlessly snaked between hills and ever upwards, I found myself anxiously watching the westward arcing of the sun. I automatically checked for the time, only to remember that I had sent my watch home with Larry, as well as my camera. The fewer distractions the better, I had decided, and so I left the cellphone home as well, much to the incredulous dismay of friends and my techno-whiz son-in-law. "What if you fall down, break a leg, get really sick? How would you call somebody? What if you see a really beautiful sight along the way? You won't be able to email a picture of it to us. And it's crazy not to wear a watch. You're sure to be late for a lot of things. Mary, be sensible".

As I was thinking about all the lifelines I had chosen to leave at home, I began to hear sounds in front of me which I could not recognize. Animal sounds, I thought, but was not sure. I stopped, scanned the horizon, the trail ahead, and the drop-off areas on all sides, but could see nothing. Frightening, low-pitched groans continued somewhere ahead of me just off the path, and another sound I couldn't identify, like wings flapping. I froze, weak-kneed and goosebumps visible on my arms. Several minutes passed as I calculated what to do. The noise increased, subsided, then increased again. Nothing for it but to proceed up the path and around the next bend.

As I came around the corner on the mountain path, I was flabbergasted by the sight of an enormous brown Griffon Vulture with a wing span about eight feet descending fast from the sky straight at me. Its clawed feet stretched forward, and the long black feathers along the tips and bottom edges of the wings were lowered like the rudders on an airplane landing. "Oh my God, I'm a goner!" and I whirled around and shielded my eyes for protection. But this magnificent Griffon hadn't targeted me. He was joining about 20 other vultures eviscerating a dead sheep 15 feet off the path. A feeding frenzy was in process. The sheep, barely recognizable except for its ripped and crimson-matted wool, was already torn apart by lethal and efficient vulture beaks and claws. Two vultures quarreled noisily over soft, oozing innards, while others snatched and pulled on spilled and scattered intestines. All the vultures' heads and white neck feathers were matted and wet with body fluids. Back legs and the head of the carcass were detached. The sight and the smell sickened me.

My Griffon Vulture, the largest in the group, swayed from side to side, and with wings spread wide and flapping, barreled forward like a tank towards several smaller vultures squabbling over the decapitated head of the sheep. I watched in horrified fascination. His competitors jumped aside as he powerfully gripped the sheep's head in his beak, then half-jumped, half-flew a short distance away with the weighty prize and dropped it. Plucking out the sheep's eye, he defiantly held it up for all to see, gulped it down and emitted death-like groans all the while.

The sounds of the birds echoing all around me were other worldly, ominous and threatening. The vultures were enormous and ravenous, their movements bounce-like as pecking order asserted itself. This was mountain life and death at its most elemental. It burned into my consciousness. I felt weak and terribly vulnerable.

Deliberately and slowly, I inched myself forward on the path and away from the scene, trying to quiet my pounding heart—trying not to look at the carnage and trying not to think of what the Griffon Vultures would be able to do to a matronly Camino pilgrim they might find comatose (or worse) along the trail. Some distance away, when I could no longer hear the terrible feasting noises, and my breathing returned to normal, I made up my mind to learn more about these incredible scavengers I'd just seen. I would Google the Griffon Vultures.

And this is a very small part of what I learned about Vultures in Spain. They do not have easy lives. They are carrion feeders by nature, just being true to their evolved species. Changing land use practices, technology and government policies aimed specifically at disease control have made their foraging and feeding difficult.

Centuries old farming practices traditionally left dead farm animals lying in the fields, and the vultures thrived, and the farmers' disposal problems were solved in a very natural and convenient way. Eventually local laws required farmers to transport dead animals to centralized locations where dead animals could be eaten by vultures. And with these steady sources of food and the occasional found carcass, the vultures thrived and populations soared. But in 2005, the government closed over 200 feeding stations for fear of Mad Cow disease, made it illegal to leave carcasses in the fields, and instituted no new measures for artificial feeding of Vultures. The populations were greatly weakened by lack of food, unable to breed and raise young.

But vultures remain a protected species. Opinions are volatile about feeding practices and there is intense international scrutiny of Spanish law. At this time, a small number of feeding stations have been reopened, using garbage from slaughterhouses. But these measures do not appear to be enough. The Vulture population continues to decline. In addition to government policies, other threats to the species include electrical wires, wind turbines (referred to as vulture slaughterhouses), illegal sports shooting, egg-robbing and poisoned baits set for foxes and stray dogs. Learning these things about vultures caused me to deeply appreciate the gift of my encounter with them while walking across the Pyranees.

But back to Day 1 of my pilgrimage. Something about my first day on the Camino and the Griffon Vulture experience took a toll on me, and I began to feel very tired, in fact, disoriented. At every bend in the road I thought the Monastery would materialize. The sun was going down fast. I no longer saw Pilgrims on the trail and I just couldn't believe that

I'd not walked at least ten miles. I was hungry. My legs ached. My pack felt far heavier than earlier in the day.

I entered a Beech Tree woods on a very steep downhill trail. It was considerably darker here and suddenly my foot caught on a root of a tree, and I tumbled down, skinning my knees and arms, and bloodying my hands. I pressed the WetWipes into use on my bruises, and determining that nothing was broken, resumed walking for what seemed an interminable amount of time. I limped along as fast as I could in the gathering dusk until I could barely see the trail, and began to seriously wonder if I wouldn't have to spend the night outdoors in the woods. Every shadow in the trees brought up visions of nesting, still hungry vultures.

These musings were broken by the sound of distant church bells, and at last the lights of Monasterio Roncesvalles appeared on the horizon. When I checked in to secure a bed at the Albergue (dormitory) and have my Camino Passport stamped with the beautiful monastery insignia, I learned that it was not "about 10 miles on the trail" from St. Jean Pied de Port to Roncesvalles, as I had so casually thought that morning, but 24.8km or 14.9 mi. Although thoroughly exhausted, a steely reserve came over me. I would not be casual with distances again on the Camino.

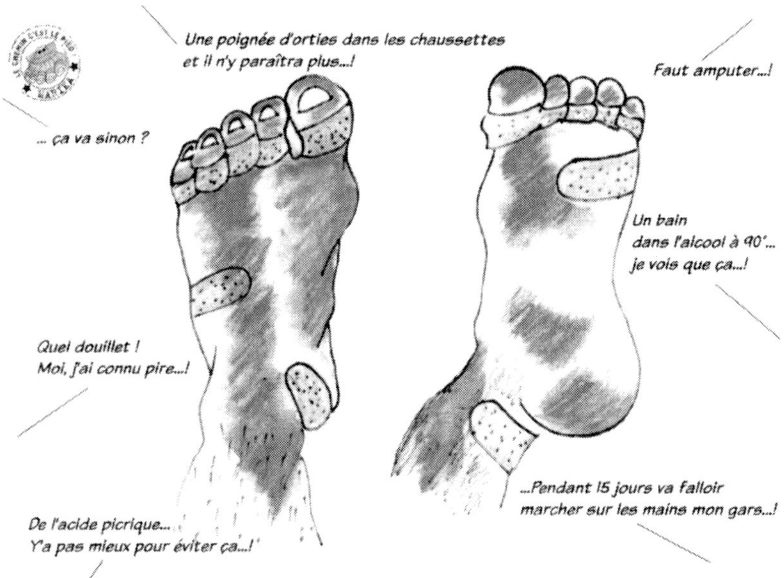

CAMINO—DAY 2

Two Falls Too Many

Postcard # 2—April 25, 2010 sent from Zubiri, Espana

Dear Elena from Grandma: I continue on the Camino towards Santiago de Compostela. Today I walked 21.9 km or 13.4 mi. It was so much beauty I can hardly think about it without tears of joy. The fields are solid yellow w. dandelions & daisies. The great woods & (birch forests) are fully in bloom with violets, buttercups, wild primroses, Lenten roses, and perhaps 20 other flowers I have never seen before. I walked unafraid through herds of cows roaming freely, sheep grazing. I walked alone but encountered many pilgrims. Today I also report 4 open blisters on big toes and bunions and two more falls, thankfully neither serious, I think only scrapes, but it makes me far more cautious.

Journal—Day 2 (Sunday) April 25, 2010—written at Zubiri

Last night in Roncesvalles I was comfortable but no sleep until 5:00am. Only snoring. At 6:00am & in the darkened dorm, I was awakened by flashlights arcing from most bunks, rustle, rustle, zip, unzip, sleeping bags stuffed into sacks, muffled voices, people heading to the bathrooms, & in about 45 minutes, most of the 120 folks were gone. Out in the dawn starting their walk. I went right back to sleep for another hour. Refreshed this am despite minimum sleep. I was the last one out of the Monastery sleeping area at 8:00am. Grounds and surroundings so beautiful. Emerged from the sacred grounds onto a simple Camino path—hedgerows with birdsong filling the air. My backpack is heavy, hangs low on my hips, the straps for shoulders requiring constant adjustment. No poles and I feel strong w/o them. Walking again with Finnish women Eivor & Gunn—not so much with them as "meeting up" w. them. Tired, but walking vigorously. Terrain like yesterday—vast higher pasture land, but many fewer farms & animals. Made it to Zubiri alone. Had 2 falls due to uneven terrain, one bad one rolling into a large boulder, hurting big toe & scratches up & down my arm. Downplayed the falls in today's postcard to Elena. Staying at Albergue Municipal—cost 6 Euros. I like its simplicity. (bathroom in a 2nd separate but nearby building) Good Pilgrim's Meal in village restaurant. Today walked 21.9km or 13.4mi.

Reflection on Day 2, written back home in San Francisco

"For He shall give His angels charge over thee, that they shall protect thee in all the ways thou goest; that their hands shall uphold and guide thee, lest thou dash thy foot against a stone."

from Elijah, oratorio and Libretto translation into English by Felix Mendelssohn, based on Psalm 91

My story of Day 2 on the Camino might appear to have a serious disconnect with the quote above, but there is meaning for me on several levels.

I wandered out of the dormitory at Roncesvalles Monastery at 8:00am on Day 2, and found the general area deserted. 119 other Pilgrims had gotten much earlier starts than I. A walk around the monastery grounds, with its infrastructure of chapels, museum, hotels, hostals and restaurants showed me how substantial the place continued to be since its founding in the 12th Century as a Camino stop and pilgrim hospital. My spirit, intuiting how sacred this place was in Camino history, settled into a sense of well-being.

My Ibuprophen kicked in, and I was barely stiff from yesterday's fall on the steep path. Today I knew exactly how far I would walk—21.9km (or 13.4 mi). Like yesterday, the terrain was high Pyranees, the sun was shining, and my senses led the way. The Camino's brightly painted yellow arrows and stylized shells were in evidence to get me onto the proper path. Birdsong welcomed my every step. Flowers of several types and colors patch-worked the hillsides. The air was sweet-smelling, except when I walked among free-ranging cattle or horses, and then the earthy cow-plop fragrance welled up from the path and reminded me of my first 17 years of life on a farm in southern Illinois. This environment was comfortable, a sort of nostalgic heaven for me.

I knew from studying my Brierley Guidebook that the path today would take me south and out of the mountains. There were more signs of civilization everywhere, especially evident as I spied the freeway frequently, and even walked a half dozen times across overpasses. While there would be a number of steep upward climbs, far more of the path would descend from the mountains. I thought of yesterday's fall on the steep path, and determined to avoid that scenario, so set my mind to being watchful, both of my steps and the views.

About mid-day, I stopped in a tiny village at a bar with a patio for a Cafe con Leche and a Bocadillo Omelette. It was a popular place for pilgrims to stop and it was interesting to observe the various ways they rested from their exertions. All gratefully slipped out of their backpacks. Walking poles were adjusted and set aside. Guidebooks were studied and the day's walking distances were discussed. There were long lines at the single restroom. Some pilgrims ate enormous lunches and some just fruit and raw vegetables. All were intent on refilling their water bottles. Style of dress varied greatly, and I was amused thinking that it was unlikely anyone would mistake us for being locals. Boots and backpacks, sunhats and khakis, trousers with zip-off shorts—even the dapper pilgrims looking a bit scruffy. Virtually every pilgrim had the symbolic Camino scallop shell hanging prominently from their backpack.

There was a sense of good humor and camaraderie as friendly conversations easily struck up between the dozen or so strangers. I was surprised at the amount of English I heard spoken. Where are you from? Are you going all the way to Santiago? How long have you walked today? Where will you stop tonight? Why are you doing the Camino? I joined in as needed to be friendly, but loved more being an observer and not having to make conversation or negotiate with a walking partner about how long or when to stop, when to leave. I mused about my decision to walk alone and determined to stick with it.

The bocadillo (sandwich) I'd ordered was shoved across the bar and I carried it outside with my coffee and found a bench to sit and eat. Lunch was composed of two 10-inch long slices of Spanish bread, filled with a delicious and perfectly done omelette slathered with butter. I finished my coffee and half the sandwich, wrapping the other half for a later snack. The crowd was thinning out on the patio. I leaned back against the wall, pulling my backpack closer for security. The sun was warm, music drifted out from the bar, and for the first time I remembered that I had not meditated that day. Nor the day before. Where were my good intentions? This was a perfect place to begin a period of Centering Prayer, but in truth, I think I had a nap in addition to my wordless and silent prayer.

I came back to myself refreshed, and with a deep sense of happiness and contentment. The Camino beckoned. I was ready to start again. Another Ibuprophen for my arthritic knees. A stop at the bathroom. Backpack adjusted. Ready to Go. And with my very first steps after lunch I realized I had blisters forming on the toes of each foot. Nothing for it but to forge ahead. Mindfulness and gratefulness, I thought, will get me through the day. Set each footstep down gently but squarely on the earth. Enjoy Now. I was walking through one of the most beautiful areas of the earth, with spiritual roots going back to the 12th Century. I was on the Camino. Living in the moment. For the remainder of the day, however, the blisters vied with the gorgeous scenery for my attention.

It is not possible to explain just how or why I took two more unexpected falls that afternoon. The several mile descent into Zubiri, my destination for the day, was steep, but the path was not unusually rocky. Perhaps I was over-confident of my ability as a hiker. Perhaps I was preoccupied with the onslaught of blisters and the beautiful flowers and distant scenery. Perhaps I was unsteady on my feet caused by the backpack with the wobbly shoulderstraps. And perhaps, I admit, it was my stubborn resistance to the advice of seasoned walkers to use hiking poles to steady and balance myself. Whatever the reason, each fall occurred, as falls do, without warning, swiftly, silently and spread over a period of several seconds.

The first fall was the more serious. On a downward descent, I found myself sliding uncontrollably on gravel, then stumbling and lurching forward, nothing to hold onto, my arms flailing. My right foot plowed into an enormous boulder, knee-high, over which I flipped, coming down hard in an area off the path, hitting my elbow and right shoulder on yet another rock outcropping. Eventually all body parts and my belongings came to a full stop. The ugly noise of falling gave way to silence. I just lay there, surrendering into my totally contorted position. I knew I was conscious and sensed that I would not roll farther into a ravine just to my left. I felt no immediate pain. No sense of urgency or panic. I just lay there, relaxing muscles area by area in my body until all was still. Letting go, collecting my thoughts and accepting and yielding to the situation.

Only then was I able to face the real issue: was anything broken? Pain now, yes, but right foot and leg, o'k. Left leg, o'k. Same for right and left arms. Fingers o'k, but badly scraped. Blood on my cheek. Pain welling up seriously now. And in spite of my predicament, I just had to laugh out loud. In my flailing forward, my backpack had been thrown over my head five feet farther down the trail. Collecting myself and getting back on the path I'll leave to your imagination. I limped on, sobered by that fall, but so flooded with gratefulness that no bones were broken that I actually remained quite cheerful until the second fall of the afternoon.

I stepped on fine rocks, feet slipping forward again, but this time my body falling backwards, and in several split seconds, I was on my back, and rolling over twice into a ditch a foot below the path. Once again surrender to the earth, silence, muscle relaxation, acceptance, gradual thankfulness that I was conscious. I realized that I was awkwardly lying in a ditch, or gulley, on my back, with my backpack directly under me. Once again I had escaped broken bones, but this time, it was a real struggle to extricate myself from the backpack straps and drag myself up onto the path. As I rested, assessing new and newer scrapes and scratches, I knew something was happening interiorly. My heart quieted. Sunshine warmed me. I seemed apart from myself. Yellow buttercups sang to me and birdsong blossomed from a distant fencerow. I was not alone.

I was o'k, but the combined jolts today of falls 1 and 2 in a short period of time took their toll on my neck and shoulders, arms and legs. As I began my final and shaky descent into Zubiri, something was wrong with my right foot. The angels in the Elijah oratorio had done a fairly good job of guiding me and protecting me from danger today, but they got all wrong that part about "lest thou dash thy foot against a stone."

Partir seule sur son chemin,
c'est aussi rencontrer les pèlerins...

CAMINO—DAY 3

The Boots That Laced Up the Back

Postcard # 3—April 26, 2010 sent from Trinidad de Arre, Espana

Dear Elena: Today was my 3rd day on the Camino trail, & the day that grandpa flies from Madrid back to you & the whole family. I walked 16.4km or 9.8mi and it went very well in spite of stiffness and blistered feet. I use a product called compeed which cushions the blisters like magic & allows me to walk on happily. The Trail today was really beautiful and varied. Sometimes I walked through meadows, or on ancient paths 4 ft wide with 10 ft high bushes, many in full bloom. Elena, there are many bicycle pilgrims on the rough trails going to Santiago and today I saw two pilgrims riding horses. Lots of animals today—so beautiful grazing in the fields. I was completely alone for several hours but walked the last two hours into Trinidad de Arre with a woman from Canada. Tonight I am staying in an ancient monastery w. a beautiful chapel & gardens, run by the Marianist Fathers. What hospitality—6 Euros. This is on the outskirts of Pamplona. Elena, will you keep my postcards and we will make a little book of them? But show every card to Amelia & Francisco, Grandpa & Nathan, & share also with Betty, Wilma & Bill.

Journal—Day 3 (Monday) April 26, 2010 written at Trinidad de Arre

This morning in Zubiri I was again awakened by pilgrims at 6am getting an early start in the dark. Luckily, they cleared out fast & I slept again until I was awakened at 7:45 as the last couple was preparing to depart the dorm. I came awake thinking I had never seen boots like the man was putting on at the bunk next to me—beautiful knee high suede boots that laced up the back. I tentatively assessed the damage of the two falls taken yesterday. More scrapes than I had remembered on my arms, hands & legs. Shoulder is tender & neck stiff. My big toe (right foot) the nail seems loose and the whole foot is sore. As well, there are 4 toe blisters. I'm cautious, yet started out after breakfast in a bar on a gorgeous day in fabulous country-side. Walked 16.4 km or 9.8 miles. Came across ancient bridge & straight into the Albergue Hermanos Maristas (Brothers of Mary religious order.) Fast-moving river & small falls adjacent. Wonderful Catholic Brother about 85 years old took me in through the gardens & a church so old. I was grateful to have located a bed, shower, rest a while and then go out to dinner alone. Walked partly today with a Canadian, but I prefer to walk solo. She is a lovely woman close to my age, also walking alone, but talking is her modus operendi, and in several hours she has laid out her life to me. Way too much information blocking the silent places buried in my mind that I hope to reach and explore. Several pilgrims cooked in the Albergue kitchen but it was too much noise and chatter for me. I ventured out in my open-toed sandals (relief) into this very small village on the outskirts of Pamplona. Enjoyed a Pilgrims Menu solo—wine delicious. Very, very tired—lower bunk again—so grateful. Toenail is looser & definitely <u>hurts</u> a lot tonight!!! I'm pumping up the medicine (Ibuprophin 600) and will probably need a doctor tomorrow. Still, I'm calm & safe & very grateful to be here walking the Camino.

Reflection on Day 3 written in San Francisco

"Wherever there is a human being, there is an opportunity for kindness."

—Seneca

About 5:45am this morning, I was awakened in the Zubiri municipal dormitory by what first sounded like four-legged creatures scratching around in the dark. But I soon realized that it was two-legged pilgrims rustling all around me in bunk beds, flashing their flashlights, stage whispering to partners, zipping and unzipping every bit of their backpack belongings, crinkling and rustling and wrestling their sleeping bags into stuff-sacks. It was annoying to my half asleep consciousness, but I struggled to the bathroom (outside and in the next building,) and very soon, virtually within minutes, the last of the early birds were out the door. A few of us remaining folks gently and gratefully drifted back to sleep in the peace and quiet. I came awake a second time about 7:45am after a much needed extra hour and a half deep sleep for my exhausted body.

As I lay there calculating how much longer I could stay in bed and still get away by 8:30am, my eye caught a man standing by the bunk next to me, lacing up a pair of soft suede boots that opened up the back and came to his knees. It seemed a difficult task to me but he adeptly laced together the back of his boots. I couldn't see his face, but observed that he was joined by a young woman who carefully descended the ladder of the bunk over me—fully dressed and ready to go. They picked up their one small backpack and left, the woman humming a little tune.

I was the last person out of the dorm at Zubiri, and as I picked up my backpack, I discovered a beautiful new pair of sports walking shoes lying by the foot of my bed. Very expensive shoes and smelling brand new, I was certain that their owner would be sad upon discovering them missing. But there was nothing I could do. I was there alone and the dorm staff had not yet arrived for the day.

I walked to a bar at the edge of town to have coffee and breakfast, delighted to find a New Yorker magazine in English. I lingered an hour reading, in no hurry to get on with the walking. I paid for my meal, walked through the adjoining restaurant to find the bathroom, and there, at a table by a window with his back turned to me, was the man with the boots that laced up the back. I had expected that the couple was long gone but they too were lingering over coffee.

I approached them. "English?" I asked. "No, No English". We all smiled and seeing them face-on, I was struck by their physical beauty. I pressed on. I pointed to the man's boots, pointed out the window towards the dormitory, then pointed to the woman's shoes. They were clearly perplexed, but kept smiling at me. Never one to be deterred, I pointed again at the man's boots, then pantomimed sleep—repeating the words dormitorio and albergue and Camino. "Si, si, Camino" they responded. Satisfied that we were making progress in this strange encounter, we all rested a bit, smiling broadly at each other.

I took out a note pad & drew a little picture of the dorm with beds, & on the lower bunk, pointed to me, and on the upper bunk pointed to the lovely young woman, then pointed to the man. They were following my gestures as best they could but began to look nervously at each other. Was I some kind of a pervert? I tried again with the picture, drawing a little pair of shoes at the end of the bunk, then pointing back & forth between the woman and the shoes. Silence. Staring. I persisted by pointing to their little backpack, then to the shoes in the picture, all the time repeating "dormitorio".

The man & woman seemed to understand at exactly the same moment. She looked in their backpack, saw that her shoes were not there, they exchanged words, and he was off in a sprint the few blocks back to the dormitory. Some 15 minutes later he returned, the lovely little shoes held aloft, and there was a sort of awkward rejoicing all around. "Buen Camino. Buen Camino." We waved good-bye and I set off happily, considerably later than I should have, but confident that I was leaving the Pyranees behind me and entering flatter land on my 500 mile trek to Santiago.

The morning's walk was glorious on paths through newly planted fields, through farms where I could see directly into the barns and storage bins, between fencerows blooming with flowering vines, sweet earth smells rising from freshly plowed fields, horses grazing, sheep dotting the hillsides, the paths changing hourly from mere tracks to farm equipment trails or to pavement through towns. My mind was clear, my heart happy, my feet cooperative, even though my little blistered toes rubbed against each other.

About mid-afternoon, I walked through a shady area of woods and rested on a stone bridge crossing a little gurgling creek. Even though it was hot, birds flitted all around. After munching on an apple and settling into a Centering Prayer meditative sit, I became aware of guitar music in the distance. I could catch snatches of the melody and very soon, coming straight towards the bridge where I was seated, was the source of the music that could not be ignored—the man with the boots that laced up the back, playing his guitar and singing. He and the beautiful young woman were both on horses, just moving slowly, just enjoying the sun and each other, just wending their way to Santiago de Compostela. We waved, she blew me a kiss and it flitted through the air towards me like a butterfly, feeling so warm and tender as it settled into my mind and heart. Gradually, their romantic music and the clip-clopping of their horses grew fainter as they moved ahead of me, and I never saw them again.

CAMINO—DAY 4

Saved by Teresa of Avila

Postcard # 4—April 27, 2010 sent from Pamplona, Espana

Dearest Elena: Today, I only walked 5.5 km or 3.3mi from Trinidad de Arre into Pamplona, where I am ensconced in a dormitory once a beautiful Jesuit Church. From my bed on the 2nd floor, I look at the great carved ceilings. Very comforting. I needed to stop here as my right big toenail is loose & wiggling back & forth. It is so sore I wouldn't even want you or Nathan near that big toe!!!! I wouldn't even want you looking at it from across the room. I saw a Dr. today but alas: she no English & I no Spanish. The walk today was very beautiful, through Pamplona suburbs & parks into the old city, all walled around. I'm staying one block from the Cathedral Plaza & the Church is all wrapped up to the top undergoing renovation. Today I watched many girls your age (5) going into school. Miss you. For better or worse, Grandma is on the Camino.

Journal—Day 4 (Tuesday) April 27, 2010 written in Pamplona

I must admit this is working pretty well to write Elena's postcard each evening over a glass of wine, then continue elaborating in my journal entry for the day. Slow start this am in Trinidad—after walking today the right big toenail is holding onto the toe by a thread. It has lifted up and out of the nail bed, resting on top of the cuticle. The toe is turning radical shades of black & blue. I'm beginning to understand this is not just a stubbed toe!!!! And yet I walked 5.5km or 3.3mi into Pamplona. The Canadian insisted on waiting for me and we managed a lovely walk to the center of Pamplona's Old City—the bridge, the medieval streets, the Cathedral wrapped in sheets for renovation. Easy to find Albergue Jesus y Maria—snugged into an ancient Jesuit Church desanctified and renovated into a Pilgrims hostel right next to the Cathedral. This dorm is unique in that architects constructed a glass balcony floor around the interior walls of the former church to form a 2nd story where I have a lower bunk, and portions of the old carved ceilings are right over my bed. I selected a bed several away from the Canadian, as she carries a sleep apnea machine which whirrs on and off through the night. I sought out a doctor at a Centre de Salud about my right foot injury but it was an unsatisfactory encounter, she speaking no English and I no Spanish. Each time she looked at the foot, she would intake her breath sharply and shake her head. No amount of sign language about the foot got us anywhere and I admit I began to panic when she called another woman into the room who, upon seeing my foot, also made the scary intake of breath. She just shook her head, wrote me a prescription for Ibuprophin (which I already carry with me) & I left, resting in a park, and feeling pain and a good deal of agitation. Experienced a strange, solitary interlude sitting on a bench, but feeling better after, limped about the charming old city of Pamplona. Great find: a restaurant filled with Spanish businessfolk, not Pilgrims, and for 11 Euros I had a marvelous Menu del Dia with wine—and after, as I neared the neighborhood of my Albergue dorm, I found a sports shop & with the help of an animated older couple who own the store, purchased a new & proper backpack which encourages me to continue the walk. Repacking will be easy. I feel unsure about my feet and whether I'll walk tomorrow, or rest another day. Still, all looks brighter.

Reflection on Day 4, written in San Francisco in 2011

"Your legs will get heavy and tired at first. But walk on and wings will lift you up."
Rumi

After leaving the unsatisfactory visit to the doctor's office in Pamplona, I hobbled in pain aimlessly for several blocks and sunk dejectedly on a bench in a lovely tree lined plaza, flower-filled, fountain gurgling, and best of all, absolutely empty of people during siesta time. I felt exhausted, anxious, unsure and without bearings. I felt afraid, almost spinning out of control—fears of every type welled up as I tried to control the pain in my foot that Ibuprophen 600 could not abate.

I slumped down. My thoughts raced and my shoulders tightened. "Where on earth was I and indeed what was I doing on this solo pilgrimage across Spain? Why did I think I could attempt this alone? And what foolishness that I should so smugly insist to concerned and helpful family and friends that I walk <u>without</u> a companion, a phone, a watch, a camera, a GPS? This walking barely three miles today with an injury was too hard, too painful, foolish even for a woman in her 70th year who spoke no Spanish. My feet and legs hurt. Where was the incredible lightness of being I had expected to experience during this undertaking?

I was beginning to see the mistake I made. There was too much uncertainty in the Camino routine—where would I eat each day, and would there be a bed for me at night? A lower bunk? I absolutely knew I could not sleep on an upper bunk—too hard to climb up with the weight I carried, and too dangerous to maneuver trips to the bathroom at night. What if I fell from an upper bunk? What if I got really sick in Spain? What if I got lost and had to sleep outdoors at night? And what if I ran into those vultures again? What if I was seriously injured? Hit by a bicycle or a car?

My mind was now in overdrive. I'd better make some big changes fast or I won't successfully finish this walk. Maybe the solution is better planning. I could leave the dorms earlier in the morning. I could dress by flashlight and start in the dark. Those pilgrims who leave dorms early are assured of getting beds that day, and they have several hours in the afternoon after finding an albergue to check in, to shower, rest, wash clothes, visit the local sites, find food, really enjoy a leisurely Pilgrimage.

I could feel my blood pressure rising. Clearly other pilgrims know the ropes, how to "manage the Camino," and I don't . . . so far this first week I'm the last to leave the dorm by the deadline in the mornings, and I seem to drag into the dorms and get the last of the beds in the evening about dinnertime. I admit I am way too slow, too full of myself, too interested in the path, birds, butterflies, vultures and whatever else catches my attention. I need to concentrate more on getting to Santiago.

An hour on the bench passed, and anxiety over the falls and pain from my loose big toenail only increased as I played and replayed my experiences of the first four days on the Camino. I worked myself into such a froth that I actually began to think I would have to give up and maybe Pamplona was the best place to do this . . . what was that old Chinese proverb? "Of all strategies, to know when to quit may be the best." I could catch a flight to Madrid today, at latest tomorrow, and from there get back to San Francisco.

My self-centered dialogue with my false self was distracted by the sound of a wooden shutter being opened in a house facing the plaza. I looked up and watched in fascination as a woman hung a cage from the open sill, talking and whistling softly to her canary until it began to whistle and trill back to her . . . I was mesmerized, charmed, soon lost in the experience of listening to their duet. The tension in my shoulders relaxed. Their music from the window entered my eyes and ears and fingertips. Gradually, light in the plaza changed, softened. Afternoon sun warmed me. Time passed, perhaps a symphony played, and when I emerged from the silent cloud of non-thinking and came awake, my body was fully relaxed. I surrendered to the scene: I and the woman and the bird and the pain in my foot were not separate entities, but one. We were the music and the trees and flowers, bricks and benches, sunlight and air, Pamplona and the Camino, all forming a single-piece creation, perfectly and divinely orchestrated components merging into a whole. All was filtered and shimmered with Divinity. I was not alone.

A poem by Teresa of Avila which I had known and loved for many years gently replayed in my heart without prompting:

Let nothing trouble you,
Let nothing scare you,
All is fleeting,
God alone is unchanging.
Patience obtains everything.
Who possesses God wants nothing.
God alone suffices.

I continued to sit quietly with this experience and Teresa's words, and the change in me became palpable, real, positively affecting my confidence and equilibrium. I felt fully awake and clear headed.

An assessment was in order. Why had my pitiful 1st week Camino concerns put me into such confusion earlier today? As I recalled them one by one, their triviality evidenced itself and I just laughed over how my giant ego got worked up because of a little pain. Gratefulness flooded my heart for upper bunks, chatty companions, blisters, falls, loose toenails, an unsatisfactory backpack, pain, exhaustion, snoring, the 6:00am noisy Pilgrims. What had I been thinking? That the Camino would be a walk in the park? A restful vacation? An easy hike for 70 year old knees?

My litany of concerns were not merely personal inconveniences but clearly pointed to authentic Camino experiences. I gently reminded myself that I had willingly undertaken this 500 mile walking pilgrimage, knowing that day after day, week after week, perhaps month after month, over all kinds of terrain, in all kinds of weather, there would be in-my-face incertitude about personal comfort and accommodations.

This walking Pilgrimage is what I had dreamed and wanted to do for over 20 years. Quit now, on the 4th day, because of a loose toenail? Not on your life!!!! I was on the Camino at last and knew with certainty, sitting on this bench in a plaza in Pamplona, listening to a little canary sing its truth, that everything I would encounter in the future would be o'k. Not just o'k, but sacred. That everything encountered so far had been sacred, even the falls. But more importantly, I understood that I had just been given, unasked for and perhaps even undeserved, the most important and graced reminder of my life: Be grateful Now. Make each moment Now. Now is eternally sacred. I felt radically reoriented.

Le plus dur... c'est toujours les premiers cents mètres !

CAMINO—DAY 5

The Big Question: Mary, why do you walk?

Postcard # 5—April 28, 2010 sent from Uterga, Espana

Dear Elena: I want your mother to teach you to call Uncle Nathan on the telephone. Tell him to come read this new card, & won't it be exciting to dial all by yourself? And you can call your papa at YouTube & your grandpapa, too. Is it fun to have Grandpapa home from Spain? Today I walked 16.8km or 10.1mi—not bad for 4 blisters & a separated big toenail. But the countryside is so beautiful. Vast plains. Steep climbs & descents. I take many standing rest stops. Walked 3 mi close by and under wind turbines w. their gentle & insistent whirring sounds. Views back to distant Pamplona all day as I climbed up & over the hills. Fields green & yellow with mustard. Hot today/no problem. I like it and usually drink four 12-oz bottles of water on the trail. The little felt heart you & your mama sewed for me & Grandpa is carried next to my heart. I want you & Nathan to pick 3 lemons, one each for Wilma, Bill & Betty. Love from Grandma Mary

Journal—Day 5 (Wednesday) April 28, 2010 written in Uterga

Walked 16.8km or 10.1mi from Pamplona. Unsure this am but repacked my new bag & walked out, buying stamps, having breakfast, & with a little persuasion from a waitress, found myself back at the sports shop to buy 2 metal hiking poles. What a difference with the new backpack & balancing poles. I was much more easily able to walk & enjoy, in fact it made the 10 mile walk to Uterga surer and more vigorous. This was with glorious views back to Pamplona, and fields of wheat & barley waving me on. These were the windy battlefields of Charlemagne as he rousted the Moors from this area. It was terribly hot today—and I grateful for a long sleeved shirt. Most spiritual was the hike up over the <u>Alto del Perdon</u> with its heart-stopping climb, vultures circling everywhere, the mysterious whirring wind turbines and at the very top of the hill, the standing iron figures of Camino Pilgrims over the ages—all looking windblown, fiercely determined and facing westward to Santiago de Compostela. Beautiful walk down other side, but pain set in and I was exhausted from the long walk and heat. Met a Pilgrim named Vincent sitting under a tree who asked me if my name was Mary. Felt certain I'd never seen him before. Concerned about my foot, he walked me into Uterga, and went to some trouble to find me a doctor's name & schedule. I landed at Albergue del Perdon (11 Euros) & had a great dinner with several women pilgrims, including the Canadian.

Reflection on Day 5, written in San Francisco in 2011

"When the student is ready, the teacher will appear".
Buddhist Proverb

My fifth day on the Camino was one of the best I could have imagined. In the early morning in Pamplona, I worked on my feet, and found that I could drain the puffy, water-filled blisters by gently pulling a thread and sterilized needle through them. I wrapped and taped all the toes together to lessen friction and to hold the loose big toenail in place and finally eased the swollen foot into its shoe. Then I set about unpacking the backpack I'd brought from San Francisco, jettisoning some possessions to lessen the weight, and repacking the newly purchased pack. I brushed and cleaned the one I'd brought with me, and said a little prayer: "let me find a new owner for this almost new pack who can really use it, more as a school or laptop bag." A janitor was sweeping the front hall of the dormitory when I went downstairs. Without really thinking, I thrust the pack at him. Tears filled his eyes when he examined it. "My son is in college and asked me for money for a pack. He will be so happy with this. God bless you, God bless you. Pray for me and my son." I smiled and walked out. Believe me, it was a blessing to be rid of the pack and to get the janitor's blessing as well.

I walked through the beautiful old streets of Pamplona, finding a cafe for a coffee, croissant and banana to fortify myself for the day's walk. The waitress who brought my food had magenta hennaed hair and an inordinate amount of make-up for mid-morning. We sized each other up. "You on the Camino, honey?" I nodded, realizing she was English. "How much does your pack weigh?" "I'm not sure, maybe 16 or so pounds." "I don't know how heavy pounds are," and she lifted the pack with one hand. "Oh, that's nothing. We have people come through here with packs three times that big." We smiled. She left to clear tables.

I set about peeling the banana and drinking my coffee. The waitress appeared again. "How old are you, if you don't mind?" she asked, squinting to get a better look at me. "In my 70th year," I replied. "Who's walking you on the Camino?" "I'm walking alone." Her eyes rolled slightly. She checked herself in the mirrored wall behind me, arranging a sassy little curl below her ear and dabbing at the corner of her lips. "I'd never let me Grandmum walk anyplace alone, much less the Camino." "Oh, I bet your grandmother would love it, the freedom and adventure." "No, she'd hate it. She's never been out of Birmingham." I wasn't sure how to respond to that, so sipped my coffee.

She started to walk away, but turned back to me: "Where are your walking poles, if you don't mind?" "I don't have poles. I don't need them." She looked at me incredulously. "Oh, yeah, you do, Grandmum!", she said, not unkindly. "You need walking poles to steady you so you don't take a fall one of these days on your arse and break a bloody hip." She walked away. I was stunned. She was one smart waitress—right about falling and definitely right about the poles. I hoisted the new pack onto my back, hooked the straps into place, gave her a wink and a wave, and left for the sports shop to purchase a bright red pair of metal hiking poles.

What a sight I was, striding in my chunky boots through the streets of medieval Pamplona, sporting a new red and black backpack with sturdy straps buckled supportively at my waist and across my upper chest. The weight seemed so differently distributed with the properly designed and adjusted pack. There was a marvelous little zippered pouch on top where I could stash immediate needs, like fruit or sandwiches or crackers, or tiny tins of delicious tuna mousse or liver pate. I felt very organized now, with my waistpack which held valuables, and this wonderfully compartmentalized backpack. I marveled at how easily I adjusted to walking with rubber tipped poles, even in the streets of a big city like Pamplona. With my wide-brimmed hat and its' drape down the back to protect my neck from rain and sun, I looked odd, but I knew I was a new and improved Pilgrim.

The long walk out of Pamplona gave me a look into the sophistication of the town, its emphasis on preserving its 1400 year old history, its medieval streets and buildings, and the inevitable blending of the very old with recent centuries of architecture. Of course, I saw no bulls running through the streets, only senior citizens out for leisurely walks on routes with lots of benches, and mothers with beautiful babies in prams, and school children in uniforms playing in schoolyards, and joggers sweating their way across the parks and University areas through which the Camino winds out of town. It took me a long time to get through the suburbs because I often stopped to admire babies and watch schoolchildren play. Often older people sitting on benches waved and called out to me "Buen Camino".

I felt so happy and lighthearted, so full of energy and enthusiasm. Of course the day had just begun. By noon I was in the country and it was hot. A beautiful range of high hills lay ahead, but to get there, I would first walk through many miles of glorious valley farmlands with feed crops and growing grains. From any vantage point on the path, I saw farmhands working the fields. These were massive farms stretching for miles, I thought, like farming cooperatives in the United States.

I thought of my older brother Pat and his wife Yvonne on the O'Hara family farm in southern Illinois. How he would marvel to see these fields and watch the farmers plow and harvest. He would have no problem with language or communicating with Spanish country people. They would know he was one of them in the way he scans the sky for signs of rain, exudes understanding and appreciation for the finer points of the farm equipment, lovingly and with humor engages each person he meets, radiates reverence for the ground on which he walks.

But while I was interested in the agriculture where I walked, I knew these farmlands were the heart of historical northern Spain. These were the very fields where battles were waged in medieval times for the usual reasons: ethnic and regional exclusion of Muslims, Jews, Basque and French; rights to land, water and other natural resources and of course religious reasons with emphasis on papal power, money and safe passage for pilgrims to Santiago. I tried to picture Charlemagne (himself an interloper in Spain) and his armies marching through these fields, feeling this heat and wind, battling the Muslims to the death in hand to hand combat.

The history of exclusion everywhere on earth and in all segments of history. As a child in the United States, I heard the stories of the family farm, the O'Hara settlement in southern Illinois given by the US government through land grants to my ancestors by name, in perpetuity. With those official land grants came good water sources, gently rolling farmland, excellent soil and plentiful woods for virgin timber and small game for food. What land grants on yellowed, crumbling paper don't tell of course, is the sad story of the American Indians and the displacement of their itinerant way of life, how they grappled with territorial exclusion from their centuries long human rights to move freely with the seasons on their Mother Earth, hunting and fishing throughout the midwest plains.

As a child, I listened with awe and my eyes widened to stories from the first 75 years of O'Hara homesteading in the 1800's—troubling stories of co-existence, bands of Indians coming peacefully through the farm, yet camping uncomfortably close to the house, their curiosity about the white women and children, the language barriers, the sheer differences in how each faction looked and acted, perceived and spoke. All those lost stories. Gradually, of course, the midwest native Americans and their way of life disappeared, dying off from bewilderment, isolation, disease, disappointment and strong government regulations. When I was a child, my father frequently found ancient Indian arrowheads chiseled from stone, usually when walking in plowed fields after a rain. I washed these little treasures my father brought home, and lined them up on a windowsill. How little did I know . . . how little was understood.

As I walked along the Camino path and mulled these thoughts, I saw that I was approaching a kind of shrine at a crossroads. I stopped to study it and even though I could not understand the details offered on a plaque with a picture, I realized it was a memorial for a pilgrim who had died quite recently on this very spot of a heart attack. How sobering. How sad and difficult for his family to receive this information and attend to all the details of their loved one's unexpected demise so far from home. But how thought provoking for a modern day pilgrim—one who prepares physically and mentally for pilgrimage, and who nonchalantly kisses family members good-bye and jauntily calls out: **I'm off Then**, as Hape Kerkeling, the European comedian, entitled his bestseller book about the Camino.

Indeed, I'm sure virtually all pilgrims leave their homes with some version of "I'm off then", with full expectations of returning home safe and sound, in better health, trimmer, with all sins forgiven and triumphantly waving a completion certificate issued in Santiago". I had to admit that I felt invincible on the Camino this first week, in spite of my falls. And I put to myself the question of my death, perhaps alone and so far from San Francisco and family. I walked on, pondering this, and came to the conclusion that I was really not afraid of inevitable death, whenever, wherever, whatever, and could only hope in that unforeseen circumstance, my family would be comforted that I had died while I was living life so fully.

I was slowly approaching the high hills over which I had to climb before coming to the next valley and the village of Uterga, where I would spend the night. The wind was not only hot but very, very strong, making it difficult to stand upright as I struggled up the steep and rocky ascent of

Alto del Perdon. Gigantic wind turbines, the power generators for most of Pamplona, were planted firmly across the hills and I could hear their mechanical whirring arms furiously churning the wind from at least a half mile away.

As the path wound closer to the wind energy turbines, I saw that some arms were not moving at all, while other machines were turning furiously. The machines are communicating with each other, I thought playfully. The scene took on a science fiction aura and I imagined the row upon row of turbines as being Martian robots defending their landing pads against my approach. I succumbed to the mind game and pressed forward, confident that my pilgrim status would win out over all their evil mechanistic ploys to keep me from passing across the mountain and proceeding to Santiago de Compostela. Even though I felt protected, I moved forward cautiously, rehearsing my strategy to cross the line of robots. If they threatened to attack me, at that crucial moment, my pilgrim gear would transform into invisible protective armor. I fantasized that the backpack would release a great ground fog, shielding me from their view, and my hiking poles would guide me on the path using undetectable cloud technology. "Santiago, protect me from all evils," I implored, as I entered the force field of the turbines.

The path led upwards passing about 100 feet from a turbine moving its arms so rapidly that the earth shook. My original strategy to fight my way through by transforming backpack and poles would not be strong enough to fight off this enraged robotic monster. There was only one thing to do: like a lamb, approach the lion. I stepped off the path, and walked non-threateningly and peaceably towards the pulsing turbine. At its base, I slipped off my backpack, dropped it submissively to the ground, lowered my poles, and sat down motionless, closing my eyes and absorbing the vibrations. After fifteen minutes of resting in the turbine's menacing shadow, and listening to its' blustering and howling and raging at the wind, I got up, passed safely away from its seismic shaking and groaning, pressed on to the top of the hill and proceeded down the other side to my destination of Uterga for the night.

It was a long day of walking. Late afternoon descent into the next valley tired me more than the morning's ascent from the plains outside Pamplona. My feet and legs burned from the heat, and raw blisters warned me to be cautious against another fall. On the road ahead, I could see a man sitting on a bench at a lookout point reading a book. I continued my approach, feeling no concern. As I came even with him, he looked at me and said in perfect English: "Hello, isn't your name Mary?" His words burned into me and I was on instant alert. I knew I had not spoken to him at any time, or even seen him in the villages or albergues where I'd slept. "Yes, it is. How did you know my name?" "I watched you approach, and I knew your name was Mary." I chewed on that response a bit, then asked "And what is your name?" "Vincent" he replied.

I nodded, then turned away and walked on, and he stepped right up to meet my pace. My mind raced to a cautionary stop: this man is very unusual looking, almost like no one I've ever seen. He's not dressed like a pilgrim. What is he doing out here reading a book? How does he really know my name? Vincent interrupted my thoughts. "I'd like to walk with you. What's wrong with your foot? You're limping. And there are bruises on your face and arms. Do you need a doctor?" He had asked too many questions at once, and I just answered wearily: "I don't know."

Using short questions and even shorter answers, we exchanged enough information for me to relax. I could see the village church steeple less than a mile away. We were headed in that direction, and I figured if I needed any protection from this stranger, we'd soon be running into farmers and town folks. I asked Vincent why he was out on the mountain on this hot day, without a hat or long sleeves. "Because I'm a runner and love these hills to strengthen my body for long runs. And Mary, I'm also the English teacher. I always carry an English book to improve my grammar. Also I like to speak to pilgrims. They often need help."

That seemed reasonable enough, and certainly not a come-on. If I'd been anywhere from age 15 to 50, I would have continued being wary. But at 70, and bedraggled as I knew myself to be in the late afternoon,

I took him at his word. "Mary, tell me about your foot," and I did. "You must see a doctor, and I will arrange it in the next village. Now Mary, tell me why you undertake this walk to Santiago?"

So he has laid it out, the big question. And maybe the unanswerable one. "I don't know, Vincent. Well, I do know why I'm here, but I can't say it exactly. It's very complicated." "Oh, you have reasons why you walk to Santiago, Mary, you just don't know that you know. Your heart knows, but you don't trust your heart yet. Head answers are easy and stupid. Ask your heart." I felt trapped by this possibility, suddenly too exhausted to go on, much less consider heart knowledge. We were now entering the village and walking by a church with an outdoor shrine to the Virgin Mary. I struggled to a seat in front of the shrine and sat down. "You rest here with Mother Mary," Vincent said. "I will go register you at the Albergue. Ask Mary why you are on pilgrimage. Ask Mary to open your heart." He jogged away.

I was astonished and annoyed with myself to be letting this funny little man take over. I looked up at the outdoor statue, chipped, weather-mottled, and I rested there in its fixed gaze. I felt like a child back in my one-room Catholic grade school in Ruma, Illinois where I spent a good deal of each school day, year after year for eight years, looking at the life-size statue of the Blessed Mother standing atop the upright piano. For several seconds, I caught sight of my child's heart. Tears filled my eyes. Too many years have passed to go this route again, I thought. After University, the past fifty years had swept the innocence away.

Vincent was by my side again, picking up my backpack. "Come and register. And you have lower bunk and nice restaurant in the Albergue." He led the way to the Albergue, oversaw registration, and told the barman that he would be back with information about a doctor. I showered, went to the restaurant where I joined other women, some whom I'd seen on the trail over the past few days. By dessert time, Vincent was back, thrust a piece of paper in my hand with a doctor's name and address, instructing that the doctor would examine my foot the next morning at 9:00am. We looked at each other. "Mary, remember that only the heart knows true reasons." As I considered this, he simply vanished, and I never saw him again.

CAMINO—DAY 6

The Man with the Cell Phone

Postcard # 6—April 29, 2010 sent from Puente de la Reina, Espana

Dearest Elena: Today I made a short but quite beautiful walk 10.1km or 6.1mi. It was incredibly hot. Brilliant red poppies bloom along the trails. Today I detoured 2 1/2 mi. by choice off the Camino to an 8-sided stone church built in the 12th C at Eunate. It was very cool temperature inside. I am staying tonight in a 500 yr old Pilgrim's Hostel—clean & friendly people, run by Padres Reparadores, a religious order of men. Out my window by my bed I see the Church steeple perfectly & 2 beautiful white/black storks have built a gigantic nest. They are flying back & forth. I walked today through miles of vegetable crops—thrilling to see so much asparagus, lettuces, leeks, artichokes, even new wildflowers by the road that I haven't seen before. I have a new blister today on my left foot that is the full length of my second toe. You would be amazed at this puffy, water-filled blister. Love from Grandma. PS I am very very happy.

Journal—Day 6 (Thursday) April 29, 2010 written in Puente de la Reina

I have just finished my 6th postcard to Elena. A good routine to sit down in a bar at the end of the day and write her postcard, then continue by writing in this journal. Disturbing dream last night about being alone in St. Patrick's grade school as a child in a bad storm. Saw Vincent's doctor this morning, who wrapped my toes like little mummies in an Egyptian Museum. It was an extraordinarily beautiful walk today, although not a long one for me . . . 10.1km or 6.1mi. Blisters on feet are bothersome & worrisome. Hot also, but nice breezes. Took a 2-mile side tour today off the trail to Eunate, a 12th Century Romanesque Church of Santa Maria de Eunate, built by the Knights Templars. Octagonal/free-standing outer porch with alabaster windows & a very sweet Madonna/Child statue in typical pose. Almost an alabaster face. Severe, yet charming inside the church and cooled by the stone walls. A wonderful 45 min. contemplative stop where I could sit in Centering Prayer. Walked into Puente de la Reina & stayed at Albergue Padres Reparadores—top floor, bottom bunk—a lovely place with the exception of a cocky little man who talked on a cellphone loudly from a bunk 8 feet from me. He was not happy when I gently pointed to the Silencio sign posted on the wall. I washed clothes, hanging them outside in a nice covered area . . . with practically no warning, thunder and lightening surrounded the town, a surprisingly huge rain fell, then hail, then cold . . . went upstairs leaving wet laundry in covered area & watched storks outside window in huge nest on church tower. Walked alone to Jakue Hotel for Pilgrims Menu del Dia, seated at a long table with about 20 other Pilgrims/many languages/great friendliness, seated across from two Spiritual Directors from Canada. Spoke of spiritual matters. They knew of Centering Prayer and pressed me for details. Feet are problematic, painful, blistered, sore, but I feel so happy. Bound feet, but unbound freedom.

Reflection on Day 6, written in San Francisco

"Be not disturbed that you cannot make others as you wish them to be, since you cannot make yourself as you wish to be."
—Thomas a Kempis—The Imitation of Christ

I awakened this morning in the dormitory at Uterga from a curious dream in which I was a little girl just like in the two or three photos I still have that were taken of me some sixty years ago. I was about ten years old in the dream, walking alone and happily across the family farm, skirting my uncle's property and then along an isolated country road and through the woods until I emerged about a mile away at St. Patrick's Church and one room school. It was thundering and had grown quite dark as I reached the school porch. I ran into the one large empty classroom, horrified to see that I was alone. All the desks were empty. The storm worsened, with high winds that shook the windows, constant rolls of thunder and lightening that lit the darkened classroom. I ran to the piano, looked up at the statue of the Blessed Mary and sobbed: "Help me, save me."

The dream seemed so real in its remembered details as I waited for the doctor who had agreed with Vincent to see me. It was a short visit, but productive in that he cleaned and disinfected my toes, and wrapped the foot quite professionally. With the dream still on my mind and the foot once again cooperative to start the day's walk, I embarked on a 2 1/2 mile detour off the trail to visit a 12th Century Romanesque Church at Eunate, reputedly built by the Knights Templars in the octagonal structural style of the Church of the Holy Sepulcher in Jerusalem.

I didn't have an extensive knowledge of the Knights Templars, but remembered from History classes something of their overall reputation as monkish like soldiers from upper class families whose role it was to guard the Church's interests, especially in protecting pilgrims and safeguarding roads to sacred sites like Jerusalem and Santiago de Compostela.

The Knights followed the Rule of St. Benedict, taking vows of poverty, chastity and obedience. They also were efficient builders of churches and pilgrims' shelters and hospitals. But stories are rife of how powerful they became, individually and collectively, not only because of their fighting prowess, but because of their political and social allies. In their role as soldiers, they were involved at various times in campaigns to evict, if not eradicate the Saracens, the Muslims and the Moors from Spain. They were handsomely rewarded for their military successes with huge tracts of land, money, castles and other properties, and from this wealth, Templar business and financial acumen flourished. For example, they created the first "line of credit", whereby Pilgrims from throughout Europe could deposit money with the Knights Templars prior to leaving home, be given a letter of credit, then withdraw money as needed along the pilgrimage route. The Knights Templars were doomed because they grew too powerful for the kings, noblemen and the Church. Fear, greed, scandal, envy and suspicion of the Knights gradually caused their downfall and eventual dissolution by the Vatican in 1312.

It was blazing hot as I approached Eunate on a path through fields. I was surprised to see that the entire place was composed of just two buildings—the church and some hundred feet away, one house used occasionally as a pilgrims' dormitory. The church of Santa Maria de Eunate was indeed octagonal, and by size standards in Spain, a very small worship building. It seemed delicate and vulnerable. A shoulder high wall was built all around the exterior of the building with one unadorned arched entryway. Just inside this wall, there was a connected porch surrounding the entire building, framed by a couple of dozen beautiful arches with impossibly thin pillars. Rounded stones were set permanently into the pathway of the porch, and as I entered the interior of the building, I was struck by how cool it was, how dark, how simple and unadorned.

The place was empty of pilgrims or driving tourists. As I walked around and my eyes adjusted, I could see that the light source came from yellowish, milky looking, thinly shaved alabaster windows set high in the roof. Besides the stone altar, the only decoration was a statue of our Lady holding the Christ Child on her lap. She held a handful of ripe wheat cut fresh from the fields. Who had brought this wheat into the church and placed it so lovingly in Mary's hands? Both mother and child wore gold crowns on their heads and permanent smiles of wide-eyed pleasure beamed directly at any soul wandering through the Church. I loved these dark-haired and dark-eyed figures, so different from the blonde and blue-eyed plaster replicas of Mary and Jesus in churches in America and much of Europe.

I sat down on a stiff little bench, slipping my backpack off onto the seat beside me. It was absolutely silent in the Church. The air felt considerably cooler than outside, and the smell inside was dry and sweet, like cut alfafa. I took a drink of water. Relaxed. I didn't decide to turn my mind to prayer. It was as though Centering Prayer descended on me through the alabaster windows, without bidding. Thoughts gradually lessened and those that rose up, I let go, without indulging them. I simply let any thought go when I became aware of it. Resting my mind in the space without thoughts. Resting my body. Resting in God. Probably thirty minutes passed in this state until I heard insistent voices and laughter outside on the porch.

It was time for me to leave the Santa Maria de Eunate Chapel, and as I left, I was amused to find several vacationers having great fun, but a difficult time really, walking barefoot on the rounded stones of the Church porch. They seemed to be startled to see an actual walking pilgrim emerge from the church and I was equally fascinated by them.

The chatty group was embarked on a driving pilgrimage to Santiago in an air conditioned car, and staying every night in a nice hotel as part of their holiday in Spain. They asked about my pilgrim accommodations, and grimaced as I told them about the dormitory beds, shared bathrooms and snoring. "But what are you doing with your shoes off and limping around the porch?" I asked. They had read that all their sins would be forgiven if they could make it barefoot completely around the porch with the rounded stones at Eunate. I really liked these automobile Pilgrims. I sympathized with their slow and painful progress on the stones, but gracefully declined their invitation for me to take off my shoes and join them. I had enough foot problems without adding plantar faciitis to the list!!!! We all shouted out "Buen Camino" and I set out alone on a narrow path leading up and over a hill.

I arrived late-afternoon at Puente de la Reina, the town at the end of my walk for the day, and easily found the Albergue at the entrance to the medieval section of the town. Greatly relieved to secure a lower bunk in a room that held about thirty people, I unpacked and prepared to hand wash some clothes. All around me were Pilgrims napping or quietly reading on their bunks.

Suddenly the door banged loudly and into the room swept a cocky little man talking on a cell phone. He dropped his belongings on a lower bunk three beds from me and proceeded to pace the length of the room, haranguing someone over the phone. This was far from dormitory etiquette. After ten minutes passed, it was clear that all the pilgrims were disturbed by the man, not just the volume of his voice, but his unpleasant tone and manner. Two pilgrims walked over to read the sign on the wall entitled Silencio and listing dormitory rules, then shook their heads and left. The man's volume increased, his arms were thrashing in gestures and he exploded in another tirade on the phone.

As the man paced and talked, he would pass close by the sign on the wall. I walked over, got his attention, and pointed to the sign, saying nothing. He grew quiet for a moment, read the sign, looked me over, then stepped directly up to my face and spat on the floor. I smiled, but held his gaze. He drew his right hand up to his left shoulder, then sliced it to his side. I stood my ground, still smiling, but quickly realized that my smile and direct gaze into his eyes infuriated him further. He turned away, continued to talk on his phone and I walked downstairs to speak to the hospitalero who had registered me.

As the hospitalero accompanied me up the steps, the little man was coming down. He began ranting, pointing at me and gesturing angrily, then turned his wrath against the hospitalero. They continued down the steps, and I went back to my bunk and lay down, interested to see how this would end. After about ten minutes, the harried hospitalero approached my bunk, and in very broken English whispered "Please, please move to other room. I have low bunk for you." "Well, is that man going to stay here?" "Yes, yes, I think so. Please move. I'll help you." Several anxious pilgrims near my bed stepped forward and encouraged me to move. The man reappeared, and determined to have the last word, said ominously and in English, jabbing his finger in my face: "You are not a Pilgrim. You are fake. You should leave now. They should put you out."

I smiled at the little bully again, lugged my stuff across the hall to a large room where indeed I had another lower bunk next to a window. It felt like an upgrade in accommodations. From my new bed, I could see the church spires directly across the street and could feel a breeze in the hot late afternoon. My escalated breathing over the encounter with the man evened out. One by one, I let tense muscles relax. I studied the scene out the window and observed two storks carrying sticks in their beaks to build a new nest. It was an enchanting sight to me to see these majestic birds swoop and dive, following the ages-old instincts to build a new nest upon an old nest, year after year.

Before I left the window at the Padres Reparadores Albergue, I observed my little friend with the cellphone down on the street about a half block away. He unlocked the trunk of a car, removed some items from a suitcase, and walked back into the building. I stepped to the door of my room and watched him re-enter the dorm room across the hall. Did I want to "settle the score?" There was that split moment in time when I might have done so—but also in the split moment, I made a personal choice between peace and conflict.

I had heard about people with a Camino Credential using Pilgrim dorms to save money when travelling. I supposed they would do that if they were tight on money or chronic cheapskates. Eager finally to dismiss the entire incident from my mind, I thought: "Oh well, everybody on earth is a pilgrim. And I'm willing to wager I've been a pain in the ass to any number of people so far on this walk. Besides, he'll drive on and hopefully, I'll never see him again."

- Ouste, pas question que tu voyages avec moi !
- Punaise, j'arriverai jamais à Santiago...!

CAMINO—DAY 7

The Contorted Crucifix

Postcard # 7—April 30, 2010 sent again from Puente de la Reina, Espana

Dear Elena: This am my socks were not dry, my feet hurt, my body was tired, so I didn't walk but stayed all day at a beautiful Pilgrims Hostel (9 Euros) wrote, rested, worked on my feet, in general I felt it was right to do. Everyday now I get out your little heart & it kisses each of my sore toes. Of course it helps. I had a buffet lunch at a very nice place & they had many desserts. I thought of you & wished you were here so we could share everything. You will love Spanish food—everything is so tasty except I don't eat eel—at least not yet. When I get home, I have some good ideas about things to make for us a tea party. Love from Grandmama

Camino Journal—Day 7 (Friday) April 30, 2010 written again from Puente de la Reina

Today I complete one week of walking but not as far on the Camino as I would like to be. Decided the feet must rest today. Because of a one-night stay limit, left Padres Reparadores Albergue and checked into nearby Albergue Jakue. Lovely property. (9 Euros) Funny! Yesterday afternoon I washed all my clothes & a BIG rain came up—not dry this am. Another reason to stay & not walk. Completely sunny today. I walked into Puente, a medieval village, bought more foot supplies. Used ATM. Stepped into Iglesia del Crucifijo (Church of the Crucifixion) Rested there, thinking of yesterday's encounter with the man on the cellphone. Startling and disturbing crucifix—Christ's arms pulled way up in a V-shape. Back to Jakue for buffet—delicious with Obanos wine from Navarre. Clothes all drying on the line and I sit & write in a lovely garden bar with grass growing between patterned concrete dividers. Evening cleared some. I used computer for an hour, answering emails to let people know I'm o'k. For hours this afternoon I had the dorm to myself before pilgrims started checking in. Wrote in spacious side rooms. The dorm arrangement here is four beds (2 bunks) as a unit divided by bamboo curtains from the next unit. Nice, cozy but still lots of snoring. Interesting to watch people cook in the evenings—mostly pasta but sometimes more elaborate meals.

Reflection on Day 7, written in San Francisco in 2011

"Let yourself do nothing, and then rest afterward."
an old Spanish proverb

Upon awakening peacefully in the morning at the Padres Reparadores, I stood at the window to watch the storks swoop and dive, working intently on building a new nest on top of the old. And all the while I watched, I was intent on my own condition—I felt exhausted. I had no energy and certainly no enthusiasm to hoist my backpack and start another day of walking. Besides, I discovered all my socks were still wet, not having dried overnight. Instant and easy decision: I would not walk today but rest my feet and dry my socks. Because pilgrims generally are allowed to stay one night only in a dormitory, I decided to move immediately to the Albergue Jakue—a nice hotel building nearby with a very spacious dormitory for Pilgrims in the basement. When I arrived at the Jakue dorm at 8:45am, it had been cleared of the previous night's pilgrims, and been made ready for the day, but the hospitaleros did not want to register me until 2:00pm. We stood there looking at each other for at least two minutes, and they bent their rules for this bedraggled and weary looking Pilgrim.

I registered with profuse thanks, hung my clothes to dry in the garden, and immediately lay down for a two-hour nap. Awakening in a completely empty and silent dormitory mid-morning was a luxurious occurrence on the Camino. A day off. No long walking. No heavy boots for me today—just open-toed sandals to allow my battered and blistered feet to heal.

I walked slowly into the medieval section of Puente de la Reina. How pleasant to have a day in front of me, with whatever would develop. The main street where I walked was very old, dating back to the Knights Templars who had used this village as one of their primary centers to protect pilgrim passage to Santiago. Even though little evidence of the 12th C was left, still the buildings were centuries old. As I studied the architecture, different floors seemed to have different styles and finishes, as if the ground floors had been built onto during different eras. I was fascinated by the many decorative shields and crests which adorned the street-front facades. How I enjoyed the leisure of the morning, visiting the various open shops and observing the bustling commerce of a coming weekend. I visited a farmacia to purchase more foot supplies, and also a bank where an ATM and my credit card made withdrawal of cash easy. I was set for another week. After two hours of sightseeing, I was ready to return to the Jakue.

On the way back, I passed by the Iglesia del Crucifijo, and felt a strong pull to step inside the church. Partway up the aisle, I was shocked and transfixed by the Crucifix hanging in front of me. I had never seen anything like this cross—Christ's feet were indeed nailed on the vertical board, but his arms were drawn up hideously above his shoulders and his hands nailed to shorter boards which formed a tight V. I positioned myself comfortably to take a very good look. The hair, the eyes, the realism of the veins and wounds, but especially that awful upward pull on Christ's arms, all caused a stillness to settle over me. I could not take my eyes away from this crucifix, and like the practice of icon gazing, the experience moved my heart in a unique way. I felt in my heart the nails piercing my hands and feet. I felt the crown of thorns piercing my own scalp. I felt I was dying with Christ. I disappeared into this experience.

Some time later, I moved to a bench in the church to rest and collect my thoughts. For the first time, I had distinctly seen and felt Jesus the Christ dying on the cross from a mother's viewpoint. Was it this particular artist or sculptor's skill that caused this reaction? Probably yes, and probably no. There was no doubt that this was a sensational rendering of a broken and vulnerable Christ on the cross, and would affect all who might study it. However, this was an unnamable experience for me. Something mysterious happened to me there—in my head? Or was it in my heart? I couldn't seem to remember who Jesus was, but clearly he was a man whose lifestyle, companions and messages were uncomfortable enough that authorities cornered him in a garden, swiftly brought him to trial, and sentenced him to die hideously on the cross.

I felt calm and accepting, but also anxious about what this powerful experience might require of me in the future.

Who was I in San Francisco? Who was I walking solo on the Camino? Who was that man Vincent who, two days ago, asked if my name was Mary and then walked with me into Uterga? Why was he so solicitous and kind to a stranger? Why had he stressed to me that truth is found in the heart? "Ask Mary to tell you," he said.

And just yesterday, who was the cocky little man with the cellphone and the car? What puzzled me about that experience was not his inconsiderate manner in the dorm, or his aggressiveness in responding to my pantomimed request to honor silence in the dorm. I was troubled by the more intangible anger in his soul transmitted through his eyes to my heart. And his searing words: "You are not a Pilgrim. You are fake."

Quand je pense qu'on descend vers le sud
et que ça monte toujours !

CAMINO—DAY 8

The Evening Routine

Postcard # 8—May 1, 2010 sent from Estella, Espana

Dear Elena: I walked 21.1km or 12.7mi today. Out & on the Camino by 7:30am, Elena, early & absolutely beautiful. I just kept walking, resting every 3 or 4 miles. It kept threatening rain, but I never had to put my raincoat on. The trail was varied today, and for 4 miles, it was a 2000 year old Roman stone trail. Of course, I had a fall—very lucky that 2 French women pulled me into upright position. Nothing broken, but my rescuers more shaken than I. That was Fall # 4, & because of MUD. Still, I count this a fabulous day. I am tired. I am in a bar eating Tapas & a salad & feeling very good. Elena, last week on the Camino paths I saw a lot of black slugs & this week a lot of very large snails. Shall I gather some for your mama to make a stew? Love from Grandma Mary

Journal—Day 8 (Saturday) May 1, 2010 written in Estella, Espana

Today quite pleased with the Camino walk, making 21.1km or 12.7mi. My feet cooperated in spite of pain & sore blisters. It was "all history" as I passed from ancient village to ancient village . . . my trusty Brierley guidebook is a lifesaver and very educational. A fair amount of walking over & alongside busy roadways and highways. This does not faze me as the cross-overs are always safe. Paths also wended through vineyards & farms with much of the day's walk on natural tracks (not paved or graveled). Some fairly steep climbing. Beautiful medieval villages of Cirauqui and Lorca. I ate tuna mousse from a tin & crackers for a solo lunch in a deserted church plaza about 2:00pm. Even took a little nap in the sun leaning against my backpack. Really fascinated by several miles path today walking on ancient & uprooted early Roman roads. Large cut/chiseled stones more or less in original position as placed 2000 years ago. The winning combination of mud and irregular stones—and down I went for another fall. Two Frenchwomen saw & ran back to me & with great effort & giggles extracted me from the mud & stones. I'm o'k, yet shaken, bruised on my arms and it didn't do the loose toenail any good at all. Still, I'm o'k, and very, very grateful that nothing is broken. Albergue in Estella pleasant, & I looked so pathetic that the hospitalero took me to a rear building next to a lovely patio, lower bunk, next to the bathroom & showers and very quiet. Lots of pilgrim bicyclists here.

Reflection—Day 8, written in San Francisco in 2011

"We journey to get to the goal, but on a pilgrimage the goal is present at every step."

Brother David Steindl-Rast OSB

My first week on the Camino had passed, and I found that my solo walk had taken on at least somewhat of a routine in the evenings. Each mid to late afternoon I would drag into the village or town I had targeted for the day, and locate the albergue. I shamelessly pantomimed my need for a lower bunk and after looking me over and checking my age from my passport, the hospitalero at the reception desk usually hustled and located an empty lower bunk for me. It's my impression that often a few lower bunks were kept empty for late arriving older pilgrims. With my foot condition, age, size and need to frequently use the bathroom in the night, it was too dangerous for me to climb up and down the skinny ladders of the bunkbeds. None of this was lost on the hospitaleros.

Once a dormitory bed was assigned, the challenge became where to put one's belongings. There were never any lockers or closets. Beds were usually about two feet apart, sometimes closer, which barely afforded enough room for personal maneuvering or a chair on which to put a backpack. Many pilgrims stored their gear on the mattresses of the beds or underneath, if there was enough room. Each day upon arrival at my bunk, I went into housekeeping mode. Shoes off. Socks to air. Essentials removed from backpack. I carried a very lightweight semi-blanket called a CabinCuddler, and I positioned it on the bed which usually had a mattress cover and a pillow, but no bedding supplies. A small hand towel I carried from home served as a pillowcase. I calculated everything I would need for the next day and rotated that to the top of my pack. Light housekeeping was mostly done for the day. Fear of someone stealing my backpack or shoes dissipated my first week on the Camino. Of course, I left no valuables unattended, but carried them in my waistpack, which was always with me. I always left my toothbrush on my pillow in case the lights were off when I returned from dinner.

After showering if the line was not too long, or a catbath, I changed into clothes I would wear the next day and set out in sandals, free from backpack and poles to find a bar or restaurant where I could sit at a table alone for some time and write before dinner. Bars were appropriate places for me to go, for they were usually quiet and relaxed in the late afternoon and early evening and I never felt out of place sitting for an hour or so before dinner. Local families often gathered there in the bar to meet friends, women brought baby strollers in—it was all a friendly atmosphere. And best of all, no one bothered me.

Writing in a bar in early evening took on a life of its own. I never wavered from the routine of finding a table alone, ordering a glass of wine, then setting up writing essentials from my waist pack. Out came a small stack of postcards and my journal and pen. Then my Brierley's Guidebook, a picture of Larry and son Nathan, and another of my daughter Amelia, husband Francisco and Elena. I added the little suede pouch shaped like a boot holding my father's rosary, and a tiny felt embroidered heart made for me by Elena and Amelia. My mother's wedding band from 1925 was on my finger, replacing my wedding ring during the walk.

This was my inconspicuous and very discreet "altar" into which I could disappear writing, and where other Pilgrims rarely noticed or visited me. I often thought that with the bread and wine, I was celebrating daily communion with my family. It was not sacrilegious, as this was sacred space and time where I contemplated with gratefulness my Camino experience. I frequently thought of Dag Hammarkjold's remark: "For all that has been, thank you. For all that is to come, yes."

Writing a postcard to my granddaughter and making a journal entry each evening helped me in a disciplined way to track time, days, total distances walked and my location on the Camino—important ingredients to internalize each day's structure and events. Using my Brierley Guidebook, I fashioned a plan each evening for the next day, based on maps, distances and towns with known pilgrim dormitories or accommodations. Particularly helpful were the elevation maps I studied to calculate and ready myself for the difficulty of the next day's trek. These activities aided understanding of the characteristics and personality of the various Spanish regions through which I passed. As well, I jotted down in the back of my journal many things I was curious about or that I wanted to remember for future reference.

As I began Week 2, I was surprised at how few miles I had walked the first seven days—a mere 57 miles—and how formidable the days and remaining 450 miles seemed until I reached the city of Santiago de Compostela. A formidable distance yet to go, yes, but I relied on an old business adage that had gotten me through innumerable large projects in my life: "The only way to it is through it." And each evening in a bar, after setting a plan for the next day, I reset my resolve to walk every single step to Santiago.

- C'est des taureaux ?
- Non, des vaches !
- Ben oui, elles sont maquillées !

CAMINO—DAY 9

2010—Holy Year or Party Year?

Postcard # 9—May 2, 2010 sent from Los Arcos, Espana

Dearest Elena: Today was beautiful—flowers blooming by the millions—and many I've never seen before!!!!! Today I walked from Estella to Los Arcos—it was 21.7km or 13.0mi. No sun today so it was cool & overcast. Tonight I will attend a special Pilgrim's Mass at the fabulous Cathedral . . . I am staying at an Austrian Pilgrim's dorm so clean & with great spirit. People from all over the world, with a fairly rowdy but friendly & good-natured group of thirsty young Brits . . . probably loud snoring tonight. Both my feet are in need of a doctor—right foot big toenail is hanging by a thread & the toe black/blue all around. To cure it, I need a big smooch from Elena. This evening a Spanish choir serenaded in every Plaza in Los Arcos. I followed them around to listen, but don't know what the occasion was. Thinking of you everyday—love from Grandma

Journal—Day 9 (Sunday) May 2, 2010 written in Los Arcos, Espana

Today as I look back, I have been filled with joy. It just pushes out the aggravation of my feet. Feet not good, but I refuse to consider stopping or worse yet quitting the Camino. Small distance outside of Estella this am I anticipated a stop at the Monasterio Irache where a fountain of wine reportedly flows for pilgrims. Alas!!!! It was Sunday & the fountain of wine was turned off. Probably better for me and my feet, but I must admit I was disappointed. Went to the Mass this evening at the Los Arcos Cathedral. Very inclusive to all religions & nationalities. Staying in an Austrian Albergue—clean, civilized, friendly. Staying here are about 1/2 doz young Brits, very early 20s, good-looking, well-dressed, attending top schools, but noisy, noisy, clueless as to dorm etiquette. They were very polite to me (my bunk was a lower one in their midst) one of them in the upper over me and the rest in bunks 18 inches away on either side. They gathered around for a talk, sitting on my bed and the adjacent bunks. Another example of cozy Camino dormitory encounters. They pressed me for details about Holy Year on the Camino, about which they appeared to know nothing.

Reflection on Day 9, written in San Francisco in 2011

"In truth, we (everybody and everything,) are all connected; most of us just can't see the glue."

Bo Lozoff from We're All Doing Time

I have particularly fond memories of my 9th day on the Camino because I felt challenged both observing and talking to five young British men in their early twenties who surrounded my bunk area in Los Arcos. I was napping on my lower bunk in the dorm when they arrived and came awake with a start as they virtually barreled into the sleeping area, bumping into things, dropping their poles and backpacks noisily, jostling onto and bouncing on the beds. From that moment on, they never stopped their joking and banter and activities of unpacking, finding places to plug in cell phones and in general behaving somewhat like bulls in a china shop. They weren't particularly loud, or obnoxious, just drenched in testosterone and unabated energy despite their day's walk.

It seemed so incongruous—I at age 70 on a lower bunk, one of them above me and four assigned to bunks on either side about 18 inches away from me. We didn't exchange pleasantries right away, but nodded and smiled. They proceeded to shower and change clothes and appeared oblivious and completely unconcerned about me being in their midst. This casual dressing and undressing of both males and females occurred to a certain degree in every dormitory, but in truth, on that day I hardly knew where to look, or not look, their briefs were so skimpy. So, I slipped on my shoes and took a little walk in the neighborhood to give them a chance to settle down.

When I returned to the dorm, I hoped they would be out for the evening, but indeed they were playing cards—ensconced on my bed. "Hi guys, how's it going? You look comfortable." They did not seem at all embarrassed being on my bed; in fact, one cleared a space on his bed and motioned me to sit there in the midst of all his stuff. They immediately asked if I would like to play a round of cards with them. "Oh no, I wouldn't want to interrupt your game, but thanks anyway."

I looked them over. These young men were clearly well-to-do, with perfect haircuts, good clothes and expensive backpack equipment. I also recognized that they were educated, but lacking restraint as pilgrims. "You're American, I can tell, aren't you?" one asked and I nodded. "And the five of you lads, you're from England, I think." They seemed to find this hilarious and immersed themselves again in their game. I was curious about this crew. Finally, one grinned at me and asked if I was having fun on the Camino. It was my turn for a big laugh, and I answered, "As much fun as a pilgrim walking alone to Santiago can have."

Their game soon finished and they threw down the cards. "When do the five of you expect to get to Santiago?" I asked. "Oh we're not actually going to Santiago. We're on a short school holiday." They explained they were walking because they heard in a pub from some girls that Camino 2010 was a big party year. They only had a week off from school in which to walk, but so far, one leaned forward and ventured confidentially, they were disappointed in the party action.

I observed gently to them that Camino 2010 was indeed a special year for Pilgrims, but I suspected that most walkers would emphasize the spiritual or religious aspects of reaching Santiago rather than on hard partying along the way.

One of the young men sitting cross-legged on my bed turned to me and asked quite seriously, "And what would be the reason that a woman would walk alone across Spain to Santiago? I'm just asking. I mean, America is a long way from here. And so is Santiago. Are you really alone? And why?" His rambling questions seemed to have a soothing effect on the young men and they shifted positions and eyed me intently. I, however, didn't feel soothed. I felt a pressured agitation when asked to explain why I was on a pilgrimage so far from home. How could these young men possibly understand when I barely understood myself?

"It's a very long story about why I am here," I began ineptly. "Actually, it's a very short story. I am impelled to walk the route. I have no choice in the matter." One young man made a drumroll with a pencil he held: "Ah, so it's your destiny, is it?" The others stared him down. I went on, realizing the maze into which I was wandering. "Destiny is a fancier word than I would use. Once I heard about the Camino to Santiago, and the millions of people who walked it over the past thousand years or so, it became my Camino, too, like a beacon, the way to go. Kind of like a way back home. I had no choice." We were all silent except for the pencil tapping out a quiet little rhythm.

"You haven't told us why you are here alone." "Well, that part is simple enough," I responded. "A walking companion is high maintenance, and for me, distracting to purpose. Silence on the walk allows important life questions to ask themselves and to be answered by the silence."

The pencil tapper grew impatient with the conversation. "I suppose you mean by life questions whether there is a God and an afterlife," to which I answered: "Yes and No. Those questions maybe, among many others of more or less importance." We all laughed. "One more question, ma'am, before we go have a drink and start the evening. What's really so special about the year 2010 on the Camino?"

I gathered my wits and told them what I remembered about "Holy Years" on the Camino. I remembered that Pope Calixtus first declared a Holy Year in the 12th Century, so from the early 1100's, set years were declared by the Catholic Church to offer special graces and forgiveness of sins for any pilgrim who made it to the Cathedral of Saint James the Apostle in Santiago. Holy Years have been fixed ever since at intervals occurring in a sequence of 6-5-6-11 years. The last Holy Year was six years ago in 2004. You can count on a Holy Year when July 25, St. James' feastday, falls on Sunday. The next one will be 11 years from now—in 2021. After that, it will repeat the 6-5-6-11 sequence. All of this is calculated on leap years, and probably other factors I don't really remember at the moment."

My audience was politely listening. Pencil tapping had stopped. But in my mind I thought: "I have about two more minutes with these young men before they bolt for a bar." I continued: Here's the deal for serious Catholic Pilgrims. To get this special church-granted indulgence in a Holy Year, they must go to Santiago and visit the Cathedral where Saint James or "Sant-Iago" is buried. They must also go to confession and receive Communion. And they must say prayers—the Credo and Our Father—praying for the Pope's intentions. That's it in a nutshell.

Of course, I added as an after thought, there are virtually hundreds of thousands of Pilgrims who have no interest at all in these beliefs suggesting that all one's sins can be forgiven by these simple actions. And those people who don't believe still make the walk—they are there for the adventure, the vacation, the activity of hiking or some personal question or problem they are solving in their minds. And those are also very good alternate reasons to go to Santiago, don't you think?

Silence from the group. The pencil tapper twirled his pencil in mid-air that I interpreted as "Get on with the story." "Just this one last thing," I added. "The hype about Holy Year 2010 on the Camino is attracting many more pilgrims world-wide than ordinary years—and it will culminate in huge numbers of people, levels of celebration, difficulty in finding accommodations, etc in the coming month of July, when all of Spain celebrates St. James' feast day on the 25th. There is likely to be a ton of partying when people reach Santiago. You guys are a little too early for party action."

I stood up from the young man's bunk to signal the end of our tete a tete. They were all friendly and thanked me for the talk. One said: "You're quite the most interesting person we've met on our walk." His compliment didn't have time to inflate my ego, for another poked him. "Actually, you mean, she's the only person we've talked to this week." They all found this hysterically funny.

As they prepared to leave for the evening, they gathered at my bunk. "Would you like to go out drinking with us this evening?" I showed them my mummy-wrapped toes. I declined their invitation gracefully. They all seemed relieved.

Pluie du matin n'arrête pas le pèlerin...
Mais pluie toute la journée fait sentir le chien mouillé !

CAMINO—DAY 10

Chilled to the Bone

Postcard # 10—May 3, 2010 sent from Viana, Espana

Today in Los Arcos I had my feet worked on by a sympatico nurse and then set out in the rain walking on some very steep/rocky paths to Viana—quite chilly all the way, but incredibly lovely countryside, flowers loving the rain. Last night in Los Arcos, I attended a special Pilgrims Mass—very moving service conducted by a multi-lingual priest, most inclusive. Afterwards he called the Pilgrims to the front, shook hands with each, blessed each of us & acknowledged our dozen or more countries. Tonight in Viana I am not in a Pilgrim refugio as all the beds were taken. It was raining & I had just completed 19.0km or 11.4 mi. I went into the San Pedro Hostal . . . very tired. Very happy. Thinking of Grandpa, Nathan, Amelia, Francisco & ELENA.

Journal—Day 10 (Monday) May 3, 2010 written in Viana

This am in Los Arcos I could not deny that my feet needed medical attention, so once again off to a Centro de Salud where a very nice woman doctor spent about 30 minutes cleaning, wrapping and dressing all my little raw piggies. There were tears flowing because of the pain. She was pretty serious & advised me to stop walking for a week . . . as I left rather dejectedly, she called me back into the room, cut bandages & tape & gauze enough for several dressings and handed them to me. There were more tears in my eyes at her kindness. She stepped to her purse, withdrew something & placed it in the knee pocket of my trousers. "Pray for me when you get to Santiago," she added. Tonight I discovered her gift to be a little tube of L'Occitane French Lavender Foot Creme & the tears came again. It is so cold out & spitting rain, but I made it 11.4 miles up, over and down several steep ascents and descents. Rough going throughout the day and once arrived in Viana all beds were taken in the Albergues. "Completo, Completo". I have taken a room at the nearest hotel, (the San Pedro) at 35 Euros and chilled & wet to the bone, was ensconced in a room only to discover no heat or hot water. The barkeep has just gravely informed me "No heat is available. All heat is turned off on May 1." I stayed, for I had paid . . .

Reflection on Day 10, written back home in San Francisco

"Outwardly, one's life may suffer every kind of limitation, from bodily paralysis to miserable surroundings, but inwardly it is free in meditation to reach out to a sphere of light, beauty, truth, love and power."

Paul Bruton

As I think back on May 3, 2010, Day 10, I remember it as my most vulnerable time on the Camino. Pain and rawness racked my feet and toes as I left the dormitory in the morning, and I had difficulty locating the medical clinic. When I finally was seated in the waiting room after filling out some clinic paperwork, my whole body was chilled and the pain in my foot was worse because of the unseasonally cold weather.

I was summoned into an examination room and motioned onto a table that felt ice cold. A woman doctor approached and examined the foot. She looked serious and called another clinician in for consultation. He probed and pushed at the toes and he, too, looked serious. I felt powerless as I could not understand the discussion between them. Every time they touched the right foot, it was excruciating. I clearly got one part of their non-stop Spanish to me—"Don't walk for a week" which they emphasized by putting checkmarks on each day of the calendar.

But in the mental and physical pain of my situation there was a gift for me—the doctor's ensuing kindness and gentle demeanor in cleaning, dressing and wrapping the toes and foot. She took extra time and trouble to prepare several days of bandages, tape and gauze for me to use. And she so extravagantly took from her purse a new expensive tube of lavender foot creme and slipped it into my pocket. These were not actions just to make me feel better, but were intrinsically and freely given to promote healing. I didn't understand these things at the moment, for I was emotionally vulnerable and preoccupied with my pain as I left the clinic.

When I got outside, it was raining, windy and decidedly colder. I hurried up the street and ducked into an empty church. This would prove to be a good place to dig my raingear out of the backpack and decide what to do about continuing the walk or settling in for a few days to rest the foot. I lowered my backpack to the chapel floor, then decided to just sit comfortably on a bench for awhile.

An old woman came into the church and settled nearby and began fingering her rosary. I watched as she moved from decade to decade, and remembering my father's rosary in my waistpack, took it out and began my own rosary. It had been years since I had gone through this drill, and it seemed awkward at first, then touchingly simple and reassuring. Over and over, decade after decade: "Hail, Mary, full of grace, the Lord is with thee. Blessed art thou among women, and Blessed is the fruit of thy womb, Jesus. Holy Mary, Mother of God, pray for us sinners, now and in the hour of our death. Amen." Over and over and over.

When I finished the whole rosary, the old woman was gone. Why on earth had I spent all this time on vocal prayers when I had given up all my childhood religious practices? And yet, I realized, I had not been praying for anything in particular, just drifting back to my youth, just acknowledging the Mother of Jesus. I shifted on the bench. My body was completely quiet, even comfortable. My mind quieted to a standstill. The church, the altar, the statues and other religious trappings seemed to disappear and reappear in my consciousness. I was not alone.

"Here I am. I intend to sit in your Presence. I intend to consent to your Presence and action within." And then I let go. Let go. I sat meditatively for another half hour or so, occasionally aware, even engaged with thinking, but always letting go of ideas and thoughts. Letting go. Letting go. If an agitated thought arose around my pain, I let it go. Concern about losing a week of my time schedule if I stopped to rest the foot, I let that thought go too—just released it. Concern about the cold weather and walking in the rain, let it go, let it go. Concern about reaching a dorm in the village of Viana eleven miles away, let that thought go also.

The doors of the church started to open and close with the arrival of several middle aged women who immediately began choir practice. One woman had a miniature Chihuahua in her purse which let out one sharp bark, then growled at every friend who came near. I took note as the woman fussed over her dog, talking baby talk and adjusting a foolish little ill-fitting jacket around its skinny haunches. She passed nuggets of doggie treats constantly to the nervous little creature, even as the women sang the first song. The organ seemed to be missing several keys and after a botched hymn and a noisy discussion among the singers, an electronic keyboard materialized from the sacristy. Choir practice began again in earnest. The little dog had escaped his carrying case and was now sleeping on the altar steps.

It was definitely time for me to head out, rain cape covering most of me and the pack. The Ibuprophen was masking the pain. I was back to my old self and began to walk on. I would try to make it to Viana. Concentrating on finding my way out of town put me in a new frame of mind. I actually found walking in the rain quite refreshing. I was heading into beautiful, mist-enshrouded countryside.

The paths to Viana were steep both up and down. And rocky, difficult as I walked hour after hour. I very carefully maneuvered wet and slick areas, especially on the descents, and several times needed to hop on rocks over little streams rushing across the paths. My walking poles anchored me at every step. Winds gusted and the downpour was steady. I saw no other pilgrims on the path but I have the distinct memory of being joyful on that walk, having strength for it, feeling it was the right thing to do despite the doctor's warning to stay off the foot. If pain drew my attention, I counted to 100 in a kind of rhythm and it passed. I'd never been out in the elements quite like this before. It seemed courageous, a real adventure.

And I suppose it was a real adventure. At a point as I reached the crest of a hill, the wind lifted my rain cape and twisted it awkwardly over my head. I dropped my poles in the mud and in wrestling with that flimsy red plastic poncho, the pressure from the backpack was too great and the cape ripped pitifully, shredding up the back. Nothing to do but walk on, the raincoat flapping and I looking and feeling like a wet red hen caught in a rainstorm and waddling towards the henhouse.

I reached Viana after my eleven mile walk soaked to the skin and chilled to the bone. I was not successful securing a bunk in either of the two dormitories, and the hospitaleros both announced, I thought rather cockily, "no, no, completo, completo." Suddenly I was completely vulnerable again and near tears. A map was thrust into my hands with arrows drawn up and down streets to a circled hotel quite some distance away. I was not a happy pilgrim. I put my backpack on, picked up my poles and headed out in the rain to find the circle on the map. I suddenly felt exhausted, discouraged, fearful and ached like I might be coming down with the flu. I plodded down streets and around dark corners. My map was soon soaked and unreadable, but at last!!! the Hotel San Pedro.

A cheerful bartender in the hotel registered me and carried my things upstairs to a little room with a bath, then left with a wave. Oh, to take a nice warm bath and dry these clothes, I thought, and proceeded to run the water and unpack my entire backpack on the double bed. And only 35 Euros for all this luxury!!! I checked on the water—it wasn't getting warm. I checked the radiators—they were cold. Hm-mmmm!!! How to turn on the heat? There were no controls on the radiator, and the water was definitely not getting warm. This would require dressing again and going downstairs to take care of the matter with the bartender.

It was not difficult to pantomime my dilemma—the bartender understood immediately, mimicking my problems back to me accurately and sucking in his breath quite sympathetically. He took me over to a calendar hanging in the entryway, pointing to the day's date of May 3. I thought I understood what he meant, but then he did more sucking and sliced his hands through the air, pointing to May 1 to indicate when the heat had been turned off for the summer. I let all this sink in. "O'k, but what about the hot water for a bath?" I pantomimed. He pretended not to understand, laughed heartily, thrust out his hand and shook mine. He turned to greet some new customers and I turned and walked to my room.

Somehow or other, I just tolerated the situation. I wasn't in any condition to make a scene with the bartender. Nor did I feel capable to leave and search for other accommodations. I endured a cold cat bath. It was too cold to go out to dinner, so I ate a can of tuna fish and some crackers, took my Ibuprophen, put all my clothes on for warmth and with stiff fingers, wrote Elena's postcard for the day and my journal entry. I'd found the little tube of Lavendar Foot Creme the doctor had placed in my pocket and solemnly anointed my feet. It warmed my skin and my heart and perfumed the air. I was satisfied with the day. I was happy and grateful for what I had. Sleep came easily.

- Bon d'accord j'ai oublié de réserver...
mais le prochain gîte est à 23 km...
Pas de quoi faire cette tête !

Camino—Day 11

The Extra Leg in my Bed

Postcard # 11—May 4, 2010 sent from Navarette, Espana

Dearest Elena: What a day today after sleeping 12 hr w/o waking. I will tell you my big surprise! It has turned quite frosty. I had to put on all my clothes & my torn rain cape, & I had to buy gloves to use with the poles. It rained & sleeted a bit; however, today I walked 21.2km or 12.7 mi. from Viana to Navarette. Cold, but still beautiful. Several of the miles were walking through Logrono, a lovely old medieval city. All the towns & villages I go through are medieval, many dating back to the 10th Century. Tonight 2 German bicyclists & I got the last 3 beds in the dorm at Navarrete, & to celebrate that good luck, we shared a wonderful picnic supper in the big kitchen. Reminded me so of Michael & Lore Weissenberger. Love to my Little Tootsie from Grandma

Journal—Day 11 (Tuesday) May 4, 2010 written at Navarette

Last night after paying for a room with no heat, I took a cold cat bath, put all my clothes on & slept 12 hours. I felt good despite the temperature in the room, so this morning on I went again in the staggering cold, with my hands relentlessly exposed walking with hiking poles. Snow on the mountains, raining & sleeting slowed me down. I walked through the lovely city of Logrono, stopping to buy gloves. Alas, the several womens' shops where I stopped had no gloves—only their spring & summer lines. I was forlorn, and a shopgirl who looked at me with pity, sat me down, slipped my backpack off, wrung her hands & tore out of the shop coming back 10 min later from where I'll never know, with 3 pr. of gloves. One pair bright red w. sequins & feathers, one shortie pair in white eyelet embroidery & 1 sturdy black mens gloves in suede with soft wool lining. It was not a difficult decision. I forked over 39 Euros (about $50) for the black ones. What relief walking in the sleet. Tonight in Navarette good luck to get last 3 bunks in a 3rd story dorm with a German couple (bicyclists). The 3 of us very compatible, and I ate in communal kitchen with them. Spoke of Irache Monastery wine.

Reflection on Day 11, written back home in San Francisco

"Walking alone does not prevent companionship and community.
—Mary Wyman

I awakened this morning after a twelve hour sleep in the Viana hotel. Body heat and all my clothes had gotten me through the night. The room was frosty. I could see my breath. My foot was extremely sore and tender, but I was happy I had walked on from Los Arcos and not succumbed to the doctor's advice to stay there and rest.

Upon leaving the heatless hotel, the weather that greeted me was overcast and more like March than May. I was barely out of Viana, when it started to simultaneously rain and sleet. Standing under a tree, I took out my ripped-up-the-back rain cape which I gerryrigged sideways to protect the backpack. It didn't work and was so futile and ridiculous that I had to laugh. I could barely move my fingers which were exposed from walking with the poles and they were red and raw from the sleet. To add to the absurdity of it all, I entered into several miles of pure muddy trail, no weeds along the side to cushion the mud, just muddy tracks and ruts. Every step of the trails through vineyards and planted fields presented gooey mud 3 to 4 inches deep. My beautiful waterproof Keen shoes were tested to the limit. The sound of each shoe going deep into the mud, then slugging and slurping noisily as I pulled it out, remains with me still.

It was a temptation to stop in the beautiful city of Logrono to recuperate from the strenuous morning's walk, but after lunch, Ibuprophen and buying some sturdy gloves, I pushed on to my target town of Navarette. I tried to concentrate on the beautiful countryside, especially the snow-covered low mountains as seen through rain and sleet. Who would have expected weather like this in May?

At one point, I walked by a saw mill in full operation to my left, with a highway to my right. I loved the noise and bustle evident throughout the area, trucks stacked high with cut trees backed into cutting stations, empty trucks ready to take out the cut boards, the industrial saws buzzing and ripping through the logs, dust flying and leftover chunks of wood falling to the ground. It looked like dangerous work—at least work that required a high degree of attention around that equipment. But then my perspective shifted to the wire fences along side the road between me and the sawmill. Crosses filled the fences. I could only take in the significance slowly. Little sticks and what appeared to be longer wood shavings from the saw mill were interwoven in the wire fences to form thousands of crosses anywhere from 3 by 3 inches to 2 or 3 feet wide.

Why? I don't know, but I can guess. One pilgrim attached sticks to make a cross on this old fence, and thousands more pilgrims through the years followed the leader. Materials blown from the saw mill were plentiful alongside the road. And I imagine it was symbolic of the Camino in some way to each pilgrim, an activity that appealed to them to stop and add their cross—to place their mark along the way. I recall another such place closer to Santiago, and also another area where thousands of little cairns, or stacked rocks appeared. So, windy and cold as it was, I too stopped, picked up sawmill detritus and formed a cross in the fence.

As I arrived at the long curved driveway of the Navarette dormitory, two German bicyclists arrived. They looked miserable and in real need of shelter. We went inside and sat down to register. No one was in sight but at least a little heat warmed the room. We were soon talking—about the weather, distances, time on the trail, just casual pilgrim conversation. They had come some 90 kilometers that day—54 miles. "I can't go another kilometer in this weather," the woman said. "I am not moving from this dorm." "Amen to that!" I answered. "Me either!!!!!!"

After 15 minutes in which the three of us began to yawn from the warmth in the room, a hospitalero showed up and announced gravely that he only had two bunks left. Hm-mmmm. He is sure, I thought, to give the two bunks to the German couple. We all looked at each other. The hospitalero sucked in his breath. "It's a pity on a night like this. Only two beds left for a party of three. What do you want to do?" The three of us ignored his question. We remained silent for a full five minutes. The man busied himself at his desk, counting the registrations and continuing to suck in his breath. I felt no anxiety; instead I was drifting into sleep.

The man stood up, raised his arm and said: "I will go count my beds again. Wait here." And up the stairs he went, returning jubilantly ten minutes later. "There is another empty bed on the third floor. You can all stay." We stirred ourselves, producing our Camino credentials and passports. He marked down our information including our ages and looked at me particularly: "Oh Senora, this is bad weather for you to be on the Camino. The weather forecast is for another week of cold and rain."

To my surprise, as we were led upstairs, the two bicyclists hugged me. The woman said: "This is wonderful news for you. We were so afraid that you would have to push on. Let's get settled and have a drink together to celebrate." I agreed to meet them in thirty minutes, but as we were led up to the 1st floor and saw the crowded conditions, people everywhere, and then to the second floor, where the two Germans would stay, I could only concentrate on the sheer tightness of quarters.

At last the hospitalero led me to the third floor where there were about 35 beds tucked into an attic—12 stacked bunks on one side and on the other side twelve singles lined up side by side, so that the full lengths of the beds were tight against each other and made one giant bed. There was not even one inch space between those mattresses. One could only access the bed by crawling in from the foot and inching forward. All this was hard to take in. I looked out a dormer window at the rain and thought of the woman in St. Jean Pied de Port who thrust the list of fancy Parador accommodations into my hand. She knew the conditions I would encounter on the Camino. I also remembered my foolish reply to her: "Oh no, I don't need that list. I'm a real Pilgrim."

My thoughts were interrupted by hearing my name called from some few beds away. It was two sisters close to my age travelling together with whom I'd had several friendly conversations over the past two weeks. It was always fun to see someone with whom there was a connection. We laughed about the coziness of the 3rd floor, the anemic heating system for which we were all grateful, and hearing that I didn't have a pillow, one woman offered up hers, declaring she never used one. Another stroke of good luck for me.

I set about personal organization but it was a real task as all backpacks were placed at the foot of the beds, lessening floor space even more. Because weather was so bad, pilgrims were not out and about in the town. Every bed had someone on it, sleeping, or reading, and one man with a guitar played some lovely and gentle melodies. I noted with amusement that the two beds tucked tight on either side of mine had been assigned to men, both napping as I unpacked my things. I calculated that when I got into bed later that night, there would be about 20 inches on either side of me to the actual person in the adjacent bed.

At the appointed time, I went to find the German couple and they immediately suggested we put together a picnic supper in the pilgrim kitchen which they deemed acceptable and very clean. We would meet there in fifteen minutes. I took a short run down the street to a tiny grocery store, purchasing the best bottle of vino tinto available on the shelf (5 Euros), a selection of olives, two slabs of pate and a long fat loaf of beautiful crusty brown bread.

I located the dormitory kitchen and staked out space for the three of us at a long pilgrims' table. Finding a corkscrew and glasses was easy. I rummaged through several cabinets and drawers in the kitchen, locating paper plates and napkins, plus odds and ends of cutlery. Tired as I was, I sensed a party in the making. The German bicyclists showed up and we were soon laying a feast, for they had brought beautiful smoked salmon, sliced sausages, several cheeses, crackers and chocolates for dessert.

What a great time we had together. How warm and genuine we each felt in the other's company. Their English was excellent and they each kept declaring how happy they were to have a chance to practice their fifth language on an American. We spoke at length about the differences between seeing the Camino on foot and seeing it from a bicycle. I was amazed as they related the short amount of time bicyclists allotted to make the ride to Santiago, less than two weeks, and they were incredulous that I had allotted 52 days from my start point to my prearranged travel date back home. They mentioned having passed by the Irache Monastery that very morning, and stopping for a drink of wine at the fountain. They were amused when I related my disappointment at having found the fountain turned off two days before on Sunday. "Oh, well," said the man, "you're sure to taste Irache wine one day," and he and the woman smiled at each other.

Good conversation permeated with many laughs. Tolerable foot pain. A satisfying picnic supper. It didn't get better than this on the Camino in the evenings. We soon finished up the bottle of wine I'd brought and cleared the table before starting dessert. I offered to make herb tea but each declined. The chocolates were set out.

The man voiced a trumpet roll through his two closed fists, then reached into his pack on the floor and produced a water bottle. "And here I present to you, Mrs. Mary, a bottle of Irache Monastery wine, fresh from the fountain this morning. This will help us digest our chocolates." He grandly poured the wine and we toasted each other:

"Buen Camino. Buen Camino." I drew my journal out of the waistpack I wore and found the message I'd copied down from the plaque at the Irache Fountain: "Pilgrim, if you wish to arrive at Santiago full of strength and vitality, have a drink of this great wine and make a toast to happiness." The woman said softly as we finished up the delicious Irache wine: "This evening is the highlight of my Camino." I could only answer "I will never forget the two of you and this evening's supper. I am so grateful for your companionship and generosity."

The three of us cleared our end of the table in the kitchen, surprised that we were the last to leave the room. The kitchen was spotless, despite the 100 pilgrims who had cooked and eaten there throughout the evening. It was 10:00pm, and the dormitory lights were out as I crept up the stairs to the 3rd floor. Only a low light coming out of the bathroom on the second floor illuminated the stairway and I could see nothing at all on the 3rd floor. How would I find my bed in the dark? How would I find my way to the bathroom in the night? Oh dear Lord, what if there is a fire tonight? I sat down on the top step of the 3rd floor to get my bearings in this packed building and rehearse exit plans. If there was an emergency, it would be clear in my mind to grab my shoes and poles, backpack and waistpack, come straight to this stairway and make my way down to the front door, guided by the bannister.

But now I had to find my assigned sleeping space. I crept along the low wall of solid beds, stumbling along and feeling backpacks until I recognized mine. I was truly afraid that a flashlight would turn on and someone would shout "Thief." I patted the foot of my bed just to be sure it was empty. Snoring resonated throughout the attic room and the stale smell of socks and wet shoes permeated the air.

I took a deep breath and gave myself a pep talk: "You can do this, Mary. Remember how lucky you are to have this bed and pillow. Oh, and forget the pajamas tonight. Just crawl in bed with your clothes on and cover up." As I settled in, I marveled at how the two men on either side of me were as close as my husband in our bed at home. There was no separation. I took another deep breath. "Oh, well, this is the Camino."

As soon as I got in bed and covered up, the man on my left rolled over and his leg suddenly jutted out from his covers and landed on my narrow cot. He continued snoring so I was not alarmed. I didn't want to disturb my covers which I'd carefully tucked in around me for warmth, so I sat up somewhat annoyed and pushed on his leg. It wouldn't budge. I pushed again. Nothing. I tried lifting it over to its proper place. No luck. I poked him hard on the leg with my elbow. Was this a bad dream? I knew I'd never go to sleep with that loose leg out from under its covers and invading my bed. My list of options was short. I got out of bed reluctantly, knelt on the foot of my bed for leverage, and lifted and pushed that leg with all my strength. It went over to where it belonged. The man made some low-throated gurgling noises, coughed and continued snoring.

I went to sleep, but didn't have a good feeling about that leg. Sure enough, after a middle of the night trip to the bathroom, I crawled forward on my bed and this time, discovered two feet comfortably resting on the middle of my mattress. At least this time I was up and not all tucked into my blanket. The man was on his left side, lying across his bed with his legs slightly curled and his feet squarely in the middle of my sleeping area. This would require a new tactic and I was too annoyed to be subtle about it. I knelt close to his feet, picked them up and plopped them over where they belonged. He rearranged himself on his side and continued sleeping heavily. I, however, stayed awake until the early bird pilgrims started dressing, sack-stuffing, zipping and flushing—all this early action to ensure that they were out on the path by dawn. That lulled me into a deep sleep and when I awakened a bit after 8:00 am, everybody on the 3rd floor was gone. The bell to signal closing time was ringing. I cleaned and dressed my sore foot, then hustled to get out of that dorm and on the path which would take me to the little town of Azofra.

Ouf ! La fin du turbin et le début du chemin...

CAMINO—DAY 12

Cold Feet, Warm Heart

Postcard # 12—May 5, 2010 sent from Azofra, Espana

Dearest Elena: Today it was so cold that I shivered my entire walk from Navarrete to Azofra & I laughed out loud when I saw that the mountains were all covered with fresh snow. It was so beautiful with all the Rioja wine/grape orchards & the purple-blue bachelor button flowers in full bloom by the road. The last few miles into Azofra were challenging but even though, I walked 22.8km or 13.7 miles. Landed at a wonderful refugio—only 2 single beds per room (very simple) & I had no roommate, so I could shower down the hall, relax, repack, work on my feet. In the communal dining room, I ate my tuna mousse, crackers, apple & cheese & drank a short bottle of tinto vino—very happy tonight—too tired, weather too bad, too cold to go out for dinner—great camaraderie as people from all over the world cooked & ate. Later, I made microwave popcorn and passed it all around. They all loved it. Love from Camino Grandma

Journal—Day 12 (Wednesday) May 5, 2010 written in Azofra

Haven't missed a day writing a postcard to Elena, then elaborating on the day with journal entry. Hope those postcards are reaching my grand daughter. Hope I don't lose this journal. This was a surprise to walk 22.8km or 13.7mi and it seemed easy until the last two miles to the Albergue with its big patio. Arrived in the rain & was delighted to find myself in a tiny room for 2, & nobody else showed up. Very tired in a very nice facility. Surprise! There was the Canadian calling loudly "Mary" as I heard myself summoned from across the hall. Actually glad to see her and that she too was weathering the cold front. After a bit of conversation, I settled into my room, showered, repacked & walked out alone to purchase a few groceries in the cold & rain. I had hungrily bought a container of soup only to discover it was actually a thick tomato sauce. Gave it away to a woman who will share her pasta with me at dinner. I have determined to break down & buy some more layers of clothes to ward off the crazy cold. Rain is beating on my windows and tomorrow's forecast is for rain. Azofra a friendly, sweet, medieval town. Alas, my feet are so cold.

Reflection on Day 12, written in San Francisco in 2011

"The little things? The little moments? They aren't little."
Jon Kabat-Zinn

The grasses on the side of the road were all frosty as I set out from Navarette on beautiful paths through stunning countryside. At least it was not raining this morning, and although clouds hung low, I could see that fresh snow had covered the distant mountains in the night. Within an hour Ibuprophen allowed me to walk easily and forget the problematic foot that I was now consciously favoring. In truth, I was limping, and concerned that my whole body was out of alignment.

For about ten miles, there were flowers blooming profusely along both sides of the path. How were these wild bachelor buttons surviving in the cold rain and evening frosts? They were that purple-blue that delighted me as a child in the flowerbeds of my mother's big vegetable garden on the farm. They bloomed late spring in southern Illinois and were prominently placed in our house on the May altar around which we said the family rosary each evening. It had been years since I thought of that childhood religious practice. I loved it then. Year after year in May, we celebrated Mary the mother of Jesus by gathering as a family around a small altar in my mother's bedroom. We assembled after supper, getting down on our knees for the duration of the five decades of the Rosary. "Hail Mary, full of grace, the Lord is with thee." Over and over and over 53 times until we were finished.

It was my job from age five to keep the vases on the altar filled during May. When I was older, I spent hours by myself every week picking flowers and arranging bouquets by color, stacking books of different sizes on the table to make platforms of various heights for the vases around our statue of Mary. Crocheted doilies covered the platforms. Mine was only one part of the ritual that made every May evening in our family an earnest and sacred event. A happy childhood memory like this one created for me on the Camino an intense experience of grateful memories—to my parents for constant love and security, a sacred sense of Another and a spiritual sense of the Divine that stayed with me for these 70 years.

Day after day as I walked the Camino, I frequently observed things in nature—like the purple-blue bachelor buttons—that catapulted me to strong, full-blown memories of another time in my life. Long-forgotten memories surfaced, people and events and things forgotten perhaps forever, but triggered by the silence of the long walk and intense observation of the collage of passing scenery.

Not all the memories were benign or simple childhood experiences. Vivid memories surfaced unbidden from every stage of my life—happy and unhappy times, pleasant and unpleasant people and colleagues, good and bad outcomes, rational and irrational decisions, fulfilled and unfulfilled dreams. And in truth, as these important memories arose, I tended to process them, then let them go. Let go. Let go.

If a serious or troubling memory surfaced, I acknowledged and thought it through. Then let it go. Many troubling memories from my Camino walk were so far in the past as to be irresolvable. Past memories are after all, in the past. What to do with anger, disappointment, grief or guilt arising and churning from an old memory? Holding on and repetitiously reworking negative emotions hadn't worked well for me in the past. Mostly over my life, I had just suppressed and buried anger, disappointment and guilt. On the Camino, I found myself being grateful for these memories and looked them straight in the eye. At this stage of my life, I was a different person than before. I liberally exercised gratefulness and forgiveness on my walk, forgiving myself as well as others in my troubling memories. Every time this grateful and forgiving response was triggered, I felt a kind of new freedom, a relief in my soul.

This process of strong memories surfacing as I walked repeated itself every single day. I remembered a saying attributed to Plato's philosophy: "Life that has not been examined, is not worth living. Life that has not been lived, is not worth examining." True enough. I attributed my memories to a natural process of walking alone, becoming the silence, observing intensely by using my five senses and coaxing open my heart whenever it automatically closed to an encounter. It was for me, I came to realize during my 48 day walk, a variation on what Thomas Keating OCSO would call "Divine Therapy."

The cold did not abate through the day, and finally I arrived at the very nice dormitory at Azofra. Check-in was easy and because of the bad weather, all the pilgrims were sitting around in the enormous lounge next to the kitchen. The little room I was assigned to had just two beds and I was delighted to learn that I would not have a roommate. What luxury after the previous evening's wall to wall beds and the visiting leg in the middle of the night. I slowly unpacked, took a leisurely shower and had an uninterrupted, meditative period of Centering Prayer.

After a brief foray to a nearby grocery store, I came back to the kitchen with what I thought was a box of tomato soup. Other pilgrims cooking in the kitchen gathered around to see what I was preparing, and we all had a good laugh when it turned out to be a thick, congealed tomato sauce. A woman cooking pasta said she would love to have it and I handed it over happily. I was under the impression that she invited me to share her pasta, and I happily accepted, hanging around and chatting with her and different folks as they fried chicken, made salads or hot cereals for dinner. I opened my half bottle of wine and poured us each a drink. She happily accepted, toasting me warmly. The woman drained the pasta, tossed it in a hot skillet with my tomato sauce, then piled it on a huge platter, sprinkled it with cheese, carried it into the dining room and began to eat from the platter. I went over and she gushed: "Delicious. I am so hungry and this just is a perfect dinner for me. She lifted her glass in a toast: "Oh, and thanks for the wine." I watched and thought: what is wrong with this picture? We clinked glasses and I wandered away.

Plan B emerged for my dinner. I went to my room, giggling all the way over how I misunderstood the dinner invitation, rummaged around in my backpack and came up with a tin of tuna mousse, some crackers, an apple and a banana. I took this down to the dining room along with two packages of microwave popcorn. I retrieved my wine and sat down across from a woman with whom I was becoming rather well acquainted. We were deep in conversation when the pasta woman brought over her empty wine glass and gestured to me: "Just a half glass more, please." I poured her glass half-full, clinked my glass to hers, and she returned to her platter of diminishing pasta.

When I observed that people had pretty much finished eating, I slipped into the kitchen and microwaved two packages of popcorn, then passed it all around and everybody had a handful. People seemed surprised and delighted. Some did not know what it was. The good feelings generated by that popcorn far surpassed the sort of odd dessert that I had offered them. In a way, my heart overflowed with happiness and gratitude that evening in the dorm at Azofra. People became warm and friendly. Nearly everybody going off to bed stopped by the table where I was sitting and profusely thanked me for the little treat.

I got up, cleared away my empty tin and banana peel and announced I was going to bed and that my feet were ice cold and had been that way all day, despite a hot bath. One woman commented that she just microwaves a towel for a few moments and takes that to bed. "Just don't burn yourself," she warned. I quickly went to my room, got my towel for a quick microwave, and went to sleep with feet as toasty warm as my heart.

CAMINO—DAY 13

Chickens in the Church—Oh My!!!!!

Postcard # 13—May 6, 2010 sent from Santo Domingo de la Calzada, Espana

Dear Elena: The Camino never ends. Today I walked from Azofra to Santo Domingo de Calzada in slogging—stick to your shoes & ooze over the top mud for 17.4km or 10.4mi. It was chilling cold, but I stopped every 3 or 4 miles in a village for a coffee or some lunch. Landed tonight in a very nice Pilgrims Albergue where the old innkeeper took one look at my pitiful self and opened up a locked separate dorm to give me a lower bunk. I could fully see the cathedral tower from my bed. Tonight I went to Church for Mass & saw the famous chickens of Santo Domingo that live in the church. They crowed all through the services. Cock a Doodle-doo. Very tired. Very footsore. Very happy. Cock a Doodle Doo from Grandma.

Journal—Day 13 (Thursday) May 6, 2010 written in Santo Domingo de la Calzada

This was a very special day & perhaps because of the famous chickens in the church. From Azofra this morning all the way to Santo Domingo was rain, cold & mud. The Pilgrims' multi-floored dorm at Santa Domingo was very welcoming & I just collapsed on a couch in the lobby, joining other pilgrims in a kind of check-in queue. The place was warm. We had to take off our shoes and stash them with our poles in an adjacent mud room. Struck up a conversation with a woman my age named Carol from Jamboroo, Australia. The old gentleman who checked us in showed us to our dorm beds on the 3rd floor via a service elevator. He kept saying with a twinkle in his eye: "sh-h-h, everybody else has to walk up." I was so grateful for a lower bunk, his kindness, Carol's no-nonsense lovely accented English. My lower bunk had full view of the Santa Domingo Cathedral tower with a stork peeking out of its nest. I went out after a rest, used the Internet for an hour (always reassuring to get messages from family & friends), then bought an XXX-Large blue sweatshirt to layer for warmth—added an extra layer of socks, & comfort at last as I headed to the Cathedral to get a good seat for the 7:00pm Rosary. Pretty interesting, although I understood little of the special event that was happening. Chickens and roosters in the church—incredible way to sustain the ancient myth of the young man accused of theft. Also stayed for a Mass with a bishop, hence lots of dressed up locals in attendance.

Reflection on Day 13, written in San Francisco in 2011

"Awesome!!!! The Best New Thing in the World."

Rachel Maddow, Newscaster, MSNBC

An aside to the Camino walk: There is a journalist in New York who is a great favorite of mine for two reasons. She is a fearless liberal, a brilliant and articulate intellectual who ferrets out truth and justice, especially in the political arena. She's tough as nails. Calls it like it is. Well-respected. Feared even for her political truth-telling.

But there is another deeply developed side of Rachel Maddow quite evident on her daily, hour-long show. I call her the Renaissance woman—beautiful in a natural way, a heart bigger than one could fathom in a journalist, warm, loyal, civil under pressure and in my opinion, she models and embodies a sense that all people on earth are brothers and sisters, despite their political views. That all life is connected. And she frequently features and celebrates the wacky event or person in life by joyfully announcing "Awesome!!!! Best new thing in the world." How Rachel would love the Chickens in the Cathedral at Santa Domingo de la Calzada and their ancient legend.

The day's walk from Azofra to Santo Domingo de la Calzada in the rain and sludgy mud tried my endurance (and shoes) to the limits and, I think, that of all walking pilgrims on the trail. I had a heightened concern about falling. The pathways through various landscapes were just consistently oozy mud—left, right and center. There was no getting away from it. It was not normal mud, but clay, glue like, capturing the foot at each step, oozing ominously up over the shoe toes and sides, then gripping the foot in place until extra effort was applied by the walker to pull the shoe out and try for another step.

To add to the general inconvenience of walking in the mud, about every ten steps the shoes collected such a massive and heavy amount of goo on the soles and sides that I had to stop and clean them by stepping off the road to find a patch of grass. I observed another pilgrim pushing the mire off his shoes with the tips of his walking poles but I didn't like the results when I tried that tactic. I already had trouble with walking in the mud with poles. The mud clung to the tips of the poles and grew into a softball size, rendering them too heavy and therefore useless even in steadying me. I finally settled on a 2-foot long stick I picked up on the shoulder of the path, held it under my arm while walking, and used it to pry the mud loose from my shoes and poles when it became intolerable.

This was slow-going and I was nervous about the time it would take under these conditions to walk the 10.5 miles to Santo Domingo. Could I possibly make it by dark? This was also the coldest day on the Camino so far. My body was chilled despite wearing <u>all</u> my clothes, including pajamas, 2 pairs of trousers, 2 tee shirts and a long sleeved tee, plus a cotton shirt buttoned up, two pairs of socks and a 4X4 foot lightweight blanket over my shoulders that I had borrowed from Aer Lingus. I looked like a giant sausage slogging down the path. The pesky winds relentlessly pierced the cotton layering. I determined to purchase warmer clothing when and if I reached my day's destination.

A stop for lunch in Ciruena bolstered my determination to reach Santo Domingo, and indeed I straggled into the old medieval section by late afternoon. I gratefully accepted a bed in a very nice dormitory holding about 80 pilgrims. I was exhausted, and could only think about showering to get warm and going to bed. But I looked out my window surprised to have a straight-on view of the Cathedral of Santo Domingo—and an enormous, precarious, absolutely enchanting stork's nest with its resident tenant perched on one of the towers. I found a chair and pulled it up to the window for a closer look. The stork was quite active, though not flying. It would stir in its nest, flapping its wings and seemed to be arranging and rearranging something deep within the nest. For the half-hour I watched, a second stork glided through the sky and perched on the nest, deposited something, then majestically lifted and flew away. This display energized me to partake in evening activities of sending emails, purchasing warm clothing and seeing whether the famous chickens were indeed ensconced in the Cathedral according to legend.

Oh, yes . . . The legends of Spain surrounding Santiago. There are dozens of these stories that have grown to support the Camino and are, in fact, part of Spanish culture. Most are allegorical tales which have incredible contrivances to illustrate solutions to moral and justice dilemmas, to reverse unrequited love, to achieve fame and fortune for a particular church or a town, or to sustain viability of religious pilgrimage routes. These stories have embedded themselves in larger Spanish history for hundreds of years. Many pilgrims over the centuries equated these stories with miracles and declared staunch belief in their validity. For skeptics, these legends are nothing more than charming but implausible stories associated with a certain time, person or place. In the early days of the Camino—late 1000's, early 1100's—this story I'm about to relate concerning the hanged man and the chickens, or slight variations of it, was being circulated throughout Europe to advertise Santo Domingo as a village of note along the route to Santiago.

What do you think, my dear Elena, about the legend I relate to you below? Is this a true story with a happy ending? Is it a story of a miraculous intervention by Saint James in the life of a pilgrim? Or is it a fairy tale which medieval public relations men in Santo Domingo fabricated to entice pilgrims to stop and spend their money on food and accommodations, and of course to visit the church, see those chickens in action—and leave money there as well?

Here's the story. A German family with a strapping young son was making the pilgrimage to Santiago to revere the saint's relics. They stopped for the night in an inn in Santo Domingo. Over the course of the evening the innkeeper's daughter flirted with the young man, and because she was older and more sophisticated, tried to seduce him and make a little money on the side. He repulsed her advances, and fled to his family's room. This so irritated the innkeeper's daughter that she conspired with a friend to hide some silver cups in the young man's backpack, which had conveniently been left outside the family room in the hallway.

The next morning as the family left the inn, local authorities were alerted, and upon frisking the young man, discovered the silver cups in his backpack. He would not confess to the crime, and despite his family's petitions to authorities, he was hanged that very day. They could not bring closure by burying him, for according to local custom, the body would remain swinging from the gallows until it rotted. Grief-stricken, the family had no choice but to proceed with their pilgrimage to Santiago de Compostela.

Upon returning from the journey to Santiago, the German family again stopped in Santo Domingo. Sorrowfully, they approached the square where their son had been hanged, and imagine their surprise to find him still hanging from the gallows, in good spirits and happy to see them. He was indeed alive and as he told them, being held aloft by Santiago himself, so that he wouldn't choke. The family raced to the authorities and found the chief official just sitting down to lunch on roasted chicken. He listened to their story and scoffed: "Your son is no more alive than this roasted chicken is alive." And at that moment, the roasted chicken shook itself, sprouting feathers and jumping all about the table, crowing and preening in front of the assemblage.

The official ran to the gallows with the family, ordered the young man's rope to be cut and helped lower him to the ground. All in attendance marveled at this miracle wrought by Santiago himself to put right a terrible miscarriage of justice. The family proceeded home to Germany with their son and supposedly spread the story of the miracle far and wide. Chickens were ensconced in cages in the local church to help establish Santo Domingo de la Calzada as the location of the story, as well as to inspire future pilgrims in the efficacy of their journey to revere the bones of Santiago, aka St. James the Apostle of Christ.

After reviewing that legend in my mind, I set off early evening for the Pilgrim's Mass and Rosary in the Cathedral. Having been a child raised on a farm, of course I wanted to see the chickens in the church. Nothing in my 70 years, however, prepared me for the events of the evening. I entered the Cathedral and immediately heard loud crowing overhead of a rooster and clucking of hens. I was thrilled. It's supposed to be very good luck for a pilgrim to hear the rooster in the church crow. I positioned myself on a side chair near the front, affording a good look at the chickens, the congregation and also the choir and altar.

Oh, those Cathedral chickens!!! There they were, displayed in quite a large cage suspended high over the pews at the entryway. Clearly visible to me, they were full-grown, full-blown red beauties, the rooster with long black tail feathers, the hens speckled and plump and ripe to seduce the rooster. I'd rarely seen more beautiful specimens competing at mid-west State Fairs for gold medals. The rooster crowed again. The hens clucked contentedly. This was quite a show.

The Cathedral was packed with 200-300 very well dressed locals who began praying the Rosary in full voice. A good number of scraggly pilgrims filled the remaining pews, some fingering their beads but most just oggling the chickens. The Rosary seemed to go on forever.

The church was warm and I grew sleepy from the melodious droning and repetitious cadence of the parishioners. Each time I nodded off, a rooster's Cock-a-doodle-doo would jar me awake, and I'd straighten up and turn my attention to the cages until I nodded again.

The Rosary ended, and a choir rose up from their seats and began singing exquisite classical church music with professionals singing solos. The rooster insistently joined in—I actually thought in all the right places. The singing was prelude to a bishop with lacy sleeves and full crimson regalia entering in procession with priests in long robes and surrounded by altar boys swinging incense. He began a formal Mass with great solemnity. Now I was curious and wide awake. Concerned even! Surely the rooster would not interrupt the bishop during Mass. Somehow, that wouldn't be proper. Priests must have some way to silence the rooster, I thought.

The Mass proceeded to the homily, which was offered by the bishop. Although I couldn't understand his words, I realized that this was a very important religious event in Santo Domingo. The bishop gave a sermon that I judged to be about 20 minutes in duration. I counted the rooster crowing seven times during the sermon. This wasn't muffled crowing in some distant side chapel. Those chickens were prominently close to the high altar. To the bishop's credit, he never missed a beat—didn't even acknowledge the rooster's efforts to collaborate with him. The rooster did, however, collaborate with the hens during that sermon. I recognized the sounds of the rooster and the hens in ecstasy, looked up, then quickly averted my eyes to those intimate moments. I observed one priest glancing nervously between the bishop and the cage, and two blushing altar boys giggling behind their hands.

After the Mass and communion I filed out of the Cathedral with the crowds, and gave one long, fond look back at the real stars of the evening—the preening and quite beautiful rooster and chickens in their cage high above the door. Absolutely bizarre the way their crowing and clucking and cuckolding had echoed throughout the Cathedral, but funny and sweet. "Awesome," Rachel Maddow would crow to the world about this ancient ritual. "Best new thing in the world."

CAMINO—DAY 14

The Mysterious Storks

Postcard # 14—May 7, 2010 sent from Belorado, Espana

Dear Elena: The rain continues!! A very kind woman from Australia gave me a bright red plastic backpack cover & I walked more comfortably in the rain from Santa Domingo this am to Belorado through several small villages, for a total today of 23.9km or 14.9 mi. Blisters continue. People from <u>all over the world</u> in the tiny little dorm room tonight—immediately around me are Koreans, Japanese, Canadians, Russians & Australians—mostly men. We all ate together tonight at a served Pilgrims Menu—most of us are walkers, but some bicyclists, who do about 90 km per day (over 50 mi) & they are exhausted. Everything today was beautiful but seeing 11 stork nests high on poles delighted me. In each were 2 stork mates sitting on eggs. How I wish we had storks in our back yard. Love from Grandma

Journal—Day 14 (Friday) May 7, 2010 written in Belorado

This am raining (of course)!!!! Carol from Australia gave me a red plastic cover for my backpack which works well in this weather. So grateful to her as there are no sporting shops to buy such things in small villages. Leaving Santa Domingo, I once again stopped in to see the chickens in the church . . . only clucking this am—the rooster was worn-out. As I left town, especially significant were the many stork nests on church steeples. Then on the edge of town, there were 11 high poles by the river, each with a platform and topped with a stork nest. As cold as it was by the water, I spent a long time at this wondrous place. Some of the nests were clearly reused by the storks year after year, just rebuilt higher for the new season. Some parts of the nests seemed old—to be stacked in layers over the years 3-4 feet high. Fascinating that the wind does not blow them away. This was along a waterway providing an excellent environment—thrilling to see storks in the nests, (presumably sitting on eggs) preening themselves and frequently to see one of the mates fly to the water, catch a fish and bring it back to the other. I've seen no stork babies yet. Tonight I am in a small one-room dorm in Belorado with bunkbeds all squished together—a real international community. Men & women share the space, & we're all mixed together in the dorm, assigned upper or lower bunks, sharing the bathroom & the showers also. Modesty is just a word, but I must admit that in the dorm itself, I mostly kept my eyes averted tonight as people undressed, showered & dressed again, all in open spaces. I think the man 2 bunks from me is quite ill. People are concerned. We ate a pilgrims' meal together tonight. I sat with a father & son—(ages 70 and 50) bicycling the entire Camino from Germany. Really wonderful people. Tonight, I'm nursing toe blisters as though they are little babies with colic. Second pair of socks do not help. Big toe is in serious need of help—it's so discolored purplish. Still, I look at these feet when I stop, or bathe, or stuff the right swollen foot into my shoe in the morning & am thankful to know and trust that Ibuprophin 600 after a bite of breakfast, lunch or dinner will allow me to nearly forget about the agony. Nothing deters. I'm actually very happy.

Reflection on Day 14, written back home in San Francisco

"The more clearly we can focus our attention on the wonders and realities of the universe about us, the less taste we shall have for destruction."

Rachel Carson

The toes were not exactly healing according to plan—I'd had blisters for two weeks on the Camino, and the morning's dressing of the feet in Santo Domingo was a truly painful session. The lovely woman from Australia came to my bunk to sympathize and insisted that she give me her sturdy plastic backpack cover as it was raining mightily. I was so grateful because my ripped rain cape was painfully inadequate and I didn't want to wait until 10:00am when stores would open.

Once out of the dorm, I stopped in a bar for an omelette and coffee, and my Ibuprophen. Fortified with protein, caffeine and a painkiller, the world took on a much brighter hue. I then walked through the remainder of Santo Domingo de la Calzada, admiring the stork nests on church steeples. I also spotted a nest in a residential area on the roof of a low garage. I hoped the owners of the property were receptive to this event that was unfolding. One stork was sitting on the nest, quite settled in. The other flew away, circling the neighborhood, then glided in and deposited what I thought was sticks. Or was it a fish? This was enchanting and I added "storks" to my list to Google when I got home.

Once in the countryside outside Santo Domingo, I approached a bridge over a river. I could see for at least 1/4 mile in either direction, and the land was flat and swampy, with beautiful tree branches hanging down into the water. Little islands dotted the river here and there. The rain was steady and the wind picked up. Mist swirled over the water. I stopped mid-bridge and my eyes adjusted. I counted 11 tall poles set in the banks of the river. On top of each pole a platform had been erected, with sides maybe a foot high. I judged the platforms to be at least 4x4 feet and on top of each was a substantial stork nest—each with resident storks. I hurried across the bridge, down a slight and muddy embankment, and positioned myself against a bridge abutment out of the wind for a good look at this astounding sight.

As I watched the storks, I began to understand a bit about what was happening. One stork in each nest seemed to keep on the move, flying out to the fields to hunt small prey or down to the riverbank to fish. Then the stork's return trip seemed to be an effort to get an overview of the land before honing in on his nest and mate, and landing on the nest in a swirl of feathers. Great stretching and flapping of wings. Preening. I could sometimes hear through the wind and pelting rain a clacking noise which I later learned came from stork beaks hitting together.

I nearly shouted when I observed one stork fly in clutching a flapping fish in its beak and deposit it into the mouth of its partner. Later, another large stork circled the nest closest to me. It was carrying in its beak a small animal—maybe a large rodent—that was fighting for its life. My heart raced. The passenger was dropped into the nest and finished off by the nesting mate. I didn't see the gory kill but I did see the stork lift its head and neck straight up several times and swallow hard.

I reluctantly left my own perch at the bridge after about a half hour. I was chilled from the wind and rain, and knew that I had to keep moving towards my destination of Belorado. But I kept thinking about the storks? Why did my heart stir each time I saw a nest?

As I walked on, old memories surfaced of children's stories which told about the stork living close to humans, being loved by humans, and then I understood. My mother had told me when I was a child in the 1940's that storks brought babies, and she had pictures to prove it. I remember drawings of white storks with black wing feathers, red legs held straight out behind them, gliding toward houses with little diaper-like slings in their red beaks, holding snug and safe infants, rosy and chubby faced and angelic and about to be deposited with expectant families.

How romantic that was for me as a child . . . how mysterious. I begged for the stork to visit us, but my mother said: "No, storks don't leave babies with women 45 years old." Then she launched into an explanation of God's will for our family—that we were only meant to have 5 children and that I was her last baby. I was confused even then about the relationship and agreements between God and the stork.

I realized while walking how authentic my mother was in her own way when telling me that story. Even though we lived on a farm with birthing animals, any hint or explanation of any aspect of sex would have been out of the question. My older siblings never had a clue that a baby was coming to our family until they arrived home from grade school in the afternoon and there would be our mother ensconced on a daybed in the living room and a new baby in a bassinet, delivered they were told, by a stork. The stork-baby connection is easy to understand in Europe, but in America, where there are no storks, the story simply spread through the writings of Hans Christian Anderson and other European writers and artists.

Since returning from the Camino walk in 2010, I have read about storks and am convinced they are a real treasure—not only in my imagination, but as highly revered birds worldwide wherever they have managed to survive. They can be found in the 21st century in much of eastern and western Europe, in Spain and Portugal, along the northern coast of Africa in Morocco, Algeria and Tunisia, in the Middle East, Asia, Denmark, Finland and parts of Russia, Turkey and Greece.

Survival of nesting storks depends on easy access to feeding areas in the immediate vicinity of nesting places. Since storks feed primarily on fish and rodents, insects, earthworms and larvae, small mammals, snakes, frogs, lizards and newts, they build their nests in valleys with rivers running through wetlands, meadows, marshes and pastures—the very topography of long stretches of the Camino. Farming patterns and extensive land usage have particularly contributed to changes in stork habitat, especially in wetland conversion to field crops. Serious hazards claiming thousands of stork lives each year include collisions with power lines and wind turbines, illegal hunting of the birds, polluted streams, rivers and pesticide usage. Organizations exist all along the Camino that have members who devote themselves to tracking stork numbers and promoting preservation of the species. I loved to think of the special interest groups of local inhabitants and legislators who ensure stork conservation. What richness to watch the stork's migrational cycles.

There are virtually dozens of stories and legends about the stork—all revering the bird and equating it with luck, kindness, harmony and spirituality. Numerous stories allude to storks being models of parental devotion, including their caring for aged storks and carrying them on their backs in migration. For example, in ancient Greece, the strong belief that storks were devoted to their aged population resulted in the philosophy of filial piety. So powerful and widespread was this idea of filial piety that in ancient Greece anyone who killed a stork was punished with death. The ancient word in Greek for stork was "pelargos" and a Greek law called Pelargonia directed (and required) citizens to care for their aged population.

The storks in Spain made a big impression on me as I walked the Camino. Each time I saw the craftsmanship of a stork nest, I was in awe. Each time I saw a stork on a nest with a mate, or standing on another part of a building close by the nest, or flying with its wingspan I judged to be 5-7 feet, I stopped and watched intently. At the time, I didn't realize how fortunate I was as a pilgrim to be seeing storks. Many pilgrims, depending when they walk the Camino, never see a single stork. Storks return to Spain from wintering in Africa in early April to the same nest and with the same mate, laying 3-5 eggs. Hatching occurs after an incubation period of 33 days, and the fledglings leave the nest at about 2 months of age. In August, storks repeat the migratory pattern, leaving northern Spain to fly to Africa for the winter. As I plodded on mile after mile on Day 14, May 7, 2010, I was endlessly interested in what was happening inside those stork nests . . . were there eggs? were there babies? Indeed, would I see any baby storks at all on the Camino?

CAMINO—DAY 15

Day of Complete Quiet and Rest

Postcard # 15—May 8, 2010 sent again from Belorado

Dear Elena: This am I went to the doctor here in Belorado for my blisters & very loose big toenail which is still carefully wrapped. After a painful treatment, I decided not to walk today, just stopped nearby & checked into a private room in the lovely little Pension Toni for a day of total rest. The owners did all my laundry every stitch & returned it perfectly folded. I slept much of the day, went out for a splendid meal, came home & kissed each of my toes with your little "felt" heart. Totally reorganized my backpack. I think I will be better tomorrow. Lots of rain beating on my balcony through today and this evening. Grandma Mary

Journal—Day 15 (Saturday) May 8, 2010 written again in Belorado, Espana

This am I left last night's crowded dorm, searched for & found a Centro de Salud Emergency Services for my foot. A male nurse with not a word of English, (and I pathetic with not a word of Spanish,) put me on an examination table covered with crumpled paper from the previous patient. He was a nice man, but vigorously and relentlessly unwrapped, treated with mercurichrome, then wrapped again the toes & bunions—all raw and painful. I could not start walking. By 9:30am ensconced myself nearby in Pension Toni to stay a 2nd day/night in Belorado. My little room is so beautiful with full bath and very quiet. I unpacked everything & gave a basket of dirty clothes to the owner who delivered them back dry & folded by 2:00pm. I was happy to pay him 12 Euros for being saved this task. I slept deeply for at least four hours, then went out to Restaurant Picias for a delicious meal . . . then a walk in the town, bought fruit and back for more organizing quietly & without the distractions of the dormitories . . . a really welcome and restorative routine change for 25 Euros. Continued this evening writing postcards & in journal, with lots of time for Centering Prayer meditative sits. The peace & quiet plus pleasant surroundings calm me and I'm even open to staying another day because of my big toe which the male nurse somewhat traumatized.

Reflection on Day 15, written back home in San Francisco

"You need not leave your room. Remain sitting at your table and listen. You need not even listen, simply wait. You need not even wait, just learn to become quiet, and still, and solitary. The world will freely offer itself to you to be unmasked."

Franz Kafka (1833-1924)

Day 15 was one of the quietest days of my life. In the morning, I spoke to no pilgrims in the crowded dormitory where I'd spent last night. I was not able to discuss my medical situation with the man at the Belorado clinic who dressed my foot, as he had no English and I no

Spanish. He just looked determined to do his job as fast as possible by energetically wiggling my loose toenail and pulling apart my toes for cleaning and wrapping. As I eased my foot into the shoe, I was in a truly weakened condition emotionally and physically. I walked out into the cold rain and wind and seriously thought about quitting the Camino at that very moment. I leaned against a storefront to collect myself and close by spotted a sign for Pension Toni. I'd read about this little place in my guidebook as alternative accommodation in case all the dormitories were full. I made the decision. I would stay a second night in Belorado. I struggled to the Pension and rang the bell.

It was all accomplished without fanfare. The owner efficiently collected 25 Euros, led me to a lovely little room with bath, even a balcony, and offered to do my laundry for an additional 12 Euros. I slipped every stitch of clothing I had with me except my pajamas through the door to him, and climbed into bed to rest and get warm. I slept for four hours without stirring until the bells on the clock in the hall awakened me.

I recall that I awakened from that deep and restorative morning sleep with waves of gratitude for being totally still, wrapped in silence, with no need to get up, be out of the room, speak to anyone. I was warm. Safe. My room, I noticed for the first time, had an easy chair and a desk. I stirred around, sat in the chair quietly, intending to sit in Centering Prayer. The unknown beckoned to me. I responded. I beckoned to it. It responded. I was caught in a kind of cloud of forgetting, just sitting patiently and with an open heart. Eyes closed. Thoughts and pain coming occasionally. When I engaged with a thought, I just let it go. Let go. Let go. And returned to my intent to be fully present to God within the spaciousness of silence and stillness. This wasn't my work to do. This was my chance to be worked on.

Mid-afternoon, there was a knock on the door, and when I opened it, nobody was in sight—only on the floor, a basket of folded laundry, still warm from the dryer. Clean laundry—another reason to be deeply grateful on the Camino. I realized I hadn't eaten that day. I went out in the rain to a very good restaurant nearby. Seafood soup and a lamb stew revived me, along with a half bottle of wine and a creme de caramel flan. I felt better. After a short walk, I returned to the pension to continue my day of rest.

I sat at the desk, writing in my journal and composing another postcard to my granddaughter. I thought deeply about my children and husband, allowing all the good feelings to surface. I didn't miss them or worry about them. Their ability to let me go off on the Camino alone allowed me to give them great space also. I did try to send a short email note home at least once each week to reassure them and of course loved receiving their emails. But I had no desire to call home to hear their voices.

I wondered how isolated pilgrims in the middle ages must have felt who were injured on the trail, or became deathly ill—with no means to contact their families. Centuries ago, walking the Camino really was a complete break from home, a truly dangerous effort, despite the inns, markets, hospitals and churches. Illness, injury, bandits and charlatans took a terrible toll on early pilgrims. And when (and if) they arrived at Santiago, they faced the long walking journey back home—sometimes it took a year for the roundtrip, with no means of hearing any news from home.

The day moved into evening in Belorado with the rain pounding the balcony windows. The owner kindly brought a heater to the room to supplement the furnace, which was trickling out a bit of warm air. It was an evening for prayer and recollection. Quiet gratefulness. I listened and waited. Pain surfaced in the foot from time to time. I had no desire to move—to even turn on the TV. Just be. Just being. Just is-ness. There was not a sound in the house, only the rain and the heater turning on and off. I was not alone.

Before retiring, I slowly repacked my backpack. My clothes were set for the next week. I studied maps, elevations, directions, calculated distances to Santiago. I studied the calendar and the number of days that were left in Spain before I returned to San Francisco. I forced myself to consider the long-term stress on my 70 year old body from finishing a 500 mile walk with a foot injury. I began to realize that night as I fell asleep, that the injury to my big toe could be a deal breaker that would not allow me to complete the Camino. Would it really be so awful not to finish? I was sanguine about this possibility—yet not anywhere near making a decision as momentous as quitting the pilgrimage. It would work out, if not my way, then another way.

CAMINO DE SANTIAGO
REDECILLA DEL CAMINO
(Burgos)

CAMINO—DAY 16

The Fifth and Final Fall

Postcard #16—May 9, 2010 sent from Villafranca de Montes de Oca, Espana

Dearest Elena: Every person who walks the Camino wears a shell like this one on his/her backpack. This has been a custom for hundreds of years. And I am wearing one also. There are many legends about the shell and the Camino. Today, I left Belorado in the rain & walked in great slogging mud for 12.9 km or 7.7mi. Fields & hills incredibly beautiful but as I got into Villafranca de Montes I slipped on a rock crossing a stream & landed in blackberry bushes with feet soaking in the water—2 bad arm scratches & an instant "goose-egg" on my shin . . . well, it took a man from Sweden & a man from France to pull me up & across a big puddle. I am o'k . . . Staying at a lovely pilgrims dorm tonight & it is storming outside. Wonderful to be safe, dry & warm. Today is Mother's Day & I know you and your papa have bought lovely flowers for your mama. I hope you are sitting on your mama's lap. She is such a good Mama. Love from Grandmama on the Camino

Journal—Day 16 (Sunday) May 9, 2010—written at Villafranca de Montes de Oca

This am in Belorado awakened to rain & stayed in bed awhile at the lovely Pension Toni—then got into gear & began a beautiful walk 12.9km or 7.7mi—a shorter distance than planned because of how muddy much of today's trails were. Still, rain stopped & started & I walked into several very small, isolated medieval villages. I always walk slowly through villages to see as much as I can of the exterior of the buildings, and the old people often looking from lace-covered curtains, tending their geraniums, sitting on steps listening to their caged birds sing. I would be afraid to put a caged bird in a drafty window as chilly as it is today. Stopped for a coffee & cheese sandwich to fortify & watched people gather in a nearby courtyard for Mass. Everybody knows everybody. Lots of attention paid to the babies. In spite of uncertain weather, many walkers on the Camino—all seem to be in a big hurry today to get through the towns as fast as possible. Coming into Villafranca de Montes de Oca, I slipped wading through a puddle where a creek crossed the path, fell completely backwards hitting my leg on a rock & landing in blackberry brambles. Feet totally soaked. Oh Lord!!! Scratches on my arm & a golf-sized goose-egg on my leg. It was fitting to the occasion & location, I am later noting with amusement, that the goose egg raised on my leg honors the Mountains of the Geese (Montes de Oca). A man from Sweden & a Frenchman pulled me & my backpack up out of the brambles—no mean feat as they had to stand in water to do it, & soon I was ensconced in the Albergue San Anton—very nice pilgrims dorm attached to a beautiful private hotel. All is o'k after a bath. (Boy, was I muddy, & deep scratches needed major attention.) Email available in hotel entry rooms. Mother's Day greetings from Nathan & Amelia & a very sweet email from Larry cheered me considerably (along with a glass of wine) as well as newsy letters from my sisters Ann & Genny. Another glass of wine as I enjoyed reading a 3 week old Time magazine in the hotel's grand lobby, and finally finished the day eating a delicious dinner in the Hotel Restaurant with Camino Pilgrim Brad—(Boys Club of NYC)—first American I've talked to in over two weeks on the Camino. We shared lots of stories about his career with Boys Club and mine with Job Corps. It was a very pleasant evening sharing similar views with a like minded liberal about youth programs and young adult education and vocational programs available in the United States.

Reflection on Day 16, written back home in San Francisco in 2011

"Would you become a Pilgrim on the road of love? The first condition is that you make yourself humble as dust and ashes."
Rumi

Rain. Mud. Cold. Variations in altitude. In my pre-walk Camino naivety, I had pictured myself in late spring walking flat and smooth Spanish paths in temperate and dry weather. 2010 proved tricky in planning for proper clothing and unpredictable in comfort on the trail. As the calendar approached the middle of May, the cold front across northern Spain relentlessly continued. I was experiencing the 7th day straight of walking in unusually cold and sharp winds and often heavy rains. It was the talk of pilgrims in the dormitories and the complaint of every bar and restaurant manager.

It was on Day 16 that I took my final tumble on the Camino and while every one of the five falls could have potentially ended the pilgrimage, this one only caused my legs to be stiff for a week and my arms and face scratched like I'd been declared the loser in an encounter with a banty rooster.

Here's what happened. As I was walking through a muddy woods with lots of underbrush on the path, I came to a stream with no stepping stones or grassy areas on the steep sides to help me cross the water. Nothing for it but to step onto rocks in the stream which flowed over my shoes and down I slipped and slid in another flailing dance—this time losing my poles, twisting sideways and landing on my backside on the bank of the path in a bed of blackberry branches that seemed to capture and hold me prisoner with their thorns. Water thoroughly soaked my shoes and pants legs up to the knee. Try as I might, I knew I couldn't get up alone.

I sat there shivering for ten minutes, unable to free myself from the thorns or gain leverage to stand. Eventually, I heard voices and soon I could see the outlines of three pilgrims coming through the woods. They came into view, spotted me sitting on the side of the road and immediately, or should I say discreetly, retreated behind some trees. Oh, no, I realized, they think they have encountered a pilgrim relieving herself along the side of the road. What else could they think with their brief glimpse of seeing me squatting in the brambles? "Hello there, hello," I called as cheerily as I could. "I need some help. Hello, hello."

The party of two men and a woman approached cautiously as they assessed my situation. Bless those two men who, determining that I was decent and genuinely in need, rushed to free me from the clutches of the blackberry bushes—men who stood in water that thoroughly soaked their feet as they each took an arm to start the rescue activity. Believe me when I relate the multiple efforts and great strain on all our body parts to get me upright and on my feet. When it was over, they examined the deep scratches on my arms and face, and the egg sized lump that had arisen on my left shin. We all stared at these injuries in awe, and somewhat admiringly, and then all of us had a nervous laugh, for it was so bizarre. I thanked them profusely, and they disappeared up the trail. I never saw them again.

It was just as well, I suppose, that my rescuers and I didn't run into each other another time. That evening in my dorm when I got out of the shower, I struck up a conversation with a young woman resting on a nearby bunk who watched me clean and disinfect the deep scratches on my arms and face. "I heard about you when I checked in," she said. "You're the woman the French guy found flopped on the bank in the water of the overflow creek. He thought first you were taking a dump, but he said he ended up pulling you out of the muck. Are you o'k?"

I considered her question carefully, curious that she had heard about my rescue that had happened only an hour earlier. "Somewhat o'k and somewhat not o'k. That French guy was great. Did he tell you that he was assisted by a really strong Swede?" She seemed surprised. I changed the subject: "I really don't understand how I got these deep scratches. And this goose egg bump on my leg is amazing. Never really saw anything like it before. And it hurts like hell." She leaned forward: "I don't understand what you mean by goose egg bumper on your leg." I replied: "Oh, it's just an American expression. Maybe British. You get a hard thump somewhere on your body, and an egg sized lump appears fast. We call it a goose egg."

My dorm mate chuckled: "Well, then, the geese have blessed you. You know, don't you, that Montes de Oca, where we are, means Mountains of the Geese?" I tried to take that in—to fit it into the day's mysteries—the blur of the cold, the mud, the water, the fall, the warmth of the hot shower, the day's exhaustion. Was I a pilgrim? Or a goose? Or perhaps I was merely a goose egg. I nibbled on a soggy rice cracker, popped another Ibuprophen 600, and slipped into an hour's restorative nap before the evening's postcard, journal writing and dinner routine.

<u>An aside, a postscript to Day 16, if I may!</u> One of the most privately asked questions by friends back home with whom I discuss my Camino experience is how on earth people handle the call of nature, the need to pee and poop on the Camino when out on the trail. How many times I came across soiled tissues on the Camino 5-10 feet off the path, usually in an area somewhat hidden, just beyond a bend in the road! Often in a copse of nearby trees. I ignored the tissues, even though I thought it gross that folks had not carried along a plastic bag to contain their personal waste. I suppose that I'd been so immersed in political correctness in San Francisco where it was "the law of the land" to pick up after your dog.

But back to the topic! Harder to ignore for me than strewn tissues was actually coming upon a person "assuming the position." Where does one look? Does one walk on by with eyes firmly fixed on the horizon? Acknowledge the chap with his pants down by calling out a hearty "Buen Camino"? Fall back and pretend to take a long look at the scenery in the opposite direction? Anything at all to avoid making eye contact.

For a pilgrim with companions, it is easier to accomplish one's outdoor business with a cooperative lookout. For the solo pilgrim finding herself in such situations, discretion and speedy execution are paramount. Just imagine how fast a bicycle can approach from the trail behind!!!! I know from experience.

CAMINO—DAY 17

Egregore, Indeed!!!!!

Postcard # 17—May 10, 2010 sent from Atapuerca, Espana

Elena: This is a picture of Pilgrims walking in the snow!!!! For 1 week it has been very cold—I can see snow on the distant mountains but <u>it has not snowed where I am walking—yet!!!</u> I am wearing all my clothes (including my pajamas)—isn't that funny? Shhhh! Nobody knows but me (and you). Today it was a bit warmer & only showers. I walked 19.4km or 11.6mi to a very amazing place—Atapuerca—which UNESCO declared in Year 2000 (year your parents were married) that the Atapuerca site and local caves are the oldest inhabited community in all of Europe. It has been dated to 900,000 years ago. And believe me, the Papasol Dorm I am staying in dates to 1580. I am looking at old, old beams just over my bed. I am also looking for spiders, but none yet. Love from Grandma

Journal—Day 17 (Monday) May 10, 2010—written at Atapuerca

This routine of writing a postcard every evening before dinner to Elena, and then scribbling away in my journal really has a value for me . . . it is a discipline on the Camino, it is a productive routine which keeps me on track and it includes very important calculations about distances walked each day, maps, timelines and definitely prepares me for the next day's plan. Last night it was quiet & peaceful in the dorm at the French Village of the Mountains of the Geese. Awakened this am refreshed. Was very disappointed to miss the Atapuerca Museum, of course closed on Monday. Ate a bit of breakfast & after a couple miles only of steep climbing, completed the day's walk of 18.4km or 11.0 mi. Stopped for an hour in San Juan de Ortega where I ate lunch from my backpack—visited and loved the Church. Series of pictures on the church walls of monks using lions to carry bags & boxes but best of all was fabulous painting of St. Jerome removing a thorn from a lion in great pain. True compassion & hospitality. Road & weather quite beautiful in crisp sunshine, but has turned cold last 3 mi into Atapuerca. This is a UNESCO 2000 designation as the oldest European human community (local caves date back 900,000 years). A very welcoming place with a pretty front garden was unfortunately "completo" when I got there, but once again, spirit was guiding me to another experience. Landed in the Papasol dormitory several blocks away—one large bunk-bedded room for 24 Pilgrims and a simple bathroom—oh my—the beams holding this place up have to be 100's of years old, but I trust they'll hold one more night. I trust. Still, I laugh out loud as I write this, remembering the US Dept of Labor OSHA (Safety) regulations I monitored and enforced for the Job Corps program. Their engineers & renovation architects would have a field day over this place. Spent time with 3 South Africans (a young couple and a quite spiritual middle-aged man. He introduced us to the concept of egregore—collective group mind & its energy—concept dates back to the pre Christian Essenes. This is his 2nd time walking in Spain, and after dinner in the nearby Papasol Restaurant, he and I talked about the mysterious egregore of the Camino.

Reflection on Day 17, written back home in San Francisco

"I command you, then: open yourself—not just to those who have a claim on you. To anyone who asks. Anyone. Because Anyone is a disguise for God."

—Deuteronomy 15:7-11

Two things remain important to me about Day 17 on the Camino. I was reintroduced to the legend of St. Jerome and the Lion, and I ended the day by stopping in the town of Atapuerca, the oldest and most significant site in all of Europe for the study of prehistoric peoples.

About mid-day, I sauntered into the village of San Juan de Ortega and stopped in the church on the plaza to get warm and to take a rest. I recall thinking that the exterior of the church was particularly beautiful and simple with its huge bell tower and three bells, and the rose window over its massive front door. I had read about the history of the village namesake, San Juan, who was a disciple of Santo Domingo. Together they helped shape the Camino over broad walking stretches by constructing churches and hospitals, hostals and supply posts for the benefit of the pilgrims. Both of these practical visionaries understood the rigors and hardships of the trails and each was responsible for designing and overseeing construction of bridges to make passage from town to town safer and shorter. Their story was fascinating to me—just two simple and honest men who followed their spiritual and humanitarian instincts to help pilgrims safely reach the goal of worshiping in the Church of St. James at Santiago de Compostela.

Sitting in the church at San Juan de Ortega, my mind wandered with a kind of kinship to the hundreds of thousands, even millions, of pilgrims who had passed exactly here in the last thousand years, in every kind of condition, with aches and pains that made my blisters and wobbly toenail insignificant. I also thought of the misfortunes of those pilgrims who started walking to Santiago, but were injured on the trail or died of illness—most likely never to be heard of again by their families. Pilgrims in the earlier centuries actually did have havens such as this where they were welcomed and cared for in illness until they could continue their journey. And of course, for pilgrims who would not continue, every hospital along the way also had a cemetery.

I was lost in these thoughts of San Juan de Ortega, patron saint of this village, and his unselfish service to pilgrims when my eyes caught the most wonderful, primitive art on the walls of the church. There was St. Jerome, in his monastery and bent over, scribing his translations of the Bible. The next painting showed a lion in great pain and agony making an appearance at the monastery gates, creating a fearsome stir among the monks. Then followed another painting of St. Jerome tending to the suffering but docile lion, extracting a large thorn from its infected paw. Finally, St. Jerome was depicted living in harmony with the lion in the monastery.

I was thrilled to examine these pictures. I'd had a "holy picture" of St. Jerome tending to the lion's paw in my prayer book when I was about ten years old, and I recall studying it during interminable sermons at the daily Masses attended in a convent near St. Patrick's Church. I nudged open the memory of me as a child in church pondering what my father would do on the farm if an injured wild beast appeared at our door. On our cellar landing hung a shotgun. St. Jerome had another kind of powerful weapon to deal with the lion: a calmness and peaceful serenity arising from a lifetime of silence and prayer and contemplation that transmitted to the wild beast and calmed it enough to allow its transformation in health and nature.

There are many interpretations of what the scenario means, what the lion represents, what St. Jerome is trying to tell us. I didn't even want to think about all those interpretations of temptation and sin. I was charmed with the scenes just as they were: these pictures represented to me kindness, hospitality, fearlessness, healing, gentleness and oneness with nature. I don't know how this story or legend got started, but I do know that St. Jerome is at least as well known for his hospitality to the wild beast as for his translations of the Bible from Greek and Hebrew into Latin. I prepared to leave the church after an hour's rest. As I adjusted my backpack, I took another look at St. Jerome extracting that thorn from the lion's pad. I was well enough aware of the visiting beasts that frequent my own life and which I meet with varying reactions from 0-10 on the Richter Scale. I had a lot to learn from St. Jerome.

As I continued the day's walk, I approached the foothills of the Sierra de Atapuerca, an area outside Burgos declared by UNESCO as a World Heritage Site. The hills of the area are riddled with caves inhabited during prehistoric times—the oldest cave dwellings in Europe, allegedly dating back to 1,000,000 years ago—certainly 250,000 years older than any other hominid site yet discovered in western Europe. For over 150 years, research has been conducted at Atapuerca by professors and students from universities all over the world. They have excavated and catalogued a rich fossil history by carbon dating bone fragments of hominids, bison, bears and carnivores, artifacts, tools and cave art.

It's surprising that the detailed record of prehistoric peoples from Sierra de Atapuerca still exists because modern man has intrusively altered the area. I learned that significant dangers to the archeological sites were posed over the past century due to mining limestone which damaged caves and burial sites. A railroad was established in the area of the Sierra to transport limestone to Burgos, further deteriorating the delicate landscapes. In addition, a military training area was established in the Sierra in the 1970's, at which point the provincial government of Burgos began active lobbying to declare the area an Artistic Monument. This led to the world-wide acknowledgement of Atapuerca as a World Heritage Site.

I was sorry I didn't know more about the archeological history of the area as I walked into the tiny village of Atapuerca. I landed at a Papasol dormitory that was quite the most fascinating of any place I stayed thus far on the Camino. I registered at a bar and was directed down a path towards a separate building.

The latch on the ancient door was a rope and a peg. I smiled, thinking of the night time security of sleeping pilgrims. I entered into a sitting room, dining room and kitchen all rolled into one tiny space, and occupied by several pilgrims reading, lounging and making tea. There were friendly acknowledgments of my arrival and I was pointed through another door into a heart-stopping dorm room holding about 24 spaces in twelve bunk beds.

The floors were ancient wooden and very worn boards that creaked and groaned with every step. The walls and ceilings were supported by hewn timbers of various sizes that supported the shape of the room. Plaster was slathered into empty spaces and chinks between the beams. Wherever a crossbeam could be inserted to strengthen the roof or walls, it had been jam-packed in, squeezed and pressured into place. I had never seen anything like this, and a queasy intuition emerged whether it was safe to stay the night. Still, I put my backpack and poles down by a lower bunk and went to find the bathroom. And indeed there was one <u>inside</u>: three sinks, three toilets and three showers in very narrow quarters, but they were clean, and relatively modern. I would stay the night. I went back to further look at those amazing walls.

A voice emanating from an upper bunk announced to me that the man at registration told him the dorm was built in 1580. Did I think the walls would hold up overnight, or come tumbling down when someone got up to use the bathroom? I connected to the male voice situated close by the bunk bed I'd chosen and we both had good laughs as we planned our escape route in case of an emergency in the night. It wasn't a bad idea, we agreed, to have some sort of an emergency plan in any of the dormitories we'd encountered on the Camino and particularly this one.

I described my tried and true version of what to do in an earthquake if caught indoors. Lie on the floor flat and facedown next to any piece of furniture—then, if the ceilings or walls collapsed, they would more likely be tangled up with the height of the furniture, giving a better chance to the person for space and air to breathe under the debris. The man was skeptical. I demonstrated the theory to him by lying down on the floor close to the lower bunk I was to sleep on that night. We discussed the likelihood of where beams and plaster would land if shaken loose. He thought through the idea and became most enthusiastic in his agreement that it was an excellent ploy to save one's life in an earthquake.

I repacked my gear for the next day, showered, then gradually made my way to the bar to write postcards and the day's entry in my journal. I felt cradled and enclosed here in Atapuerca—like I was a very old soul visiting a place where I'd been before. I sensed a mysterious relationship to this area of Spain with its well archived archeological digs.

I tried to make a comparison of Atapuerca and its earliest peoples with southern Illinois where I'm from originally and the Indian nomadic tribes that wandered through my ancestors' farmlands. Fewer than ten miles from our farm is located the famous Modoc Indian Digs, intensively studied sheltering caves cut into bluffs and carbon dated back some 8,000 years. And only about thirty miles from our farm lay the world famous Cahokia Mounds, the largest archeological site in the Americas north of Central Mexico. Cahokia was a powerful Indian cultural center on the floodplains of the Mississippi River, a large complex city of 20,000 people—a trading society with monumental public works, burial grounds, agricultural fields all thriving a full century before Columbus discovered America. Both great mysteries—Cahokia Mounds, close by St. Louis, Missouri, and Atapuerca, located near Burgos, Spain, both meriting UNESCO World Heritage designations. And the unanswerable mystery in both places—why did the peoples and cultures disappear over time? And the sites fall to ruin?

I ordered another glass of wine. This required serious consideration. Back in Illinois, I always experienced amazement at the alleged ages of the two archeological sites, the tools, art, fossils and artifacts. "Imagine," I would muse in my provincial way, "8,000 years ago men, women and children were wandering through the area now southern Illinois." But here in a bar in northern Spain, sitting in the village of Atapuerca, my mind was bedazzled, radically amazed when I compared the north American midwest sites to this northern Spain site carbon dated to 1,000,000 years ago.

I couldn't really take in that span of time. What two-legged and four-legged creatures crawled, evolved and walked here in the Sierra de Atapuerca? Perhaps hunting and foraging on the very site where I was spending the night? Homo erectus? Homo heidelbergensis? Homo antecessors? Neanderthals? What astounding evolutionary groanings birthed the various stages of the western European hominids who deposited their meager artifacts in the Atapuerca caves?

I pondered these things alone through dinner in the adjacent restaurant, then carried the remainder of my wine back into the bar sitting area, where I found the pilgrim from South Africa scribbling notes at a table. We shared our similar thoughts about Atapuerca, and he used the term "egregore" to refer to how similarly we thought about the area and its history. I was not familiar with the term egregore and he explained it as "a state of group mind or group spirit" by a body of two or more people engaged in cooperative thinking or activity usually in the context of strong emotional or energetic influences and resulting in a group identity. He spoke of the strong egregoric relationships he felt with pilgrims all along the trail, even though he walked alone. He thought the term went back as far as the Essenes in the time of Christ and was a religious term.

"It may be a religious term," I replied, "but I see that "egregore" or group mind as you call it could be applied equally to the political and corporate worlds of today, to sports, to the military branches, to racial divisions, to any group who follows a particular interest—whether the goal is good or evil. Every evil movement in history, for example, African Apartheid or the European Holocaust or American slavery, probably emerged with individuals subscribing, buying into the ethics or mystique of strong authoritarian, directive or cultish leaders—and outsiders observing, watching, then awakening to the larger group's strong energetic influence. We discussed various examples from our vantage points as an American and a South African and soon began to dissect the concept of the egregore of the Camino.

There was no doubt in our minds that the Camino was a powerful example of my fellow pilgrim's "word for the day". My friend continued: "For a thousand years, history showed Pilgrims by the hundreds of thousands stopping—dropping what they were doing and heading towards Santiago. And powerful attractions certainly existed for pilgrims throughout the Camino's history, from as early as the 10th Century and still existing today in the 21st Century. In the very earliest days, the Catholic Church presented enticing relics and icons which drew pilgrims into a collective interest around participating in the Camino—planning, praying, risking, walking, seeing, touching, all for the purpose of receiving upon arrival the Church-issued Indulgences—having one's sins forgiven at the Cathedral in Santiago."

I loved this man's intensity. I took a different tack. I agreed that group mind continues on the Camino—but "today, it is a different era, and people walk with many motivations besides religious and spiritual ones. Contemporary Camino egregore is seductively and powerfully crafted and marketed by numerous books and how-to guides translated into many languages, by tourist organizations and web technology. The Camino is big business for the Spanish economy, and continues to be supported by the government for the income potential to the hospitality industry, restaurants and bars, souvenir shopkeepers, churches, the availability of albergues, refugios and town dormitories to keep the pilgrims coming and to house them at modest costs—all this constituting the group mind of the people connected to the Camino and who profit from its sustainability."

The man was growing agitated—his head was shaking, sometimes in agreement but more often in disagreement. He seemed shocked that I would put an economic and touristic spin on the Camino. He leaned across the table: "No, no. I will not believe it. There is an ancient and deeply ingrained spiritual egregore of the Camino that arises spontaneously in the minds of all pilgrims. It may not be Catholic, or religious in any sense of the word, but it is there anyhow, and every pilgrim discovers it."

We looked at each other and quieted. This was a profound and respectful moment. I had no way of knowing whether all pilgrims experienced the Camino in some sort of a spiritual way as he believed, but I was open to the idea. After all, I was personally experiencing it daily.

"Look," I said, "we're not at odds here. I am simply suggesting an economic egregore that fortunately exists in place and is motivated to keep the Camino going and alive . . . and because it's there, with its myths and mystiques, its shopkeepers and accommodations, the modern pilgrims walk—but with hodgepodge motivations. You are suggesting an innate and cellular spiritual motivation. I don't know about that, because most pilgrims are hard-pressed to categorize or even express their personal motivation for taking this long walk. Yes, the year 2010 is designated as a Holy Year and certainly offers certain benefits to the religiously oriented pilgrim, but for the secular walker with a personal agenda, or a tourist's agenda, it seems to be all in the hike, all in the day to day experience of seeing the beautiful country and growing tired each evening, of finishing the chosen route, and being able to say one has arrived in Santiago and that one now possesses a diploma to prove the walk was completed. I personally struggle with my own motivation for being here. I don't know if there is some innately spiritual motivation in all pilgrims that even they don't understand."

At this point, the light dimmed over our table by the long shadow of the barkeeper who was waving a big key in his hand and motioning towards the door. He presented a bill for the two empty bottles. We all laughed, realizing that the evening's wine was the third conversationalist at the table.

The Camino's egregore did exist, and was, we agreed to agree as we paid our bills, a mysterious, mystical and transformative element in our lives that had for many years beckoned each of us to participate as walking pilgrims. "You have made me think of the Camino in new ways tonight, and I thank you for your company," the man said. I smiled: "And you, my pilgrim friend, have made me a believer."

We walked out the door into the cold midnight air. A slightly sweet fragrance filled the little entrance garden—not honeysuckle, but like honeysuckle. A Milky Way of stars poured across the sky, and a sliver of moon hung low. Ancient silence so intense I could taste it. Nothing stirred. Here, visible to us, was the original Compostela—the field of stars. Was it any less visible and awe-inspiring hundreds of thousands of years ago to the earliest inhabitants evolving on this segment of Planet Earth? And a mere 1000 or so years ago, these same stars, moon and heavenly planets beckoned and guided the earliest Christian pilgrims slogging their way to Santiago with sore feet to see and touch St. James' holy bones and have their sins forgiven.

It was enough for me to know that in the 21st Century, May 10, 2010, in the little Spanish village of Atapuerca, this South African and I were just two of those pilgrims across the ages, walking to Santiago. We stood there, lost in thoughts, then shook hands, and I never saw him again.

CAMINO—DAY 18

Walking and Visiting with Jane

Postcard # 18—May 11, 2010 sent from Burgos, Espana

Elena: I picked this card especially for you because he is such a funny fellow—mechanical & ringing his bell to mark each hour. Today was an amazing day but kind of hard—The walk from Atapuerca to Burgos was 11.6mi & tonight my feet hurt. I had a lovely tapas late lunch/ early dinner at 4:00pm with a sangria pitcher full of fruit . . . so tasty & it revived me at a plaza café as I studied the exterior of the Burgos Cathedral. The best part of today was it did not rain. I was so grateful to walk freely without fear of falling in the mud. Elena, I think of all the churches I've been to in my life, the Burgos Cathedral is the biggest & most beautiful. I know you will see it one day & enjoy its treasures. Just know that I carry the little heart that you & your mama made me. Love from Grandma-on-the-Camino

Journal—Day 18 (Tuesday) May11, 2010 written at Burgos

At last I've arrived in Burgos, a big city by Camino standards. But what a very cold walk it was (19.4km or 11.6mi) from Atapuerca. The road out of town was lovely, a bit by the freeway & a lot in the countryside but problematically muddy. I seemed totally alone today on the trail—I never met another pilgrim, until the outskirts of Burgos, but my sister Jane seemed to be so insistently speaking to me in poetry, first Carl Sandburg, then Gerard Manley Hopkins. Outside Atapuerca the path cut sharply up and across a very steep hill bound on one side by military barbed wire fences, and by public open space on the other. Thousands of tall stalks of almost blooming white flowers & amazing little ground-level purple powder puffs about the size of a 50 cent piece. Lots of Lenten Roses blooming. Steep climb with fog drifting in and out. An other-worldly place, I thought. A very tall cross next to the military zone fence. Rocks in formation created a cross on the ground and spelled out the word <u>God</u>. In the swirling mists I could just make out a huge labyrinth formed with rocks nearby the path. I stopped, entered the labyrinth and distinctly heard Jane's voice: "The world is charged with the Grandeur of God." No one was there. Complete quiet. Reached the labyrinth's center in tears, then back on the circular path outward to the Camino. Continued walk towards Burgos, soon entering a several mile city approach through an industrial zone. Jane's voice again: "I am in a perfect state." Spires of the Burgos Cathedral dominated all—so imposing—the most beautiful exterior Cathedral I've seen. Albergue adjacent up steep steps—not difficult to find as pilgrims looked at me and pointed the direction. I am on the top floor and happy to have a bottom bunk. Ate outstanding Tapas chosen from a huge selection & with a pitcher of Sangria filled with fresh fruit. A real treat. Tour of the Cathedral overwhelming. Very large picture of St. Elena disfigured as a martyr. Oh, My. Spent an hour walking around the Cathedral Plazas and in the church. Another hour on email. Feet very, very blistered and painful.

Reflection on Day 18, written in San Francisco in 2011

"The world is charged with the grandeur of God.
It will flame out, like shining from shook foil;
It gathers to a greatness, like the ooze of oil
Crushed. Why do men then now not reck his rod?
Generations have trod, have trod, have trod;
And all is seared with trade; bleared, smeared with toil;
And wears man's smudge and shares man's smell: the soil
Is bare now, nor can foot feel, being shod.
And for all this, nature is never spent;
There lives the dearest freshness deep down things;
And though the last lights off the black West went,
Oh, morning, at the brown brink eastward, springs—
Because the Holy Ghost over the bent
World broods with warm breast and with ah! bright wings."

God's Grandeur by Gerard Manley Hopkins, SJ

My memories of May 11 are clear and truthful to me, but they will not be to everyone. I recognize and admit the story that unfolds as I write this is edgy, mysterious, mystical. My sister Jane has been dead for 3 years now, but as I walked on May 11, 2010, I felt her presence so strongly that I heard her voice, talked with her, asked her questions, saw her in spirit, but not in body. She recited the Hopkins poem to me on the Camino, as she had on several occasions over a period of sixty years.

Here is our story before the Camino. When I was two years old, Jane, the eldest of five O'Hara siblings, left the farm in southern Illinois and went on scholarship to a private girls' high school in St. Louis, followed by four years at Webster College. She excelled in school, but was lonely for her family, and returned to the farm as frequently as possible for weekends and vacations.

My earliest memory of Jane was intense excitement at her visits home. I crawled up on her lap and begged her to read stories to me. And read aloud to me she did, generously and patiently, before I could read and long after I became proficient in reading. She liked fairy stories, fiction, Shakespeare, poetry of all types, the St. Louis newspaper, the funny papers, Life Magazine, Mad Magazine, Classic Comics—whatever was at hand, or that she was studying, she would read to me. I was enchanted with everything about my oldest sister. She was expanding my little girl horizons.

One day when I was about 8 years old and Jane about 20, we were out in the garden helping our mother pick strawberries. I loved summer vacation, because Jane would be home for a few weeks. I busied myself picking hollyhocks and larkspur and zinnias for household bouquets. As Jane examined my basket of flowers and the pans of strawberries, she stood up and recited God's Grandeur, the Gerard Manley Hopkins poem she had studied that year at college. Rather quietly, but with authority: "The world is charged with the grandeur of God. It will flame out, like shining from shook foil." The remaining 12 lines of the poem rolled off her lips.

Our mother was attentive. I was stunned. "What does that mean?" I asked. And Jane proceeded to tell me in simple words, using the flowers, the strawberries, the fields surrounding our farmhouse to illustrate the grandeur of a God-created world. It was a defining moment in my 1st decade of life, as she gestured inclusively towards herself, our mother, the vegetable garden, the resident mockingbird singing out its little heart on the electrical wires—and then to me—"yes, Mary, you too are God's grandeur flaming out." My eyes were big. Jane shook her hand back and forth as she repeated "like shining from shook foil." My heart was pounding. I understood the powerful lines of the poem. I dissolved in love.

Over the next 60 years, this particular poem would be the touchstone of the relationship with my sister. I venture that every visit, every telephone call, every email would include some private reference by one of us to some line or other from the Hopkins' poem. We lived on opposite sides of the country, but we kept in touch, frequently discussing the poetry my sister wrote throughout her life. I can say with complete honesty that there was never a disagreement with each other. We were soul friends.

Jane became seriously ill. While en route from California to Florida to tell her good-bye, I learned of her death from my daughter and a kindly airline employee as I changed planes midway in the trip. With tears and a shattered heart, I settled into the remaining 3 hour flight to Orlando. I calmed my mind and body by breathing deeply, thanking God for Jane's gentle life, for her friendship, her husband, beautiful children and grandchildren, her sweet love and loyalty for her brother and three sisters which we felt so deeply each time we connected. I remembered the good times, and there were many, but my sister was gone. I told her good-bye, and entered into the silence of Centering Prayer.

I commit these memories to paper because it is the brief history of two sisters as I experienced it. I fully know that skeptics will read of the close relationship pre-death, then dismiss the Camino story I am about to tell as one of imagination, of an exhausted walker whose memories were triggered by solitude and landscape that evoked ideas and lines from a familiar poem. Maybe so. Maybe not.

Now back to Day 18 on the Camino. I was climbing the steep hills outside of Atapuerca on my way to Burgos. Low fog lay across the valleys below. In spite of the deep chill in the air, flowers were rampant on the path and both sides. I heard Jane's voice: "The fog rolls in on little cat feet. It sits looking over harbor and city on silent haunches, and then moves on." I was instantly alert and looked around. Nothing in sight. Nobody on the path. Where had these words from Carl Sandburg come? Then I heard Jane laugh and say: "I taught you that poem when you were a little girl. Don't you remember?"

I did not answer. I walked on, more curious than afraid, concentrating on each step as I reached the top of the hill and level ground. I stopped to steady my breathing and take in the area. A forbidding high fence with barbed wire separated the Camino path from a military encampment. Signs on the fence showed symbols of No Trespassing. My side of the military fence definitely seemed to be the safer, as I stood next to a tall wooden cross placed incongruously on the Camino path. A bit further on, rocks had been placed on the ground to neatly form another cross and to spell out the word "God." I was not alone.

The fog and mists swirled in and blanketed the clearing where I stood. In a nearby field, I could just make out part of a labyrinth, its circular spirals traced with stones from the path. I entered the narrow opening, slipped my backpack to the ground, and slowly began making the circles and turns. I heard Jane's distinctive voice again: "The world is charged with the grandeur of God. It will flame out, like shining from shook foil. It gathers to a greatness, like the ooze of oil Crushed. Why do men then not reck his rod?" I dissolved in tears as I heard these words. Reaching the center, I heard this: "My dear sister Mary, I know why you walk the Camino."

I probably stopped in the open area at the top of the hills for an hour before I started the descent to Burgos. The fog had lifted and the steep path down offered an inviting view to a pilgrim—surrounding farmlands, the city at a distance, the spires of churches, but also a somewhat daunting walk, with its several miles of industrial outskirts to navigate before reaching the Cathedral. There had been talk among the pilgrims at the last few overnight stops about saving time and wear and tear on the body by taking the bus from the suburbs of Burgos into the center of town and skipping a very boring portion of the Camino.

No bus for me. I would walk. Far from being boring, I found the suburban approach to Burgos interesting and informative about the Spanish way of life. The freeways and secondary roads managed to connect to every part of the city via overpasses, interchanges, special driving lanes, stoplights galore—all filled with honking horns and speeding trailer trucks, busses, trollies, lorries, taxis, private vehicles and vans. After walking in the solitude of the hills and countryside for weeks, I was a bit disoriented, so took special care in crossing the busy commercial streets. I remembered constant admonitions to my children when they were little: "Look both ways. Cars go squish." As adults now, I knew my children would be horrified if they could see me navigating these busy roads. Cars might go squish, indeed, especially on distracted old lady pilgrims.

But nothing deterred me from this several mile approach to Burgos. I could see first hand large factories, showrooms, small distribution centers, corporate offices, TV and radio stations, used car lots, appliance outlet stores, what America might call strip malls, bars, restaurants, fast food, the occasional high rise apartment building, church, bakery, movie theatre. Yellow Camino directional arrows pointed the way, but were harder for me to spot. What an anomaly for the ancient Camino to pass through this industrial area, before reaching the medieval center of town. But how could it not pass through? This was Burgos sprawl—a phenomenon evident in any large city in the world, and I liked it for the change in scenery from the countryside and as insight to Spanish way of life.

The extended walking on pavement tired my legs. I found a church just off the road and sat down on an empty bench to rest and close my eyes. Almost immediately I heard Jane's voice: "Generations have trod, have trod, have trod; And all is seared with trade; bleared, smeared with toil; And wears man's smudge and shares man's smell: the soil Is bare now, nor can foot feel, being shod."

I was sanguine about this visitation. I thought about the words I'd just heard. I was in an industrialized area, for sure, and the ideas fit the general location, but I was also sitting in a church. Was this Jane's idea to jolt me awake? Had she hit the nail on the head by quoting these lines while I sat on holy ground? Was it institutionalized church that was seared, bleared and smeared with toil? Smudged with man's smell? Would the Jesuit poet Hopkins roll over in his grave to hear this heresy?

Jane had two more messages to deliver to me on Day 18, and they came late in the day, as I completed my tour of the Burgos Cathedral and sat quietly in a side chapel. I was exhausted by the day's walk, the intimate and emotional connection with my sister. I wanted to pray but my body was filled with tension. "Jane", I began tentatively, "are you here? Are you o'k?" Immediately I heard this back: "Yes, Mary. I am in a perfect state. You will understand only when you join me. Don't be afraid." I relaxed, intending to sit in Centering Prayer. Intending to be receptive to God's presence. Letting go of thoughts. Letting go. Letting go.

Some time passed when I heard Jane's gentle and supportive voice for the last time: "And for all this, nature is never spent; There lives the dearest freshness deep down things; And though the last lights off the black West went—Oh, morning, at the brown brink eastward, springs—Because the Holy Ghost over the bent World broods with warm breast and with ah! bright wings."

I wanted desperately to answer Jane, to engage with her, to hold onto the experience of her presence, but reluctantly I let go, and entered the reality of sitting alone in the Burgos Cathedral. The experiences of Day 18 on the Camino as I have described them drained me fully, and I sat in the silence of the side chapel until it grew dark. An attendant tapped me on the shoulder, pointed to his watch and then to the nearest exit. I returned to the dormitory reluctantly, carrying this powerful and unique experience in my heart for the remainder of the Camino walk and to this day. I can't offer a sacred vow that this mystery unfolded as I relate it here, and yet, I cannot disavow that this was my word for word experience.

CATEDRAL DE BURGOS

PATRIMONIO DE LA HUMANIDAD

CAMINO—DAY 19

Mornings on the Camino

Postcard # 19—May 12, 2010 sent from Hornillos del Camino

Dearest Elena: I left Burgos this am at 7:30, walking for 20.5km or 12.7mi, and arrived here at 2:00pm. I am slow today and stop every 4 or 5 miles for a coffee & to take my backpack off. Still miserable cold. A man advised me to take my shoes off at rest stops to relax my feet and it makes a world of difference for the next stage of walking. Today muddy a big part of the walk. Have entered an area of Spain called the Mezeta—flatlands of cereal-grain crops, and really beautiful. I wanted you to have this card because there is an old tradition of hospitality to lions & this man seems to be cuddling this lion. I really miss you Elena. It's not a sad "missing" but a happy one to think of you at the Crayon Box Spanish school. While I am walking everyday I am thinking of you & your mama & papa, of Uncle Nathan & of course of my dear husband Larry, your Grandpa. I show many people your picture, because I always have it propped up as I write in the evenings. Love from Abuela Mary

Journal—Day 19 (Wednesday)—May 12, 2010—written at Hornillos del Camino

Last night in the Burgos dormitory I encountered for the 3rd evening an Asian woman who moaned through the night long and pitifully in her sleep—quite loudly. I was aghast that someone shouted out angrily in the darkened dormitory: "Will you shut up!!" This am I saw her—nothing I could do, but bless her from a distance. Feet fairly awful this am but after draining blisters and wrapping them, I was off from Burgos. Today I walked on the Mezeta & because of the rains, it was very muddy in parts. Stopped frequently (every 3-4 miles) to rest. I see that I actually covered 20.5km or 12.7mi. The country flatter in most parts although steep climbs into and out of some villages. Descents are treacherous in the mud. I never expected such variations in elevation on the Meseta. I rolled into Hornillos, upright & footsore & found the Albergue was "completo" but wait!!!! Be patient, several of us were admonished, and sure enough, kind souls opened the adjacent Town Hall, stuffed tight with bunk beds and one tiny bathroom. I once again had a bottom bunk & was grateful for a bed at all. It started pouring rain & I spent the late afternoon and evening in the warmth of a bar/ restaurant across the street from the Chicken Fountain, which I'm assured is very famous in these parts. Delicious lunch sharing a table with people from Madrid. Afterwards, talked to multiple people from all over the world with foot and leg problems . . . a beautiful young Japanese girl with a sprain confided to me that her mother did not know she was walking the Camino alone, but thought she was in South America studying Spanish for the summer. "But it is o'k. My brothers know where I am." And I talked to a young man from Berlin suffering badly from a painful rash on his calves from "too many km day after day." My own feet are dressed & bandaged & require painkillers to keep going. Blisters are simply not healing & entire big toe is black and blue. But, I'm happy to report, those Ibuprophin 600's are pretty effective at their job. Really, it's this weather that is getting me down. Spaniards are aghast at the extended cold, rain, sleet & snow for this period in May. It's all they talk about!

Reflection on Day 19, written back home in San Francisco

"If you are irritated by every rub, how will you be polished?"
Rumi

My overwhelming impression of mornings in the Camino dormitories was that they came too early, too noisily, rousing me from deepest sleep. Anywhere from 5:00am on, there was rustling, padding about, yawning, soto voce conversations that couldn't wait between companions, great flushing of toilets, flashing of flashlights, stuffing slippery sleeping bags into stuff sacks, zippers zipping annoyingly back and forth, back and forth, buckles buckling. And then, it seemed to me, it just went quiet. I and a few others inevitably went to sleep for another hour or so.

Dormitories had a consistent rule that pilgrims depart with all their belongings by 8:00am. Therefore, for the late sleepers, bustling about began in earnest by 7:30am. As soon as I awakened, I violated the 'no eating' rule in dormitories by secretly nibbling on a rice cracker with water before taking Ibuprophen.

For me, the most challenging part of every single day was coaxing my right foot into cooperating for the day. The big toe stayed a lurid purple with overtones of black and blue from the falls the second day of the trip. It was sore, painful, swollen every morning. And then there was the matter of the loose big toenail which was lifted from the nailbed and floated around, connected by two or three tiny strands of tortured flesh. That toenail had to be wrestled and wrapped into place each morning. I did this "footwork" sitting on the edge of my bed, bent over rather uncomfortably because there was never enough room under the upper bunk to sit up straight.

Blisters plagued most walking pilgrims—nobody seemed immune. I pierced mine frequently with a needle and thread drawn through to drain fluid. Then each toe had to be wrapped separately and eased first into a protective sock, then into the shoe. Often, I would look up and find other pilgrims peering at my morning foot regimen, either with compassion or barely disguised horror. I always gave them a cheery hello.

In reality, I had blisters running the length of the toes on both feet from Day 2 to Day 43, when a kindly woman looked at my feet and then brought me Vaseline. She insisted that I rub my toes every remaining day of the trip with this before putting on the socks, and that the blisters would heal fast and not return. I was skeptical, but polite, bought a small tube of Vaseline, and indeed the blisters began to heal by the end of the last week of walking.

And so each day on the Camino started in a similar fashion. With my teeth brushed, feet wrapped, and plan for the day clearly in mind, I prepared to leave the dorm. I rustled my own stuff into the backpack, zipping to my heart's content—and I think without bothering anyone else. I was careful about lifting the pack from the floor onto my shoulders in one move, so carefully lifted it from the floor onto a chair or table, stooped down and backed into it, adjusted and buckled the straps into place around my waist and above my chest. Finally, I buckled on the waistpack which kept my valuables secure on my person and very importantly, immediately accessible. I would win no fashion show for pilgrims, but it worked for me.

Almost all pilgrims who walked with poles left them at the front doors of the dorms in big bins. I always slid mine under the bed for safekeeping. I did not want to be the last out of the dorm some morning with not a pair of walking poles in sight. I'd come to realize that I could only continue the walk if I walked with two poles. I adjusted my hat that was none too attractive but it was perfect for me with its large front brim for sun and rain protection, a tie for under the chin and a drapey cloth that covered my ears and the back of my neck. A final look around for belongings, and I was off. Every single day I gave myself the same little pep-talk prayer: "Sweet Jesus, my brother—This is my job today: to walk. May I enter the next dorm in at least as good a shape as I leave this one. And may there be a bottom bunk for me. Amen."

The minute I vacated a dorm, located the directional arrows and set out walking alone each morning, my mood bloomed. I felt renewed, excited and curious about whatever the day would bring. What I would characterize as joy inevitably swept over me. I am not sure why I felt so happy every morning, even in bad weather—just irrepressible happiness welled up at everything I saw and felt. Perhaps it was my normal personality asserting itself. Or perhaps I willed each new day on the Camino to be fruitful. Thich Nhat Hanh said, "Waking up this morning, I smile. Twenty-four brand new hours are before me. I vow to live fully in each moment and to look at all beings with eyes of compassion." As for the backpack's weight, the pesky feet and the considerable pain and bruises I had endured, they were along for the adventure, just like I was, and so we tolerated each other.

CAMINO—DAY 20

Poppies Blooming in the Snow

Postcard # 20—May 13, 2010 sent from Castrojeriz, Espana

Dearest Elena: Do you remember the card I sent you that had Pilgrims walking in snow? I sent it to you too soon, because today I walked from Hornillos to Castrojeriz (a total of 21.2km or 13.2mi) much of it in the snow & frosted wheat & grass along the road. Cold, cold, cold, but beautiful . . . and the last part it rained, rained . . . I was so happy to arrive at Castrojeriz—I am staying in an unheated dormitory for Pilgrims—people from all over the world & it's so cold in the dorm that I'm sitting in a nearby bar drinking wine, waiting for my dinner, & missing you. It is very warm in here & I'm glad to be doing my daily postcard to you and my journal here. I never expected to be cold—only way too warm in the month of May. Even the Spanish people are surprised at this cold & very wet stage of weather. Anyway, I'm happy to be doing this Camino walk & very grateful. Here in the bar a friendly cat is sitting on my lap. Grandma's freezing on the Camino

Journal—Day 20 (Thursday) May 13, 2010—written at Castrojeriz

Today I awakened, out at 7:30am in the rain, no BAR open for coffee, so just started walking, soon discovering that the rain drops were becoming snowflakes, oh, my!!! The wheatfields & then all the rocks and plants along the road & all the ridges were soon snow-covered. The wind howled. The grasses all frosted & stiff. Poppies in the snow. It was beautiful. After several miles I detoured by ½ mile off the road, stopping at San Bol, an amazing old church turned into a hostal for 12 pilgrims. Although closed, I was welcomed in for coffee, pate & bread by the hospitalera from Hungary, who was very kind and warm hearted. The circular pilgrims' table stood under a beautifully painted dome and the place emanated sacred vibrations. Gregorian chant softly played. Fortified as much by the spirituality of the place as the coffee & pate, I walked on, having another coffee in Hontanas, because the tiny village was as medieval as it gets . . . like a movie set. Leaving this village, it was terribly muddy, slug, slug. And believe me, I was careful. Muddy all the way here to Castrojeriz, walking a total of 21.2km or 13.2 mi. Arrived at Albergue Casa Nostra, nice interesting building but very cold without heat. Heated water in a cooking pan to wash up. So once again I spent the evening in a bar drinking a half-bottle tinto, visiting with pilgrims who stopped by my table to say hello, and would you believe a golden pussycat has come and settled onto my lap as I write. Delicious ensalada mixte and lentil stew with vegetables and sausages on the menu for dinner.

Reflection on Day 20, written back home in San Francisco

"Tibetans say that obstacles in a hard journey, such as hailstones, wind and unrelenting rains, are the work of demons, anxious to test the sincerity of the pilgrims and eliminate the fainthearted among them."

Peter Matthiessen

The walk from Hornillos to Castrojeriz was definitely the most uncomfortable physically of the 48 days I spent on the Camino. As I left the village of Hornillos, I ducked out of a chilling rainfall into a doorway to eye the snow on the nearby hills. The scenery was beautiful, but it was freezing. I'd only been walking 10 minutes and already my feet were cold and the pain of my ripped toenail and blisters was nearly intolerable. "Honest to God, I thought it would be hot mid-May. This is just too much for me," I said out loud.

For the first time, the idea of a little bus ride between villages seemed appealing. Who would know? Who would care? Who would blame me, given the weather? My little sinking spell passed quickly enough, and I trudged back onto the path and into an hour long rain that subtly became sleet and snow-flecked, then a full-on snowfall. I could feel the various precipitations pelt against the two pairs of summer cotton trousers that I wore over my pajamas. I felt and heard the sleet and snow against the crown of my hat and the long cloth that hung down and protected the back of my neck.

Little snowpacks formed in the folds of my badly ripped plastic poncho, now and then careening down to the ground like miniature avalanches. The knuckles of my gloved hands were stiff from the cold and ached like an arthritic attack. My ears were frosty, my nose runny. This was misery. I also grew nervous that snowfall would obliterate critical yellow arrows necessary to keep me on the straight and narrow path. I had a vision of becoming confused in the snowstorm, dying of hypothermia, and being found a week later—a frozen clump of matronly pilgrim 100 yards off the path, clutching a postcard and my journal.

I was facing into the storm, intently watching every step on the muddy path. The wind intermittently gusted the snow up under the brim of my hat and steamed up my glasses. "O'k, this is it! I'm going back and find the bus," I thought, and stopped to take off my gloves and wipe my smeared glasses with a tissue. I put glasses and gloves back on and picked up my poles, preparing to return to Hornillos. There, right at my feet and to the side of the path, were dozens of wild red poppies in bloom. They were heart stopping!!! beautiful—the red blooms, the silvery green stems and leaves in the snowflakes. How could it be that poppies would bloom in this weather? I almost missed them. I would have missed them if I had taken the bus. Instant gratefulness warmed me.

I studied the scene. The falling snow created an artistic picture that might have been painted by Van Gogh. All the elements of his genius were here in the way he illustrated movement—I thought of his whirling night time stars, his windswept waving wheat. And here for me to see on the path framed and frozen into a kind of pointillism—tiny dabs of falling snow—daubs of dancing reddish poppies, grayish clouds hanging low, frost-covered bushes shimmering, adjacent rutted puddles rimming with frosty sleet. My senses engaged . . . The poppies flashed their neon color in the wind. I smelled their redness, tasted their frozen scent. Felt their stiff and awkward sturdiness braving the wind. I relaxed my grip on the handles of the walking poles. Time stopped. I was not alone.

After savoring the sheer beauty of the scene, there was no longer a question about going back for the bus. I moved on towards the day's goal of Castrojeriz, feet creating a new kind of icy crunching sound with a catchy little rhythm. The mud and sludge seemed to be firming up—freezing, I supposed. I stopped twice that day at shelters to rest and get blessed relief from the cold. I didn't see any more poppies.

When I finally reached Castrojeriz—a total walk for the day of 21.2 km or 13.2 miles, I was too exhausted and numb to notice at first that there was no heat in the dormitory where I settled in for the night. The water in the bathroom wasn't icy, but too cool for me to shower. I went to the tiny kitchen, boiled water in a large cooking pan on the little gas burner, and carried it to the bathroom. Dipping my towel in the hot water, I was able to bathe, but more importantly, warm my face, arms and hands, torso and legs. I seated myself in one of the toilet stalls, then placed my feet in the pan of bathwater. My body endured shooting pain in my ice cube toes, then gradual relief. Bodily tension from the extended exposure to the cold somewhat subsided. I finally stopped shaking involuntarily.

When I finished my cat-bath ablutions and returned the pan to the kitchen, a very nice Irish American lady from Boston was humming loudly and bustling about, scraping carrots and quartering anemic looking tomatoes, frying onions and garlic on a gas burner, and consuming a hot drink that suspiciously and deliciously smelled of bourbon. When she saw the pan in my hand, she made the sign of the cross. "Oh Jesus, Mary the Mother of God . . . That's just the pan I need to make pasta for my husband and my sister. Are you finished with it?" And she reached eagerly to take the pan. I lowered it to my side and held on firmly, smiling broadly at her: "You can have the pan. I'm not cooking tonight but here, let me clean it out for you first." I chuckled as I emptied the bathwater, thoroughly scrubbed the pan, then dried it and handed it over with a flourish. I left the hummer in the kitchen preparing her pasta sauce and went to explore the dormitory.

I was on a mission searching for extra blankets. I located a stack of woolen ones set out on an upstairs chest. Sorting through them proved futile, as none felt, looked or smelled very clean, but I selected the heaviest one I could find, and gratefully arranged it over my pathetically inadequate bedroll which I carried. In weather like this, it was not the time to be picky about blankets, or worried about bed bugs.

I settled in a drafty library/sitting room and glanced through a Spanish weekly magazine. A tabloid as trashy as any Hollywood rag to be found in an American grocery store checkout line, I thought, and even without knowing Spanish, I could read the pictures. Here was a plump starlet who had dieted herself into a bikini. And on the next page more love handles. Love triangles. Love quadrangles. Page after page of the "other man." The "other woman." Red carpets here, there, everywhere. Tummy Tucks. Face Lifts. Botoxed laugh lines. Multiple adopted children of famous stars looking cranky and shell-shocked being herded through airports. Shocking necklines. Shocking skirt lengths. Baby bumps. Recognizable English royalty hissing at each other. Spanish royalty attending a glamorous musical gala.

I threw the magazine aside. I did not come to Spain to look at tabloids. My feet were getting cold again. "This damn cold weather is just too much," I announced to nobody in particular. The smells from the pasta sauce bubbling away in the kitchen reminded me I was famished. It was time to find a warm Bar that served dinner, write a postcard to Elena and scribble a journal entry for the day.

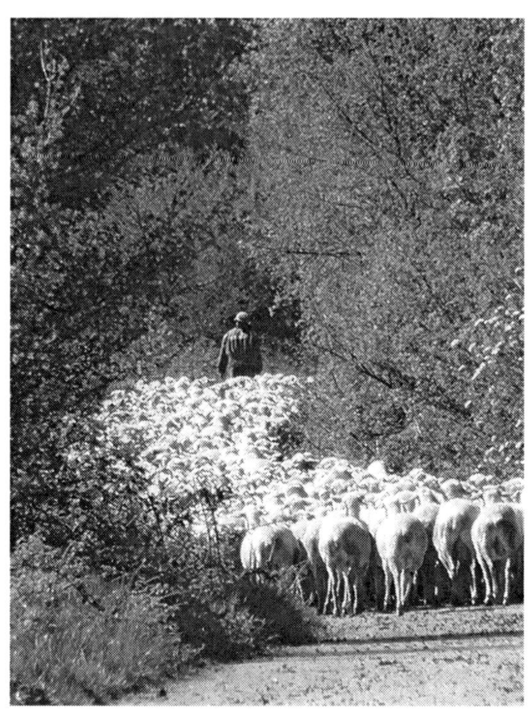

CAMINO—DAY 21

And You? Why do you Walk the Camino?

Postcard # 21—May 14, 2010 sent from Boadilla del Camino, Espana

Elena: I simply cannot believe the weather I'm experiencing—cold, chilling winds, rain. Now this am it was sunny—but by 2:00pm it was overcast, then chill spitting rain into Boadilla del Camino—I felt lucky to be able to walk 19.1km or 11.5mi. When I arrived here I was given a mattress on the floor of a kind of barn "living room". Then a young man appeared who worked there & said to me: "You are too tired to sleep on the floor." He picked up my things & took me to a lovely semi-private dorm room with only 3 bunk beds & I got a bottom one. It was a mysterious encounter!!! I picked this postcard picture of the sheep following the shepherd because I have walked with sheep on the road several times. Dogs help the shepherd keep the animals together. Love from Grandma

Journal—Day 21 (Friday) May 14, 2010—written in Boadilla del Camino

This am promised & delivered sunshine for about 4 hours on the Camino, but then cold, then overcast, then rain & wind all the way into Boadilla del Camino. I am very tired after this 19.1km or 11.5mi walk. Walking out of Castrojeriz was fabulous—beautiful little town—long and narrow, then winding paths that cut across the farmland and steeply ascended a mountain with breathtaking views into the valleys and amazing birdsong . . . including my favorite cuckoos calling from fence-rows. The descent down onto the Meseta was very slow, very steep. Staying for the night at a memorable place called <u>En El Camino</u>, a family-run Albergue where because of sheer numbers and full house, I was taken to a side building & given a place on the floor. The son came in, picked up my things & not minding at all 25 other pilgrims sitting & waiting for their mattresses to arrive, led me back to the main house and to a small private room. 5 older pilgrims joined me. Ate with about 60 pilgrims in the dining room for a delicious 'set menu'. Afterwards, a dozen of us sat together, finishing our wine and talking until nearly midnight. The topic dominating all: <u>Why are we walking the Camino?</u> I took copious notes.

Reflection on Day 21, written at home in San Francisco

Engrave this upon my heart: "There isn't anyone you couldn't love once you've heard their story."

Anonymous

The walk on the morning of Day 21 was beautiful, and I began to have hope of a change in weather. Walking westward from Castrojeriz, the sunshine warmed the farmlands, and the snow on distant hills melted rapidly. The sunshine also brought out the energy of the birds and I heard their song from trees and bushes, and observed them flitting and feeding along every fencerow. The cuckoos seemed particularly sensitive to the warming sun and their gentle calls ricocheted from pasture to pasture. The path crossed miles of tapestried farmlands, then crisscrossed up a steep and rutted path to the crest of a mountain.

At the top, views in every direction were breathtaking, especially down onto the Meseta. These were the flatlands of northern Spain, and considered by many to be the hardest stretch of the trip especially if the weather was either intensely hot or cold. I'd been warned amply in my Camino readings about how boring the Meseta could be for pilgrims, with nothing of interest to see or to eat. I didn't believe a bit of it. The Meseta looked gorgeous from the mountaintop. And besides, walking on flatlands would probably give my blisters and injured big toe a chance to heal.

It was a formidable walk down the mountain, and the weather changed rapidly over the course of two hours. Sunshine and warmth faded into gray cloudiness. A chilly wind came up and by the time I was actually walking on the Meseta, it started to rain hard. After a total of 11.5 miles, I was grateful to roll into Boadilla del Camino and find a place in an Albergue. There seemed to be confusion as I settled into a chair at a circular registration table. Too many soggy pilgrims. Too few beds. With each two registrations completed, the lovely young hospitalera would scurry off with the pilgrims and their belongings, then rush back in about ten minutes to work with two more souls. It was a slow process and I felt uneasy about whether I'd get a bed or not. There was one thing I knew: I could not walk further. I was too exhausted.

During the wait, I grew to like the place. It was evident that it was run by a close-knit group of people—a family, as I learned through the evening. I could observe from my place at the registration table, a small shop, a bar, lovely artwork and a restaurant on the first floor. There was a great flurry of late afternoon activity by the staff, and all seemed so friendly, effortless, joyful even in the work of serving pilgrims. The aroma of roasting meat—pork, I thought, and sauerkraut, filled the first floor area. I would eat here tonight, even if I didn't get a bed. I had a very distinct feeling that this was a special place on the Camino.

When finally I was registered, I learned the good news/bad news. I would have a place to sleep for the night, but—it would be a mattress on the floor of an adjacent building. The young woman walked me outside to the other building, carrying my backpack and speaking Spanish to me non-stop. There were many pilgrims in the enormous room to which she took me, lounging on chairs with backpacks at their feet. But there wasn't a mattress in sight. She deposited me in a chair next to an empty space on the floor that she pantomimed to be especially reserved for me. Seeing the glazed look in my eyes, she elaborately and enthusiastically pointed at her watch, gesturing that a mattress would be brought in just one hour, at 5:00pm. I smiled weakly at her, not at all sure I understood a bit of what she said. For good measure, she made a fist, displayed her fingers, and counted out loud from 1 to 5 in Spanish, tapped her watch again, and disappeared through the door.

What could I have done? Left because there was no bed available for an hour? And where would I go? It was raining outside, nearly dark. I felt weak from the sheer effort of thinking about sitting upright for an hour. A man came in and somberly joined a woman sitting a few feet from me. "The other albergues are completely full," I overheard him tell her quietly. "No possibility for us to move. We're lucky to have this spot." Hearing his assessment of the situation, I became grateful to be in out of the rain. I sat as comfortably as I could in the hard little chair and turned my attention to the silence of the room. I intended to be available to my place in the universe that evening. I disappeared into the sound of the rain on the windows, the chill in the air and perhaps even into sleep.

I felt a tap on my shoulder and a man who worked at the Albergue—a member of the family, was standing by my chair. "You are too tired to sleep on the floor. Come with me." He picked up my pack and guided me to the door. "Hurry, Hurry. I'm supposed to be working in the restaurant." And without another word, I was led past the poor souls waiting for their mattresses, back to the house, up some stairs to a side room with three bunk beds and my pack deposited on a lower bunk. "Rest for awhile, then come downstairs at 7:00 for a delicious pilgrims' dinner." He closed the door and was gone. I took a warm shower, then collapsed on my bunk to sleep for an hour. When I awakened, I had been joined by 5 older pilgrims settling in. All of us were compatible, and all very grateful for this tiny room with beds and a bathroom nearby in the hall.

At 7:00pm, I made my way to the cavernous dining room where dozens of pilgrims were coming in from the bar and various rooms, grouping themselves at long tables. Everyone was warmly welcomed by the staff, and I was directed to join a group of a dozen pilgrims at a smaller table, all speaking English but representing multiple nationalities. We awkwardly introduced ourselves. There was a man from Germany. Another from Hungary. A woman from Canada. A man from Italy. A woman from Sweden. Two women from Japan. A man from Korea. A man from Brazil, a woman from Spain, another from Belgium and I, the only American at the table. I observed each tablemate carefully. All but one seemed open and friendly, eager even to talk and laugh. I was thrilled with this mini international community.

Wine was poured from several carafes on the table and toasts were warmly offered via clinking glasses. An enormous crockery tureen was brought in from the kitchen and set in front of me. The waiter walked away. The middle-aged man from Brazil said "This is an honor for you. Please serve us. You are the grandmother of our table." I cooperated by ladling out bowls of hearty lentil and sausage soup. Thick slices of homemade bread accompanied the first course. The room quieted in appreciation of the delicious and warming food. Second servings of the soup were passed around and our waiter carried the empty tureen back to a sideboard. "There is a small delay in the kitchen—30 minutes until the main course," he announced, clearing the bowls away.

Conversation around the table in English began again and seemed to go on forever about the rain, the snow, ice cold feet, hands, noses and ears. Horror stories were exchanged about personal discomforts of walking in cold weather. Two whole weeks of miserable chill seemed to be the only topic about which the collective table could speak. I marveled at the facility with which every person spoke English. Listening to all this intently, I wanted to hear more about each person, and less about the weather.

Never one to be shy, I finally stood up and clinked a spoon against my glass for the attention of my tablemates. "Hello again, Mary here from California. I am so happy to be with you in this nice warm albergue this evening. I have two proposals for our table. Would you like to hear them?" Hans, on my left, rose up magisterially and said: "And Mary, what would you do if we said we didn't want to hear your proposals?" Everybody laughed. "Oh, I would give them to you anyway." Another toast was raised. "I propose no more discussion of the weather tonight during dinner." I observed reactions. People were nodding in agreement. "And my second proposal is that Hans refill our wine glasses." This got a round of applause. The ice was broken in more ways than one.

By the time the waiters carried in steaming plates of roast pork, conversation was moving beyond the normal pilgrim exchanges of home bases, occupations, blisters and how far we'd walked that day. Hans had launched into a ramble about the current state of the German economy. I gave him my attention, but he was going on and on. I could hear around me other snippets of private conversations that included the state of Spanish television programming, accessibility to the internet on the Camino and at the other end of the table, raised voices arguing pro and con about ordination of women as Catholic priests. Intense curiosity piqued about the lives of these randomly placed dozen souls at the table.

Conversation stopped as we assessed the laden plates delivered from the kitchen and set down in front of us. Thick, succulent slices of roast pork were fanned out across a bed of sauerkraut. A small mound of steamed red cabbage separated the meat from a generous portion of roasted potatoes and red peppers. The aroma was intoxicating. The Brazilian quickly stood and offered this toast: "With bread and wine and good companions, the Camino is walked." We solemnly raised our glasses and drank. Then, making the sign of the cross over the food, he slowly continued: "Bless each of us You have assembled here, O Lord, and all these gifts, and the farmers who raised the food, the vintners who grew the grapes, the cooks who prepared this meal, the servers who brought it to us and those who will wash the dishes. May this food and drink nourish us to walk the Camino and that evermore we may be your hands and feet on this earth. Through Christ our Lord, Amen." I thought "That Brazilian is probably a Catholic priest, and with a good measure of Buddhist thrown in."

The food was delicious and bounteous. The 12 pilgrims at our table continued to share stories, tell jokes, raise toasts to each other. I felt a great oneness with these strangers with whom I shared the food and wine. "The intimacy of the shared Camino dinner hour," I mused as I looked around. Even the one reserved looking woman warmed to the deepening sense of camaraderie. I would probably never see these people again, but for tonight, we were not 12 pilgrims, nor 12 apostle companions to St. James, but one with him.

The restaurant was clearing out. Almost all pilgrims were gone—heading off to bed, or to the bar, and still we twelve sat talking, lingering through dessert, through coffee. Our waiter cleared the table, and encouraged us to stay where we were and visit. No one made a move to leave and Hans ordered carafes of wine from the waiter. I rose to my feet. "I have another proposal, and this is a really, really good one." People were fully attentive. "I propose that the 12 of us change places and sit between people we haven't talked to yet. Exchange information. Maybe tell why you are walking the Camino."

I expected a very mixed reaction to this end of evening proposal. Maybe some resistance or scoffing. Or begging off and going to bed. But with one motion, all the pilgrims arose. We walked around the table, making eye contact, smiling, and not at all awkwardly, seated ourselves again in new places. Conversation began in earnest. The carafes were delivered. The wine was poured. The atmosphere mellowed. Storytelling began.

As I was assuring my new seatmate that I had walked multiple times across the Golden Gate Bridge in San Francisco, and that it was indeed safe to do so, the two Japanese women stood and clinked their glasses for attention. Even when we all stopped talking and looked at them, they continued clinking their spoons against the glasses. With all eyes turned on them, they blushed deeply, then put their hands over their faces. The Brazilian immediately stood and said, "I think we have another proposal. Tell us what you would like to say?" One started tentatively: "Please forgive our poor English. We have only one request, and that is to know why we are here." The other continued "Why does each and other walk the Camino? This evening I have learned very many stories. It is a good chance for us to hear from pilgrims. Please tell us."The other repeated her sister's sentence: "Yes, a good chance. Please tell us."They bowed and sat down.

We pushed our chairs back from the table and into a circle. Hans offered to begin. I slipped a small notebook out of my waistpack and took notes as discreetly as I could. For more than two hours, I scribbled away as we spoke in the quiet restaurant about why we were on the Camino. A few people seemed very sure of their reasons and told us directly and confidently. Others were a bit self-conscious, perhaps unsure of what to say, or embarrassed by the activity. Some appeared tentative—more guarded in describing why they walked to Santiago de Compostela. But all spoke and most with a kind of passion that arose from pain.

It was not an easy exercise. It evoked emotion in every person at the table as the stories were told. A pilgrimage of deep religious conviction was described. Pilgrimages of thanksgiving for favors received or being saved some great sorrow. Pilgrimages of discernment over life decisions. Pilgrimages of grief—grave illness, death of loved ones. Disappointment in love and marriage. Pilgrimages of Loose Ends: loss of jobs; interrupted studies; boredom or depression; adventure or touring or athleticism. This quote from The Sharing, by Edwina Gately, a favorite poet of mine sums it up: "But in each brave and lonely story, God's gentle life broke through . . . And we heard music in the Darkness and smelt flowers in the void."

This intimate depth of personal sharing had not shown itself during the casual dinner conversation, but being surfaced so abruptly among friendly and trusting pilgrims at the end of the evening evoked cooperation, palpable, heartfelt compassion and love among us. It had been a risky exercise among Camino pilgrims, but on this occasion, it resulted in deep insight into the human condition, warm support for each other, agreement, laughter, anger, angst, tears, and at least for that concentrated time, understanding and oneness within the pilgrim family.

Camino—Day 22

Closer to the Truth

Postcard # 22—May 15, 2010 sent from Villasirga, Espana

Dear Elena: Your Grandma in her 70th year keeps on going, although the feet are still bandaged. Today I walked 20.7km or 12.4 mi on fairly stoney paths. Walked for several windy and cold miles along a canal so beautiful (just like on the picture) & crossed these old Roman "dams" or "locks". Into Fromista, a medieval town with stunning churches (12th, 13th & 14th Century) & finally in the rain again, into Villasirga where I am ensconced in a private hostal eating tapas & resting my feet!!!! I think a Pilgrim's feet are always sore. Extra love today from Grandma on the Camino, enough for you to give kisses to the whole family.

Journal—Day 22 (Saturday) May 15, 2010—written at Villasirga

I slept very soundly in my lower bunk last night. This am sought out that young man who had rescued me from the mattress on the floor and slipped him 5 Euros for his extraordinary kindness. We connected, like a mother and a son. Last night's pilgrim group dinner at En El Camino was delightful, and today, twice reviewed notes I took, blessing each person as I recalled their looks, their mannerisms, their stories. Saw many storks and stork nests today, always perched on Church steeples and posts & monuments. No baby storks yet, at least visible to my scrutiny. Feel like I'm nesting too, on the Camino, and about to give birth to something new. Cold and windy walk into Fromista along a gorgeous canal & over Roman bridges & aqueducts that still serve irrigation functions. Stopped & watched men open & shut ancient irrigation valves. One came to me and asked that I take his request for return of his wife's health (coma) to Santiago for him. Fromista churches fantastic—(San Martin, 1066) & the other San Pedro (with museum) playing classical Church music. Lots of Pilgrim statues and monuments in and around the churches. Bought stamps at TABAC in order to continue sending Elena's postcards. Walked on to Poblacion de Campos where at 1:00pm as I was walking through the village, the church bells rang hundreds of times. No people. The church locked. I don't understand why. For the last two miles into Villasirga walked together (and separately) with several debonair and very entertaining older Brits walking stages of the Camino over several years. (Pelosi Connection in San Francisco) Once in Villasirga, they kept on walking, and I, having walked 20.7km or 12.4mi. took a heated room in Las Cantigas Pension (30Euros) very nice—next to Church of the White Virgin (Santa Maria la Blanca.) Spent an hour in this magnificent old church catching up on the day's prayers, thinking about last night's dinner partners again, and the man with the wife in a coma. Feeling pure gratefulness to have gotten this far on the Camino. Settled in a bar as close as possible to a space heater occasionally wheezing out a breath of warm air on my feet. Ate tapas early tonight with good wine. On the Spanish TV weather map the little symbols for snow and rain are being replaced with little round suns—all the folks at the bar took note and began animated discussion—I think, I hope, I pray that this means the weather is about to change for the better. Feet are extra sore but with a soak and after a massage using the l'Occitaine Lavender foot crème the nurse gave me in Los Arcos, I'm somewhat recovered.

Reflection on Day 22, written back home in San Francisco

Ti-ts'ang asked Fa-yen, "Where are you going?" Fa-yen said, "around on pilgrimage." Ti-ts'ang said: What is the purpose of pilgrimage?" Fa-yen said: "I don't know." Ti-ts'ang nodded in agreement. "Not knowing is nearest the truth."

From the Zen Book of Serenity

I was late leaving the dorm in Boadilla del Camino on Day 22, and didn't catch a single glimpse of last night's tablemates. But they were on my mind and their stories appeared in my dreams. I sat in the restaurant with my morning coffee, and pored over the notes I had taken the night before as each of the twelve of us at the table tried to articulate why we were making a pilgrimage to Santiago. As I read the notes a second time, each person's story and face came into sharp focus.

Out of all the pilgrims from last night's dinner, I could really only remember Hans' name. He told us he was retired from an appliance manufacturing company in Germany, and therefore had a lot of time to pursue sports and leisure, especially hiking with his friends. He wanted to win a bet with his neighbor that he could walk the Camino from Roncesvalles to Santiago in 28 days, beating his friend by one day. Around the table, we were dazzled, incredulous that it could be walked that fast. "Winning a bet is not a very good reason to be walking a pilgrimage," he observed. "I'd rather be doing it slower, seeing things, not starting at 5:30 each morning and ending in the dark. This is the only time I've talked to people since I've left. But a bet is a bet, and I'm going to win this one. There's money on it."

Sitting next to Hans was a handsome man from Hungary. He started confidently. "Everything is good for me, life is good, no worries—but you see, I have a little crisis. My girlfriend is pregnant. She's happy, I'm happy, but she wants to get married. I don't think that's necessary. So, we have this little disagreement and I'm walking the Camino. It is a big decision in life for me. I need some time alone. Maybe I'll know what to do when I reach Santiago. Maybe not."

The woman from Sweden shot a venomous look at the man from Hungary. "Stupid. Stupid. Any man who gets a girl pregnant is stupid and cruel. I'm up to my chin in this problem right now. Her voice cracked with emotion and pure anger. My husband has gotten our daughter's friend pregnant, and wants to divorce me. I did not suspect any of this. I'll never give him a divorce. Look at me. I am 56 years old. He is 63. She is 27. I am so angry I can't breathe Swedish air. So I walk everyday to keep from killing my husband. Maybe I'll just keep on walking after Santiago straight to Finisterre and into the sea. Then he could marry her." We were all shocked at her intensity. She began to cry and one of the women moved her chair closer to her and another handed her a tissue. From the corner of my eye I saw the Brazilian man slightly raise his hand to make a discreet sign of the cross in her direction. No one spoke for about two minutes. I was pained as I scribbled her words into my journal.

Finally, I heard the voice of the lovely Canadian woman. "I want to speak next, because I am also very angry and confused. I lost my job of 11 years, 8 of them as a supervisor in an automobile manufacturing company. Actually, I was fired because I had an affair with a manager in another department. The company got rid of me by reorganizing my department. They cut out my position, gave me severance pay. But I was fired, and everybody knew it. My lover won't see me anymore. Of course, nothing happened to his job. The men are always protected. So I have no job. I'm depressed. I have a little money and a lot of time. I wanted to get away, and I heard about the Camino. It's a change of scenery. Something different for me to do. Maybe my depression will lift. I don't know. I'm not even sure I will go all the way to Santiago."

I shifted in my chair to get a better look at my companions. "Good Lord," I thought. "I hadn't expected this candor. So far, this is an earful. Who knew there was such drama on the Camino? Where is this exercise going to lead?"

The two Japanese women both raised their hands together, then laughed and pointed to each other. "You go first." "No, you go first." "O'k, I begin. We are sisters from Japan," and the first bowed slightly to her sister, encouraging her to continue. Her sister followed the cue and told the group: "Yes, we are twin sisters from Japan, and we are not married, like others at this table." Another slight bow to the other twin, who continued: "No, we are not married, and we do everything together. For example, we live together, take meals together, work at the same company, but different departments, and we even travel together." More bowing. "Yes," the other continued, "we travel together, like in Africa, New Zealand, America and Europe, but this time we have a big reason to walk in Spain." Another bow. "Yes," the other lowered her voice: "we have a big reason. Last year I was baptized as Catholic. Most of our family was very, very unhappy. My sister is thinking about what to do." A deep bow, and the other continued: "Yes, I am not completely clear about Catholic faith. I am studying if I should be baptized." The other sister continued: "When I joined the Catholic Church, I read many books. I learned about the Camino, and thought it would be spiritual to walk with all the pilgrims from a thousand years. Very Buddhist. As is usual, my twin sister accompanies me, even though she has not yet decided on baptism." Bowing to the right. "Yes," the other said. "We walk to Santiago together. My sister wants to stir her fervor by seeing the relics of the bones. Maybe I will be lucky and St. James will help me decide to be baptized." They remained silent for several moments, then bowed deeply to all seated at the table and sat down.

Following the example of the Japanese women, the Korean man stood and bowed to us. "I am from Korea, the most beautiful of the Asian countries. It is popular for Koreans to walk the Camino. Very big honor. Very hard work and stamina to make it to Santiago. I walk this year with no pay because my supervisor walked all the way to Santiago and his diploma hangs on the wall next to his desk. He received a big promotion when he returned. I think this is a good way for me to get a promotion also. My company is very famous all over the world. You are all welcome to visit Korea. You will not be sorry to spend your vacation and your money in Korea." And he took his seat at the table.

None too soon for the Korean to be finished, I thought, as my pen was running out of ink and my hand ached from the rapid note-taking. Seven had spoken, five more to go. And what on earth am I going to say to these people when it's my turn? I can't think of a word to say. I dug another pen out of my waistpack in time to record the next story.

The Brazilian began slowly and thoughtfully: "I have known about the Camino all my life. There are many people in Brazil who have participated in its sacred mystery. Even as a young man, I wanted to come to Spain, to walk the Camino. It took a long time for me to save enough money and get six weeks of free time to come here. And for why? For why have I done this? I have grown restless in my work, afraid of making mistakes. Afraid of people where I work. Afraid of lies and accusations. Afraid of change. But I can't hold back my changing." His shoulders slumped, I thought, and he looked very tired.

Everybody at the table was attentive. He nervously finished his cold coffee. "I am a Catholic priest for 32 years. When I was ordained, things were simpler. I was filled with love for the church, for being a priest, for saying Mass, for working with the people. But now there is corruption everywhere and abuse. Vatican rules are unrealistic, shall I say—on the sexual life and women being ordained. So unrealistic. People are leaving the church. And for why? For why do they leave the Church? Because the Church imposes man-made rules on its followers. Would Christ have forbidden a woman to minister to the people? Would Christ have turned away a homosexual? Would Christ have forbidden a priest to marry? There it is. I walk the Camino in confusion about who I am. The work I am doing. I walk for why? To regain my vocation. I'm confused. I will ask for my sins to be forgiven when I reach Santiago. Forgive me. What I have told you I have never told another person." He smiled at us so sadly. "May St. James bless each of you in your needs and guide you safely on the path. May each of you experience Christ's love. May each of you be Christ's hands and feet on earth." And the Brazilian priest humbly raised his hands and blessed his fellow pilgrims.

The middle aged woman from Belgium leaned forward in her chair. "I will go next," she said with authority, speaking slowly and distinctly.

"Thank you for your blessing and your story, Father. Like Jesus, one who is a truth teller is always on a difficult and uncertain path. One who tells the truth and lives it may well be carrying a heavy cross, may well be crucified by unbelievers, may well be turned away by his own people. Thank you for reminding us that Christ and his message was very different from how Christian institutions have structured themselves." She let this sink in and seemed comfortable with the silence she had created in her wide-eyed audience. "And thanks to all of you for your honesty in telling us why you walk the Camino. My story is very different, and without crisis or drama. I am a religion teacher in a Catholic College in Belgium for 8 years. This year, I have been accepted for a doctoral program in Theology in the United States. It is my lifelong dream to study in America. So I walk on the Camino because for a short while I am free before my studies begin. I am happy. I am filled with thanksgiving and gratefulness. This evening, I am renewed in spirit and hope, and yes, love also, because I am sitting here with the 12 of us. For me our Pilgrim number is significant. Santiago himself, a simple fisherman, was one of the 12 Apostles chosen by Jesus, the Christ. Are we in some mysterious way also chosen by Christ for some special role in this world? When Father blessed us just now he said 'May each of you be Christ's hands and feet on earth.' I like that definition of a Christian. But I would enlarge it. Whether one is a Christian, a Buddhist, a Jew, or Muslim, Hindu or whatever tradition, isn't that our role? To be the hands and feet of the Great Absolute? To lose our ego and drama and to serve our brothers and our sisters?

There was complete silence in the group. Everyone seemed stunned—lost in thought, or perhaps in translation, dazzled by the Belgian's story. The woman from Spain sat forward on her chair. "I think I'll go next. Right now, I am very sad about my religion. All my life I have loved Jesus and Mother Mary, the Catholic Church, ceremony, rituals, prayers, feast days and saints, especially our Spanish mystics, Teresa of Avila and John of the Cross. I was in a convent for four years, but that was not my vocation. Now I have spent 23 years working in a hospital, mostly as a surgical nurse. All my life until two years ago, I had a loving relationship with God. Everyday I went to Mass and said the Rosary. Even with a busy schedule, everyday I meditated on Scripture. My greatest joy was to sit in silent prayer three times each day. I actually felt God's love nourishing me, felt like I was guided in decisions, like I was a favorite child of God. God was the source of my strength in a difficult job. But now, I am like a dry sponge with no water. I don't have connection to God. He disappeared from me. I feel nothing, nothing, nothing at all from God—no guidance, no love, no relationship. Why has he abandoned me? Everyday I go to Mass, say the Rosary, meditate on Scripture but I feel no love, nothing from God. It is a crisis for me. That's why I walk the Camino. I am looking for God. He has lost me."

Silence in the group. I felt completely overwhelmed, weak, almost like I might faint from the weight of these unexpected stories. Then the man from Italy spoke up. "It's getting late, so I'll make my story short. I was in prison for 8 ½ years. It was pretty serious crime for some people, I guess, and while I was there I had a lot of time to think about life—about my sins. None of my life was exactly religious, but it was o'k. I made a bargain with God: 'You get me out of prison by 2010, and I'll walk the Camino for you during Holy Year.' So you see, both ends of the bargain are kept. I got out of prison early and back to my family. I have papers to leave my area for a few weeks. God will forgive my sins when I reach Santiago and I'm honored to be here tonight with you."

The Italian had made it short and sweet, and now it was my turn. Why was my mind a total blank? Everybody looked at me, and I said "Honestly, right now I don't know why I am on the Camino. For many years I have been filled with the idea that I must walk to Santiago. Love has pulled me here. The person I have been is dissolving in that love. Maybe like a caterpillar, I will turn into a butterfly. Thank you for your companionship tonight. I will never forget you." And the evening ended.

Just reviewing these notes at the breakfast table brought the previous evening's intimate discussions and my brother and sister pilgrims clearly into focus. It was hard to believe even in morning's light that 12 out of 12 people spoke English, and that 12 out of 12 would articulate their Camino stories and reasons for walking to randomly met strangers around a restaurant table at an albergue. I couldn't wrap my mind around the dynamic that had coaxed these people to speak. I wondered how they individually felt this morning about last night's stories they heard at the table.

"I'll probably never see them again. They're long gone this morning. We're scattered to the winds," I thought, and pushed on. I was eager to begin the day's walk to Villasirga because I would walk along canals and aqueducts built in Roman times. The country was flat, the sun was out and although it was cold, I felt an incredible lightness of being as the first few miles slipped by uneventfully.

The smooth walking path ran straight and flat with a fast flowing canal along one side. Planted trees lined the paths at set distances and birds gravitated to them for shelter and to the canals for water. I often heard croaking of frogs and occasionally caught glimpses of them splashing into the water from the banks. Despite the cold weather, rampant wildflowers bloomed along the path and between the tracks separating crops in the fields—sometimes even insistently blooming out of cracks in the concrete sides of the canals. How good it felt to be out in nature walking with energy, letting last night's stories slide away.

Occasionally, I'd pass men working at the aqueducts to release water into irrigation troughs that were channeled into fields. I'd seen irrigation done like this in Idaho where my husband's family lives—the technology so essential to crop yield. It was hard to think that these Roman canals along which I walked were in existence before America was discovered in 1492 by Spanish explorers. I also remembered from visits to Idaho, that no community traced with canals was immune to the tragic drowning of young people who dared to swim in the fast moving water. How many Romans and Spanish, perhaps even Santiago pilgrims, had come to similar fate from swimming in these channeled waters?

I stood on a small bridge, stopping to watch several men struggle to open an irrigation valve. The mechanism seemed stuck, uncooperative to their efforts to pry it open with hefty wrenches and hammers. I don't know Spanish, but I think there was considerable cursing at the thwarted project. Suddenly, one of the men spotted me standing on the bridge. He gestured to the other men, who quieted and we all stared at each other. "Camino?" he called up to me. I nodded. The man broke away from his group and scrambled up the embankment and quickly approached onto the bridge where I stood. He spoke to me rapidly in Spanish. "I don't understand," I said gently, wondering if he wanted money, or was trying to warn me of some danger. He repeated his message more urgently, jabbing his finger in the direction I was headed, and I thought his eyes were pleading with me. He seemed troubled, intense, desperate even.

I looked around for help. Two pilgrims were approaching on the path and as they reached the bridge, I asked if they spoke English. "Oh yes. Are you having a problem here?" I nodded, "This man wants to tell me something, but I can't understand it." One pilgrim turned to the man and asked him in Spanish what he wanted to tell me. Gradually, through translation, I got the terrible story. The man's wife lay in a coma in a hospital for one month, victim of a car crash which killed two of his four children. He wanted to walk to Santiago to beg the saint for return of her health, but couldn't leave his two children at home, his wife in the hospital nor his meager field job. Would I go for him? Would I plead his case to bring his wife back to health when I arrived at the Santiago Cathedral?

Two of the workers from the viaduct made their way onto the bridge and put their arms around his shoulders protectively. The man began to cry. I didn't have a clue how to respond to what seemed a futile request. How could I take this man's prayers to Santiago? I slipped my backpack off and to the ground. Then I approached him, and gestured to the two pilgrim translators to come near. The six of us gathered into a tight little circle. I looked at him intently as he collected himself and wiped his eyes and nose on his shirtsleeves. "I will not reach Santiago for many days, but I will carry your request and lay it at the altar in the Cathedral."

I felt how awkward this was—how feeble my response as it was translated to the man and his friends. I took the man's hand and heard myself say: "Here is what you must do everyday as I am walking to Santiago with your request." I nodded to the translators who spoke my words to the man. I continued: "Everyday go to the hospital. Take your wife's hands and tell her how much you love her and want her to speak to you—how much the children need her and are waiting for her to be well." These words were translated to him in Spanish. Finally, I added "Be loving and gentle with the two children. Hold them everyday. Let them see their mother while she is alive. I will deliver your request to Sant Iago as soon as I arrive."

The translated words seemed to sink in and the man began sobbing. He sunk to his knees and his friends lifted him gently, led him off the bridge and back to their project at hand. The two helpful pilgrims lifted my backpack from the ground and gently adjusted it on my shoulders. Finally, because there were no more words to say, they turned and walked away on the path.

As I watched them leave, I felt my strength diminishing. After some minutes, I walked on with this unexpected burden of the man's story and his request to me. I felt its weight on my shoulders and in my heart. I wished I'd never seen him, heard his story, or offered to deliver his request to Santiago. Why hadn't I kept my mouth shut? I'd placed myself in such a ridiculous situation. What on earth could I do with this obligation? Walk into the Cathedral and blurt out the man's request to the statue of St. James? Seek out an English speaking priest and pass the request along? This was exactly the kind of involvement I didn't want on the Camino.

Even though it was clouding up, I stopped at a bar in Fromista for a coffee and lunch and tried to forget about the morning's encounter and the foolish promise I had made. I located the Cathedral, went inside, sat on an impossibly tiny and uncomfortable chair by a side altar, and slipped off my shoes. There in my mind flashed the man's face again, those pleading eyes with tears streaming down, pinning his hopes on my taking his request to Santiago. He displayed such faith that I could be his courier to the Divine to bring his wife back to him. I hadn't seen faith like his since my mother Irene was alive. How completely she believed in vocal prayer and was devoted to all kinds—petitionary, praise, thanksgiving. She prayed always and in all ways and for all things good—rain, crops, food to eat, health, water, safety, her husband, children, the neighbors, studies and exams, birth and death. I heard her say many times: "I pray everyday for a happy death." I couldn't understand that, and actually thought it sounded crazy. Tears formed in my eyes. "Mama, you were so sweet and simple, so humble in your faith. So close to your God. What should I do about this man?

I rested with this question for awhile, then took out the journal from my waistpack and a pen and wrote a page which I titled <u>To Saint James—A Petition from the Man at the Canal</u>. At least it would be ready in case I wanted to follow through when I reached my destination—just in case the right moment would present itself at the Cathedral in Santiago. As I finished my task and put away the journal, several women came into the church where I sat, shaking their wet umbrellas. It was time for me to leave. In the vestibule, I wrestled into the remnants of my ripped rain poncho and set out in the chill for my destination of Villasirga.

CAMINO—DAY 23

The Weather Changes

Postcard # 23—May 16, 2010 sent from Calzadilla de la Cueza, Espana

Elena: Today from Villasirga to Calzadilla I walked 23.3km or 14mi. I started at 10:00am (very late for me) & got here about 6:15pm, walking very slowly and I absorbing the gorgeous countryside that looked for the first time like southern Illinois. Best of all, it was sunny all the way and warm for the 1st time in 2 weeks. Bird song was tremendous, flowers & fields so beautiful, my spirit so happy and peaceful. Walked alone . . . today saw few pilgrims. The 1st 10 miles no pain, just walking, but the last 4 miles seemed long. I had no choice but to come here to stay. I seem to be getting stronger each day, leg muscles really firming. Tonight I had a Pilgrims Menu—white bean soup & roast chicken, vegetables, dessert & wine. Delicious. It is not difficult for a pilgrim to eat well & inexpensively. Missing you, Elena & everybody else—family, neighbors and friends we both love.

Journal—Day 23 (Sunday) May 16, 2010—written at Calzadilla de la Cueza

What a luxury it was to have a private room with bath last night. Slept so well & awakened at 8:30am, down for breakfast, then back to the room to "pray over" my feet & work on them. Rubbed Rosemary Irene on them & then began walking. Not bad, not much pain this am. I'm grateful for the gorgeous day, of course the 1st time in two weeks. The trail is flat today, a very welcome change from the past weeks. After one hour walking, could take off my sweatshirt. The warmth of the direct sun massaged my neck & shoulders. Slow walk through Carrion de los Condes & then onto more old Roman roads, only this time the original roads have been preserved and are currently used by local traffic. Rocked on top, and raised from the flatlands about 7-10 feet as the Romans originally designed. It was a long walk today, 23.3km or 14.0 mi. The air delicious, the land flat/rolling slightly like southern Illinois, but with mountains in the great distance, snow-covered, wheat fields tall & beautiful, "heading out" & now many fields of purplish grasses, poppies, bachelor buttons, rapeseed's yellow flowers, daisies, ferns, moss, wondrous birdsong & for many, many miles, rows of new & mature poplar trees planted along the road. Love those trees. How could I be so happy? And tonight in Calzadilla, anticipating a Pilgrims Menu and a good sleep in my lower bunk in an enormous dormitory.

Reflection on Day 23, written at home in San Francisco

Be praised, my Lord
For all your creatures, and first for Brother Sun,
Who makes the day bright and luminous.
And he is beautiful and radiant. With great splendor
He is the image of you, Most High.

St. Francis of Assisi, from the Canticle of the Sun

How well I remember the blessings of my 23rd day of pilgrimage. Two weeks of sharp winds, the incessant chilly rain, the sucking mud on the trails that kept the pilgrim's pace slow and unsteady day after day—these were dissipating, and the mood of the Camino gradually lifted. Pilgrims began to relax and seemed friendlier—so grateful to walk or bicycle in the warmth of the sun. Barkeeps and hospitaleros were jollier and more energetic. The whole somber mood of the two weeks was lifted. And all because of Brother Sun.

I sent my extended family a brief email from Calzadilla de Cueza on May 16:

"Needless to say, I am on the move, but slowly, slowly. The feet are in denial now, and I coax them along in the morning . . . a good night's sleep helps a lot. The weather pattern of cold has broken. Today is the first time in two weeks that I walked comfortably and that the sun warmed the countryside and firmed up the awful mud. More later, as I am fine, extremely happy with the walk. The Camino is a huge adventure, as well as a much larger undertaking than I had anticipated.

Love from Mary"

And imagine my delight to get an immediate reply from my sister Genevieve O'Hara in St. Louis before my paid hour was up at the internet shop: "O my dear sister Mary . . . Thank you for the word that you are still on the trail. When I have time, I worry mightily about all the things that may befall you . . . robbers, charlatans, wild animals, pitfalls right in front of you. The croup, sciatica, and chilblains. Do you have medals, scapulars, amulets and holy water? Be sure to drink plenty of it. Here's a snippet of a psalm for you:

Send your light and your truth
Let these be my guide
Lead me to your holy mountains
To the place where you dwell.

Love from Genny"

And I was able to email this snippet of a poem right back at her—Hey, Genny: Remember that Kabir said something to the effect of "Why run around sprinkling holy water? There's an ocean inside you, and when you're ready, you'll drink."

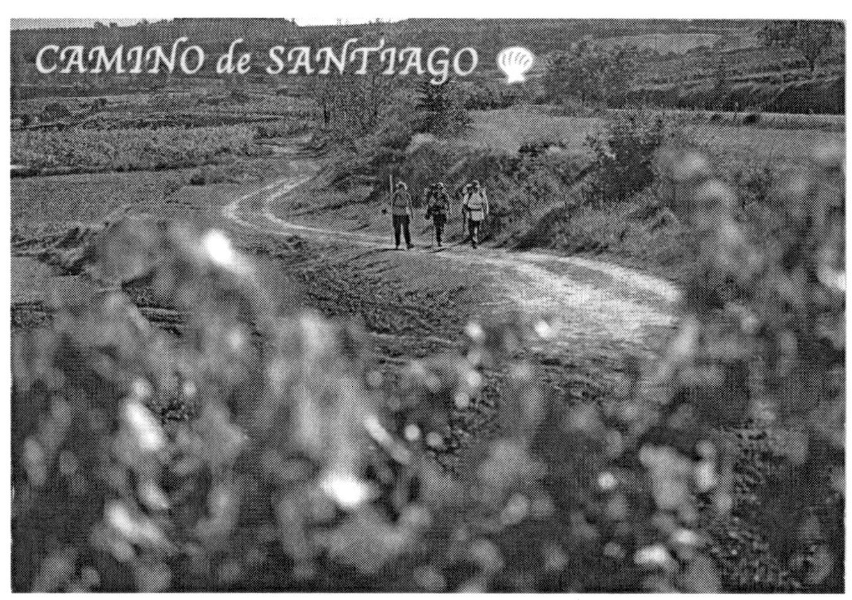

Camino—Day 24

250 Miles Down . . . 250 Miles to Go

Postcard # 24—May 17, 2010 sent from Sahagun, Espana

Dear Elena: Today was truly wonderful. The cold weather seems to have left the north of Spain & it was gloriously blue & warm, even hot today as I walked simple trails through farmland and woods from Calzadilla de Cuesta to Sahágun—21.6km or 13.0mi. Millions of wild flowers by the road & dominated by brilliant red poppies. Elena, the most exciting thing today was that I saw two bright lime green lizards that darted across the road—Each was 12 inches long. Ask your mama to show you a ruler with 12 inches so you can picture how big the green lizards were!!!! In the town I'm staying tonight there are many storks—so beautiful in flight & sitting on their nests. Today for me is the best as I'm at the half-way mark—250 miles walked out of about 500. Keep these postcards of my trip, & you and I will make a scrapbook while we eat m & m's. I love you—Grandma

Journal—Day 24 (Monday) May 17, 2010—written at Sahagun

Left Calzadilla this am by 7:30am and walked several miles before breakfast—coffee, egg sandwich & an apple. Rested carefully every 2-4 miles today, stopped & walked a small labyrinth. Stopped to watch small birds perched on top of poplars, to listen to cuckoos, to watch storks flying in the countryside and sitting on their nests on Church towers. Thrilled to watch 2 bright neon green lizards dart across the road—each a foot long. When I see these things, my mind expands, my heart responds, my whole body quickens with interest and delight. Stopped in a deserted plaza in San Nicholas at noon for lunch—spread out on a bench, backpack off, poles leaning nearby, shoes off, and a canary in a nearby window sang its little heart out for me . . . Cecilia Bartolli could scarcely give a concert so magnificent as this . . . I remembered back how I loved and owned canaries in my twenties, & I determined to get one back in San Francisco. The walk today was very soothing to me as I pass the half-way mark & determine that 10 or so miles per day will get me to Santiago de Compostela by June 11. The weather so clear, warm, even hot, as I walked 21.6km or 13.0mi. Sahagun's Albergue Viatoris very nice. Two beautiful hospitaleras greeted me with lemonade & carried my backpack to a lower bunk in a spacious building, with a large patio, clothes drying area, nice bathrooms, and a charming kitchen. Once again, I turn virtually all clothes over to them to wash/dry—only 12 Euros. Observed in the dorm a woman lying on a massage table all covered up and several young women carefully tending her. I sent her a silent blessing from a distance for whatever ailed her. Many restaurants, but a walk through a small grocery shop with a good wine selection prompted me to buy an Italian pack—one part dried spaghetti with an attached package of prepared sauce. Mushrooms, I thought, and a carrot, onion and tomato to add to the sauce, and a good red wine. Tonight I'll cook. Finding the kitchen empty at 7:00pm, I leisurely cooked while sipping wine, and the dish was ambrosial with the addition of fresh vegetables simmered in the sauce. A young man came in, popped a pizza in the oven which he called the cooker, and sat at the kitchen table. He opened a notebook and meticulously stroked Chinese characters. Felt a wave of love for him and his diligence as I remembered Amelia sitting for hours lettering her Chinese homework from 6th grade through high school. By 8pm the kitchen was humming with activity & conversation was lively. There's always someone thrilled to be offered a glass of wine and I shared my bottle with several pilgrims. I'm sometimes aware of people not having much money on the Camino, and although very good wines can be gotten inexpensively, wine nevertheless is a luxury for some walking their pilgrimage on a budget. Back at my lower bunk, I was greeted by a group of ten Italian male bicyclists just arriving—all flash and dash in their colorful, silky and very form fitting biking gear—one ensconcing himself above my bed and the other 9 in the adjoining bunks. Although they were adorable, it was all too much energy for me. I walked out into the bustling neighborhood, found a restaurant, ordered dessert and started writing in my journal—just grooving on my astonishment that I was half way to Santiago.

Reflection on Day 24, written at home in San Francisco

"You can only go halfway into the deepest forest; then you are coming out the other side."

An old Chinese Proverb

I clearly remember the excitement of reaching the half way mark of completing 250 miles on the Camino path to Santiago de Compostela. It certainly was not a feeling of pride or accomplishment, for I felt slow as a snail. It was, however, a distinct dawning that I was no longer heading towards the halfway mark, but coming out on the other side towards my 500 mile destination. That the dream of making a walking pilgrimage was not just about arriving in Santiago, but day to day, one mile after one mile, sore foot after sore foot reality, and that I was gifted with the grace and enthusiasm and stamina to keep going. Whether or not I made it all the way to Santiago was becoming immaterial—I was where I was at the end of each day, and today, I was half way there.

I remember that gratefulness became a palpable walking partner with me—just as though "being grateful" was integrating into my personality, and cellularly into my body. This feeling permeated my senses. It seemed that I tasted nothing, saw or smelled or touched or heard nothing that did not register on me as pure gift, grace, a blessing. I was definitely moving into a steady mental state that only months before, I might have smiled about in another person as being "pious and cloyingly precious." But there it was—I found myself grateful as steady state of being.

As I made friends with the idea that I was halfway to Santiago, I came to realize elements to my pilgrimage that I wanted still to explore. One was a close mental examination of various stages of my life. I would try to do this in remaining days while walking, be disciplined enough to observe the passing scenery, stay on the right trail, and still delve deeply into the people, places and experiences of my life. At this half way mark, I determined to be more attentive to the spiritual, however it would manifest, to pray more, sit in meditation, breathe the silence more consciously, so that I could be more open to others as occasion or need might arise.

CAMINO—DAY 25

The Man with the Brochure

Postcard 25—May 18, 2010 sent from El Burgo Ranero, Espana

Dearest Elena: What a day!!! I walked 18.8km or 11.3mi from Sahagun to El Burgo Ranero and it was hot, hot after 2 weeks of chill & steady rain. Mountains in the great distance are snow covered. I walked along the highway on an ancient Roman path, alongside which were lovely poplars offering shade to me. And Elena, I saw another 12-inch green lizard and guess what, frogs sang to me over & over from the streams of water. Croak-croak! And I croaked right back to those froggies. Poppies bloomed red & orange just for me & they bobbed amidst all the other wild flowers. Saw a stork on a church steeple sitting on an enormous nest. How could I not be happy? Barn swallows by the thousands flit through the sky in great sweeping waves. Grandma's on the Camino.

Journal—Day 25 (Tuesday) May 18, 2010—written at El Burgo Raneros

This am as I started off from the dorm I said to myself "o'k, sweet Jesus, where will my bed be tonight? I know you have a plan." And just at that moment a somewhat annoying man in a car stopped & gave me a flyer for what he called a new pilgrim's hotel on the highway. I stuffed it in my pocket to be polite and on I walked, resting frequently, including airing my feet after lunch. It was very hot, though at a great distance the mountains were snow-covered. Alas, when I got to El Burgo Ranero, a distance of 18.8km or 11.3 mi from Sahagun, I was exhausted, and found by frustrating trial and error that there was not a single room to be had in the several albergues, and not a hotel room either. Pilgrims were everywhere, lounging, sitting at cafes. I talked to a few folks I recognized, then sat down on a bench under a tree, knowing I could not walk 13 more km or an additional 7.8 miles to Reliegos, the next village. I stayed very calm & unworried, closed my eyes & soon was deep in Centering Prayer. After 20 minutes or so, I opened my eyes and it came to me in a flash: what was on that flyer the man handed me this am? I dug the crumpled flyer out of my pocket, studied it, then ran into the nearest bar to ask directions. Bingo!!!! Very nearby, I learned. I walked on with an enormous smile on my face and sure enough for 32 Euros, I had a beautiful room with a large bath. I soaked in the tub for an hour. My foot (right big toe) is really black & the skin around the toe looks deeply troubled. I cannot understand why it's not healing. But I have a room & a bed, and as I write this, I'm happy, happy. Sure enough, I saw the man who gave me the brochure at dinner.

Reflection on Day 25, written at home in San Francisco

"When God closes a window, you'll find a door will open."
Anonymous

I clearly remember the man I met on the morning of Day 25. I was walking on a path adjacent to a road, no other pilgrim in sight, when a car stopped, and a man just a few feet away leaned out the window and tried to give me a brochure. I wasn't interested, smiled politely and walked on. He drove alongside slowly, talking to me and gesturing with the brochure—weaving along and not watching at all where he was driving. I waved him off. He drove up a bit farther, stopped and got out of the car, and stood in front of me, blocking the path as I approached. He opened the brochure and tried to show me the pictures. I said firmly: "No Spanish. Only English." He shrugged, "Well, why didn't you say so? American, aren't you? I used to live in Albuquerque with my Mexican cousins. So here's the deal. There is a new hotel for Pilgrims on the highway. You'll pass right by and can stay overnight. It's new and perfect for you. Very clean. A good restaurant. Perfect for you—not like those crowded albergues filled with bunk beds. I'll give you a discount."

I took the brochure and because he stood in my way, pretended to study it. I was annoyed that I was being delayed, and annoyed further that the brochure clearly showed a highway hotel with the parking lot filled with gigantic trailer trucks. As though I would stop at a place like that for truckers! I elaborately folded the brochure and put it into my pocket. "Looks good," I said. "Thank you for letting me know about this," and I stepped around him and walked briskly away. My targeted town for the day was 11 miles on walking paths and I needed to keep to schedule.

The aggressive man and his brochure immediately faded from memory. The countryside was beautiful, sunny and warm, birds singing from every planted tree along the raised paths. For the first time I observed flocks of barn swallows filling the air in great numbers, swarming the sky like a darkened cloud—sweeping in unison first to the right, then upwards and then diving as though directed with one mind. Frogs were croaking in full chorus and I was beginning to hear cicadas. Clearly, we were all feeling the change in weather. I even felt that the storks were sitting on their nests in calmer fashion than I previously observed them. Were the eggs about to hatch? Maybe there were actually baby birds in the nests but so little I couldn't see them.

I straggled into El Burgo Ranero after the 11 mile walk, very happy but exhausted—hot and tired, feet and legs aching. The tiny town at first seemed welcoming. The bars and restaurants were filled to the brim with music and pilgrims, every outdoor table and bench occupied. I approached the first albergue—"completo." Then the second. Then the third . . . All voicing the refrain "completo, completo." I then visited smaller private places with rooms to rent: "completo, completo." It did not take long to exhaust all possibilities of a vacant bed for the night.

Discouraged, I sat down under a tree to consider what to do. I studied the guidebook—the next town was nearly 8 miles away. I would have to walk there, I supposed, but first I would rest. Rest and trust to make the right decision. I finished my bottle of water. Rest and trust, and be attentive for the next stage.

After perhaps a half hour of Centering Prayer, I opened my eyes slowly, rose to my feet and resigned myself to walking 8 more miles. I was adjusting the straps on my backpack when instantly, in an intuitive flash and a flurry of activity I didn't yet understand myself, I was scrambling to find the brochure in my pocket. "I'm sure this won't help," I thought, "that man said the hotel is on a highway and the path today cut far away from the highway." But still, I ran into the bar with the brochure and showed a waiter the little map, pointing at the hotel, certain he would say it was miles away. He looked, shrugged his shoulders, and pointed out the door, then wiggled his fingers back and forth like a person walking, and said: "15 minutes."

I remember well the 15 minute walk from the edge of town to the highway: it was all pain and joy. Pain from the toe which was throbbing, and the stiffness from sitting under the tree for a half hour, but oh the joy of seeing that hotel truck stop just ahead, its neon and garish signs beckoning a weary pilgrim like a shimmering oasis appears to a parched desert traveler. It was a truck stop, no doubt about that. As I approached, I could count at least 40 enormous cross country, cross continent trailer trucks lined up in rows by the gas pumps, and many more stopped for the night on the sides of the massive parking lot. The brochure had looked nice enough, and I figured whatever the eventuality, I could handle it. I checked in at the bar of the hotel and noted many well-dressed travelers there having late lunch. Soon I was ensconced in a lovely, spotlessly clean room. Air conditioned. I was safely in for the night. And very grateful for the tub in which I soaked my foot and the bed where I napped for an hour.

I wandered down to the restaurant for dinner at 7:00pm, but was barred from the door by an apologetic waitress who declared the doors would only open at 8:00pm. I went to the bar to wait, amused at the formality of a truck stop's restaurant dinner schedule. The bar was busy, filled with men and women travelers, plus lots of men who looked and smelled like truck drivers who had just showered, shaved and put on clean plaid shirts.

I worked my way up to the bar, bought a glass of wine, then in order to distance myself from the busy scene, walked outside into the warm evening air, seating myself on a bench by the door of the gift shop. The sky was cloudless and clear with a slight tinge of sunset pink. For a half hour, I was lost in watching the sun set behind the distant hills—changing in color from that early tinged pink to an extraordinary blaze of red-orange and purple.

A man came out, rearranged some chairs, then sat down next to me. "Hello, are you staying here at our hotel?" I recognized the man's voice immediately. I nodded. "How did you hear about us?" he asked. "Oh, I was just leaving Sahagun this morning on the pilgrims' path, and a man in a car stopped and gave me a brochure. He was from Albuquerque, New Mexico. He said I should stay here. He even got out of his car to be sure I took a brochure." I smiled at him. The man looked at me sharply, then laughed in recognition. "Well, I knew you'd need to come here, but you didn't seem to want to hear about it. Sometimes I have to be firm about these things."

I asked the man out of curiosity how he knew I'd need to come to this hotel, but his cell phone rang just then, and he stood, shook hands with me and disappeared into the gift shop. I let my question to the man slide away . . . his answer wasn't important. I knew in my heart what the true answer was.

The sun was just dipping behind the hills, subsiding like the events of the day. I could begin to see stars . . . maybe planets, and an outline of a moon. A slight breeze was stirring. Well-being and love filled my heart. The Camino had provided bounty for me today—a beautiful and easy path, great weather, a lime green lizard, frogs, mysterious barn swallows so beautiful in flight, storks nesting quietly, a bed for me in a hotel, and anticipation of an excellent dinner in a nearby restaurant. I was grateful for it all, but especially grateful for the man with the brochure. Our morning's encounter was no mere coincidence on the Camino. I smiled as I remembered a saying within the 12-Step program: "Coincidence is one of the names of God."

CAMINO—DAY 26

The Scarf That Moved on the Path

Postcard # 26—May 19, 2010 written at Mansilla de las Mulas, Espana

Dear Elena: Oh my, what a day! It was so beautiful like this card. There were poppies in bloom along the entire road 20.1km or 12.1mi. The trail was smooth with trees planted every 20 feet. Great to have a bit of shade on a hot day. I left the hotel this am, walked back through El Burgo Ranero (Little Village of the Frogs) to a grand froggy symphony chorus telling me good-bye. Most impressive frog voices—sopranos, altos & tenors. The walk today was filled with armies of ants crossing the paths energetically traveling in columns to the other side. Another lizard, this one brown, hustled across the path, but here's the best ever!!!! I saw a few yards in front of me what I thought was a brown scarf lying on the path. Up closer, I was charmed to find that it was about 1000 brown fuzzy caterpillars inching along like a caravan so close together they looked like a piece of clothing, but moving. I watched mesmerized for a long time, guarding that moving scarf in case a batch of bicyclists came roaring by. The town where I stay tonight means "Hand on the Saddle of the Mules". I am looking for Mules.

Journal—Day 26 (Wednesday) May 19, 2010—written at Mansilla de las Mulas

This am left El Burgo de la Ranero (Little Village of Frogs) and walked to Mansilla de las Mulas (Hand on the Saddle of the Mules) a distance of 20.1km or 12.1 mi. It was a perfect day, although I slept as soon as I arrived. 1st time that happened. But up late afternoon to find bananas & yoghurt drink for breakfast, bank for cash withdrawal (works perfectly every time I need it.), internet, talked with Hollanders at a bar. Delightful trio who are walking the Camino in stages, year after year. Then took a long walk alone in the town, finding a beautiful restaurant—classical music filling the rooms and courtyard—delightful dinner of gaspacho, then merlu (fish), asparagus & polenta, and strawberries & cream for dessert. A half bottle of very good tinto vino. Love it the way it's always served here—slightly chilled. Must research the caravan of caterpillars crossing the road, over 1000 in tight formation moving as though one caterpillar . . . where, why, what was going on? Feet better today after last night's long soak in Hotel Avia, but legs got very tired today . . . 20km or 12 mi. seems about all I can handle . . . will I hold out? Hold up? It really is day by day and it's that way for everyone, really. Where am I? I often say to Elena in her postcards "Grandma's on the Camino". Leon is coming up—another big city after this intense country experience.

Reflection on Day 26, written back home in San Francisco

Study nature, love nature. Stay close to nature. It will never fail you.
—Frank Lloyd Wright

On Day 26, I was determined to move a bit faster than usual, as I hoped to walk 12 miles and get to Mansillas de las Mulas before every bed was taken. As I walked from the truck stop hotel back through El Burgo Ranero to pick up the Camino path, the frogs were performing in full morning voice, their croaks coming from all directions, but mostly from a big pond at the edge of town.

My disciplined start didn't last very long and I was soon sitting on a bench immersed in the variations of froggy pitch and volume. The overall effect was quite beautiful to hear. Glorious froggy solos emerged from nuanced chorus oratorios. At times, all voices subsided into deep silence. I could just pull from memory parts of the poem by Robert Frost called Pea Brush.

The frogs that were peeping a thousand shrill
Wherever the ground was low and wet
The minute they heard my step went still
To watch me and see what I came to get."

It must be fascinating, I thought, for the inhabitants of the Little Village of the Frogs to know the habits of the frogs, their life cycles and mating patterns, how they reacted to changes in weather and temperature. I smiled as I thought of how some townspeople would probably not find this froggy cacophony charming at all to listen to 365 days per year. With frogs so bountiful, I wondered whether there were laws protecting them, or were they "open season" and their little legs a regular dietary staple for the inhabitants of the area.

I started the beautiful trek again, walking for miles along young trees planted by the path. How beautiful this trail will be in the next 10-20 years as the trees mature, I thought, providing shade to pilgrims and shelter to the birds. How visionary of the locals to plant hundreds of trees in this area—and so effective in improving air quality environmentally. Wildflowers continued to brighten the fields despite the recent cold weather and I was delighted with the beautiful grasses growing right up to the paths. For miles I watched tiny birds, maybe finches, that flitted about, landing skillfully on the tips of the grasses, swaying and balancing almost comically.

A brown lizard appeared ahead of me on the path, frozen in position. I too froze in place and we looked at each other, but only for a few seconds. He couldn't stand the tension between us, or perhaps it was the very large shadow I cast across his path, or perhaps it's simply in the nature of lizards to keep to their tasks at hand, but he was off in a flash, racing across the road and disappearing over a perpendicular drop into a roadside ditch. I loved that little four-legged fellow and wondered how he'd react if he met up with those neon green lizards I'd been seeing the past few days.

Every hour or so, I would come across great colonies of ants, usually in the process of crossing industriously from one side of the road to another. Perhaps it really was industry I was observing: often single files of ants would march forward following a leader, each carrying bits of leaf or what looked like gravel—maybe it was food. I liked to think they were stocking up some wondrous, newly built underground colony, pioneers in a new dynasty. I was often puzzled that ant holes were dug right on the path where so many pilgrims walked and bicycles whizzed by. Once, a dozen columns of ants marched in a tight formation to the other side of the road in a rhythmic pattern, not carrying anything, but like an army, I thought, intent on moving through enemy territory. There seemed to me to be deliberate intelligence manifested in the activity of the ants. But not always. As I watched, a half dozen bicyclists rolled over three long columns of ants crossing the road, their wheels massacring hundreds of ants and leaving the remaining ants in panic and disarray. The bicyclists certainly didn't see the ants, and the dead ants certainly didn't see the bicyclists.

In the afternoon, bicycle traffic picked up on the trail. Bikes whizzed by at considerable speed, given the unevenness of the track. I became more watchful as I often didn't hear them approaching from the rear, and more often, the bicycle pilgrims didn't call out their friendly "Buen Camino" until they were even with me or just past.

In late afternoon, and not long before I arrived at Mansilla de las Mulas where I would spend the night, I spotted something on the trail ahead of me. Somebody dropped something on the path, I thought, a brown sweater or a scarf. I approached, thinking I would hang it from my backpack and take it into the next town, perhaps even finding the owner. As I reached down to pick it up, it moved and I could see that the brown mass was not cloth of some type, but brown fuzzy caterpillars, maybe as many as a 1,000 of them bunched together, all touching each other, crawling over each other and moving across the path as though operating with one primal urge or one mind.

I was astounded at this sight. I'd known about "processionary caterpillars" in western Europe that march along in single file, head to tail, sometimes travelling long distances before burrowing into the ground to live their next stage of life. But this "scarf of swarming caterpillars" was entirely different and completely unknown in my experience. About 3 feet by 3 feet, this shape was amorphous, constantly undulating, changing color as the bodies packed together and moved along, the long brown and black hairs on their beige caterpillar bodies rising and lowering as each little being thrust itself forward in unison with the group.

I took off my backpack on the side of the road, and knelt down to get a better look. I could see hundred of little eyes, thousands of tiny legs and all involved in a sort of planned but frenetic action to move somewhere—from my viewpoint, at least from one side of the road to the other. I knew instinctively not to touch caterpillars, for some are very poisonous to insects and inflammatory to human skin. I picked up a stick and poked gently at one flank of the mass. It began to writhe and twist, frantic from fear. I threw the stick away. I announced solemnly to them as they calmed down: "I promise I won't do that again."

What on earth was happening here with these massed caterpillars? Where were they going, and why? Were they travelling in unison to protect themselves from predator beetles or lizards or birds of prey? Were they huddling together to protect themselves from cold? Maybe, but they were in far more danger from pilgrims. Some walking pilgrims came along. "Is everything o'k with you," they asked, seeing me seated on the ground. "Oh yes, I'm just guarding these caterpillars until they get to the other side of the road." The pilgrims barely glanced down, showing little interest in the science lesson at their feet. They swigged a drink of water, shared a snack of trail mix. One stepped off the road to pee, and another actually smashed with his boot 3 of my caterpillars that had gotten separated from the mass. I was relieved when the humans headed down the path.

I wasn't finished with the caterpillars quite yet. They were on the move, constantly squirming forward in one direction. I predicted it would take at least another half hour for them to be safely off the path. Leaving now was more convenient to my walk, but it would leave the caterpillars in distinct danger of not reaching their goal. I stayed seated on the path, watchful, yet lost in the migratory mystery of my temporary companions.

Sure enough, I could hear the bicycles and the bicyclists before I saw them. About a half dozen approached, riding two and three abreast. As they saw me seated in the path, they slowed, alert, curious, and carefully approached me single file. They saw I wasn't hurt, and turned their attention to the brown mass of caterpillars. Immediately, all left their bicycles and got down on their knees for a better look. I couldn't understand what they were saying, but it was evident they were very appreciative of the scene before them. They took pictures of the migration, gestured and measured, argued and agreed. One took notes and drew a little picture of the scene.

The caterpillars were nearing the safety zone from humans on the path. It was time to go. The bicyclists had not made an effort to talk to me, but it was clear that they did discuss how my sitting there had prevented their hitting the caterpillars. "French?" one asked me as they were leaving. "No. I'm American." He furrowed his brow, stuttered a bit, and slowly formed these sentences: "Thank you for sitting here in middle and saving the lives of tiny creatures. This is very beautiful event for us to see such nature. And may I say very good, creepy action on Camino." And the six of them rode away, so typical of other Camino bicyclists with the left hand on the handlebar and the right arm half-raised in recognition. "Buen Camino," their voices of farewell individual yet fading in unison.

I picked up my pack and poles, made the necessary adjustments, and took one more look at my little brown, hairy caterpillars. They were safe now, halfway down the bank supporting the path, still tightly massed, and one flank struggling over a large clump of dirt. I just had to laugh out loud as I walked on about my bicyclist friend calling the massed movement of the caterpillars both beautiful and creepy. I hoped he meant that it was a beautiful and unusual scene, and not a creepy one. Still, I thought, if a horror movie were ever made about the Camino, there could be a scene of enormous, mutant clumped caterpillars lying in wait on the path to snuff out unsuspecting pilgrims.

Camino—Day 27

Watching and Being Watched on the Camino

Postcard # 27—May 20, 2010 sent from Leon, Espana

Dear Elena: Today, after walking for 20.5km or 12.3mi, I arrived in the important Spanish city of Leon. I'm exhausted!!! I arrived at an Albergue run by Benedictine Nuns, got my lower bunk & collapsed for a nap. The walk today was partly in glorious countryside where I saw lavender butterflies fluttering-by, but for many miles it was the industrial approaches to Leon—a city of 200,000 and it was only big trucks & fast cars buzzing by. But after a nap & a clean-up, as the Brits say, I went out for a Pilgrim Menu & a long visit to this cathedral shown on the card. Oh my, it is grand & I sat in the Plaza for a long time, watching the early evening promenade. I made a 1-hour, walk-through tour of the Cathedral. I think of you everyday. Grandma's on the Camino . . . more than half way but still a very long way to go. Love, love, love and I send you one little kiss for each little finger.

Journal—Day 27 (Thursday) May 20, 2010—written at Leon

Today my Brierley guidebook suggests that Peligrinos take the autobus from Mulas into Leon, but I chose to walk. It was a long slog of over & along very busy freeways. Some countryside. I continue to love being on the Camino, whatever the circumstances, but the last few miles of pavement & hot sun got to me, plus I got a little lost finding the Benedictine Albergue, hidden away, tucked into a little alley. About a half dozen older people separately approached me and helped me find my way. But here I am writing in the Nuns Chapel, having attended their Vespers & evening Mass, and feeling stronger. Late this afternoon I indulged in an excellent menu, the waiter more than solicitous. I had ordered a white wine with the fresh steamed asparagus course, and fully expected to drink that throughout the meal, but the waiter was talkative, (he had spent a year living in Brooklyn) and insisted that he bring me a tinto vino that would complement his mother's lamb stew. I waxed poetic over the stew, and the next thing I knew, the waiter and his mother were bringing me tastes of several of her desserts, and a pear liqueur to wash them down. They were crushed when I refused a coffee. They both sat down and we had another glass of wine. I think they were just happy to speak English and rest from their afternoon lunch duties before the whole routine started again at 8:00 or 9:00pm. I paid for nothing extra, but left a substantial tip. They insisted I come through the kitchen to see the mama's domain. It was a lovely encounter and I walked away happy in body & soul. Took a long slow walk through the medieval section of Leon . . . so old, yet modernized to make things livable. I sat in front of the Leon Cathedral for a long time, also took the entire interior walk through—very impressive overall. Side chapels typical of other major cathedrals. This was an excellent day, though I must admit that overall exhaustion is setting in. All Pilgrims must feel it. Maybe it's more pronounced that I'm in a very big city.

Reflection on Day 27, written back home in San Francisco

"If the only prayer we ever say in our lives is 'Thank you,' that will be enough.

—Meister Eckhart

It was lovely to think on Day 27 that I was getting closer to Santiago. I might just make it after all, I thought as I walked the hard pavements for several miles through the approach to Leon, the largest city on the Camino. The traffic and heat made me buzz by late afternoon and I was eager to find the albergue run by the Benedictine nuns. The city was beautiful, and distracting, filled with streets and alleys that all seemed jumbled up as I studied my map. Determining that I was hopelessly lost, I kept on walking in a daze, looking for yellow Camino arrows.

Here is what happened the last hour until I reached the Benedictine Convent. Just as though I were being tracked on a GPS by the older inhabitants of Leon, I was approached by elderly citizens over and over who would say: "Camino?" and I would nod and show them my little map. They pointed the way, speaking to me in Spanish, and often shaking my hand and patting my shoulder. They seemed so kindly, so gentle. We looked at each other, smiled. I thanked them and walked on.

Who were these guides when I was so exhausted after walking 12.3 miles? And why were they always there just when I couldn't determine direction and thought I was lost? Could they possibly be organized to assist lost pilgrims? I couldn't believe it was a coincidence that I was approached a half dozen times that mid-afternoon.

I think these older folks were highly sensitized to Camino walkers trudging through Leon. When they saw me—close to their ages, carrying a backpack and limping a bit, they simply stepped forward to guide a pilgrim, to point the way, or sometimes even walk with me to the next yellow arrow. I was as curious about them, as they were about me. One of the men who pointed the way, pulled a rosary out of his pocket and placed the crucifix gently on the palm of my hand. A woman opened her purse, withdrew her rosary, and touched first her heart with the crucifix, then touched it to my heart. Encounters with these old Camino watchers and the yellow arrows are burned into my memory.

After finally settling into the albergue and resting a bit on my very welcome lower bunk by a window with a breeze, I set out somewhat revived for a late lunch/early dinner, locating a restaurant just before 4:00pm, selecting the place by the printed menu on the door and the generally pleasant interior. I was the last customer served before the restaurant closed for the afternoon, so all was quiet with relaxed service.

It was an unusual experience for me in that I talked at length to the waiter and his mother, the head cook, about their lives, my Camino and family and life in San Francisco. She came out of the kitchen with tastes of extra desserts for me, took off her apron and sat down at the table after her son told her how much I liked the Lamb Stew. They spoke about cooking as a profession and the unrelenting demands of owning a restaurant, how exhausted the mother was from cooking between 60 and 80 meals day after day for lunch and dinner. The mother said she'd never been to Santiago but would like to go someday to see what all the fuss was about.

I suggested the woman could take some time and walk to Santiago from Leon. "Oh, I couldn't do that", she said. "My son could never keep the restaurant going by himself, and besides, I'm too old to walk there. I would have to take a bus tour. I'm 53 years old. I'd never make it walking." We looked at each other. After an awkward silence, she added: "Well, you seem to be on your feet. I guess we're about the same age." I blurted out "No, we're not the same age. I'm 70." Immediately, I wished I hadn't told her my age. She grew silent, looked at her son, pushed the dishes around on the table, brushed crumbs from the cloth. She seemed confused and embarrassed. She pointed to the bar, and her son jumped up and brought another bottle of wine.

She cheered considerably and soon we were conversing again about our lives. I departed the restaurant through the woman's kitchen at her request, she so proud to show me her refrigeration system, her stoves and microwaves, her dishwashing equipment, her storage areas. She introduced me to the kitchen staff for the evening shift. Both of them hugged me and sent me out the back door of the kitchen into the cool evening air with their heartfelt Buen Caminos. I countered as I turned with a heartfelt thank-you to both of them. Some yards away, I heard the waiter call out "Pray for us when you get to Santiago." I turned and waved, but thought: "Oh, no, another obligation."

I felt pulled in two directions—go back to the albergue and rest before Vespers, or walk in the medieval section of Leon and visit the Cathedral. Tired as I was, I opted to walk, to partake in the evening activity that was near frenzy around 6:00pm—workers stopping to shop for staples and bread, tourists picking up their pace to see the sights while it was still light outside, students walking determinedly with armloads of books and rumpled looking pilgrims carrying backpacks. I was delighted that the Cathedral stayed open another hour. I went in, getting an admission ticket and brochure, and spent the hour just walking to see the bare minimum, the aisles, the altars, the side chapels, the overwhelming art and grillwork and gold leaf, the statues and crucifixes, the awesome height of the interior arches and ceilings, the long side passages, the stained glass windows, steps down to lower levels, pipes for the organ reaching up to heaven. Suddenly I was exhausted and could go no farther.

Once outside, I settled onto a bench in the Cathedral Plaza and observed the 7:00pm scene to be slower than an hour before. Now Leon inhabitants were out meandering, promenading leisurely, shopping, sitting in cafes having drinks and tapas. Groups of Asian tourists were being discreetly guided through the streets by little flags held high by leaders. Elderly men and women sat on the benches, leaning on canes. Children were playing games in the enormous plaza, running and hopscotching and jump roping, walking hand in hand, sharing sweets. I often could not spot any adults with the children or watching from afar. What freedom for the children. I was mesmerized with the musicians who materialized into little groups and played in various areas of the enormous surrounding plazas. It was growing dark and the lights were coming on in the streets. I got up, foot sore and muscles stiffening, and hurried back to the albergue for evening Vespers and Mass.

Only a few pilgrims gathered for the evening services. The nuns sang the chants and songs behind grillwork, and the priest moved methodically through the Mass. I could barely follow it, such weariness descended on me, yet I wanted to be there, to hear the singing, to see if pageantry would emerge, but no, it was all Benedictine simplicity performed this sacred night as for the past several hundred years. I was so grateful for the simplicity of the service.

I stayed in the chapel after services for an hour, writing a postcard to Elena and the day's journal entry until a nun tapped me on the shoulder and gently guided me to the door. As I passed into the courtyard of the albergue where I was staying, I noticed a large group of young people gathering in the lovely little park called Plaza Santa Maria across the street. How nice, I thought, that they have a gathering place like this park. Little did I know that their music and partying would continue until 4:00 am, a Thursday night University student tradition that would awaken me several times through the night, their singing and laughter and high spirits wafting through the open windows of the muggy dormitory.

Camino—Day 28

From the Nunnery to the Winery

Postcard # 28—May 21, 2010 sent from La Virgin del Camino

Today I was so tired in Leon that I only walked 10.1km or 6.1mi to a small village called La Virgin del Camino. I got here at 1:00pm, checked into a private hostal & slept for 2 hours. A long soak-y bath and an excellent afternoon meal. Now, I picked this card for you of the Virgin & Baby Jesus because Jesus has just had a bath and is getting ready for his Mama Mary to read to him before he goes to bed. Today, I walked by dozens of "Bodegas"—funny little caves dug into hillsides, well fortified with doors & supports—and it's here that some people age their wine for a long time. I like seeing all these different things, Elena, but when you travel to Spain you will understand so much more than I because you speak Spanish like your Papa Francisco. Still, I manage with smiles & sign language. Love, Grandma

Journal—Day 28 (Friday) May 21, 2010—written at La Virgin del Camino

This am I awakened very early to the hustle and bustle of the dorm. Last night it was noisy on the Plaza Santa Maria outside my room. I learned that Thursday night is Students Night and the city is very noisy very late. This am I attended a 1 hour sung Prayer by the Benedictine Nuns (complete with nap) & then set off walking through the busy Leon streets, out of the city and proceeding only 10.1km or 6.1mi. to this small village of La Virgin del Camino. Was given a drink of wine by a man working in his underground wine cellar. Checked into private Hostel Central (20 Euros) very clean, nice & immediately slept for 2 hours. Great lunch. Slept another 2 hours. A soaking bath, good for my feet which are not great—at least not the right foot. Pain & some swelling. Still, my spirits are good and after this light day of walking, I'm feeling better. No regrets for what son Nathan calls my "Epic Quest". I hope mightily that Nathan will be drawn to walk the Camino some day.

Reflection on Day 28, written at home in San Francisco

"This day is a renewal, every morning the daily miracle. This joy you feel is life."

Gertrude Stein

I remember with thankfulness, some amusement and a bit of embarrassment my experience on Day 28 in the Benedictine Chapel in Leon during the nuns' one hour morning prayer service. The chapel looked so different from the night before at the evening services. I settled in a little before 8:00am on a bench, backpack at my feet. "What a glorious way to start the day," I thought, "blessed with an hour to pray before starting my walk." The nuns began chanting behind the grille. The sun shone in through stained glass windows, casting long pastel-colored panels across the sanctuary and the chapel walls. The air was cool.

I marveled at the nuns' sweet voices coaxed out of the silence in the chapel. Back and forth, back and forth, the silence encouraged the nuns to sing, and the nuns cooperated, then beckoned the silence to return. Now and then, an old, old woman from the neighborhood who sat near me would cough and hack several times into her rosary and black shawl, and make a peculiar hissing noise in her throat that as it echoed away, enhanced the silence. But then, even my own body entered the rhythm in the chapel—I was being invited by the stillness—and I answered yes with an intent tenderly offered to be open to the presence and action of God within. Muscles relaxed, thinking quieted. Time passed. I was not alone.

I awakened abruptly, straightening myself from my contorted position, and realized that I'd fallen asleep. I had the feeling that a long period of time had elapsed since I'd entered the chapel. I was the only visitor present. There was the steady rhythmic sound of an elderly nun methodically sweeping the sanctuary with a long handled broom, and three nuns in long habits glided about changing linens on the altar and arranging fresh flowers. When I stood to leave, adjusting my backpack, a friendly nun carrying a large decorative key approached and accompanied me to the door. I awkwardly started to apologize for falling asleep. She just smiled at me. She patted my shoulder, touched my hat, placed the key in the lock and I heard it click as I walked down the steps on the other side of the closed door. She knew a Pilgrim needs her rest.

I was curious about how long I'd been snoozing in the chapel. I stepped into the courtyard of the albergue next door where I'd spent the night. Activity hummed as pilgrims were already lining up to be registered. I approached a friendly soul for the time, and her wrist watch displayed 10:30am. I'd been in the chapel for 2 ½ hours, most of that time sound asleep to make up for the noisy evening in the park across the street.

I hurried on with my walk through the city, refreshed in spirit, but somewhat exhausted still in body. I engaged with the mid-morning sights and sounds of the busy downtown area of Leon. At an outdoor coffee shop, I drank a café con leche standing at a tiny raised table and munched on a long twisted pastry. How could I be both tired and deliriously happy? Consulting my Brierley guidebook, I changed my plan for a long day's walk and targeted the village of La Virgin del Camino only about 6 miles away. I continued following the yellow arrows painted on sidewalks and lampposts and soon emerged on paths cutting through fields, once again out in nature, smiling and carefree.

During the walk, I saw multiple cave-like structures dug into hillsides and covered with dirt on top—all of them with low doors to enter and with big locks attached on the outside. Some had little ventilation pipes sticking out at various angles. I was curious. As I studied one of them, I saw a man about 30 feet from me, just off the path, unlocking and entering one of these caves. As I approached, I could see that he had placed a basket by the door and was busy unloading things and carrying them into the cave.

I couldn't see the interior as it was too dark, but I stood nearby the entrance until he noticed me and I gave him a big smile. He looked me over shrewdly, then softened into a smile, determining, I thought, that I was not out to rob him blind, but a clueless pilgrim who didn't know about "wine caves" or recognize one when she saw it. I smiled again and shrugged my shoulders. He smiled and shrugged his shoulders. Then, from the basket, he picked up cheeses wrapped in cloth, showed them to me, and speaking rapidly in Spanish all the while, turned and carried them inside. When he returned carrying four bottles of wine and placed them carefully in the basket, I was still standing there. More smiles. He began to explain again in Spanish, gesturing with his hands and arms, laughing, shoving his hat way back on his head, picking up a bottle, showing me the type of corkage, then gesturing for me to enter the little cave with him.

At the time, my curiosity got the better of me. My mother's admonitions 60 years earlier against entering unknown places with strange men didn't surface, and I stepped into the cave with the man. The air was many degrees cooler than on the outside. My eyes quickly adjusted to the diminished light and on two sides, I could make out racks from floor to ceiling filled with wine bottles. On the third side, open shelves held a few small wheels of cheese, some wrapped, others unwrapped and with thick rinds. A large tank rested on a small table, and the man spoke to me at some length about its contents, but I simply could not understand. I examined all carefully. I was fascinated by the damp smell—it seemed a combination of rain-soaked earth, aging wine and cheese ripening.

Finally, the man raised one finger, beckoned me outside and quickly uncorked a bottle of wine. He raised the bottle to his mouth, took a slow sip, then another, then a long drink. He handed me the bottle, gesturing for me to drink. I declined, but he stepped inside his cave, bringing out a stained and chipped mug and poured me a generous taste. "Good Lord, what am I doing drinking with a strange man in the middle of the day out in the countryside of rural Spain?" But I raised the cup, tasted the contents, tasted again, then drained the cup saying: "Ahhhh, delicious!"

It was time for me to go . . . I thanked my generous and gracious host profusely, declined another cup of wine, shook hands with him, and never saw him again.

Canicule du matin n'arrête pas le pèlerin...
Mais canicule toute la journée fait sentir le cochon grillé...!

CAMINO—DAY 29

A Bit of Camino History over Breakfast

Postcard # 29—May 22, 2010 sent from San Martin del Camino, Espana

Dear Elena: Today was scorching, and still I loved the walk—(18.1km or 10.9mi), flowers by the bazillion, frogs in ponds & waterways & best of all, in the heat now nearly all day I hear the cicadas chirping & buzzing. Now birds only in the am and early evening. It's hard for them to sing in the heat. I stop in every town & rest. I'm drinking about two liters of water per day (plus coffee & wine) . . . I can't get another swallow down. Elena, tonight will be a real adventure for me. I have to sleep in the upper bunk . . . oh my, this is very hard for me!! I'll tell you how it goes . . . I hope I don't fall down from the bed onto my head. This is because there are many, many pilgrims on the trail now and everybody wants a bottom bunk. I meet everyday people from every continent and frequently Koreans. My sore toe has been injured for one month now & the big toe stays purple as the flowers.

Journal—Day 29 (Saturday) May 22, 2010—written at San Martin del Camino

Today walked 18.1km or 10.9mi and all in hot hot sun. Today begins my 5th Week on the Camino—hard to fathom. Felt rested after great sleep in the private Hostal. Coffee and a good talk this morning with 2 American tourists who knew virtually nothing of the Camino. I arrived at 3:00pm in San Martin which is early, still only, only a top bunk which I took. Oh, my! I have practiced climbing up, but still coming down is the devil. The problem for me is how close the upper bunk is to the ceiling as I climb up & try to hoist myself safely and crawl onto the bed. Horrible. A chair is no help in these tight quarters. A bit nervous about the whole "bathroom in the middle of the night" thing. It didn't help that the woman on the top bunk across from me told me of her fall from a bunk bed only last night & she has an ugly big bruise to prove it. I feel a little odd today from walking in the heat. I need a better strategy . . . more water, more stops. Today began drinking sparkling agua gaz and taking my shoes off at every stop as the feet sweat, & socks & feet need airing. Not so hungry but realize that fuel must be attended to . . . banana, salad, and now at 7:00pm will have a menu prepared here at the dorm by a bustling Mama. Not exactly light, pasta & pork steaks, salad, bread & wine. There are mountains in the distance, and I start walking towards them tomorrow.

Reflection on Day 29, written back home in San Francisco

"The thoughts of my devotees dwell in Me, their lives are surrendered to Me, and they derive great satisfaction and joy enlightening one another and speaking about me."

Chapter 10, Verse 9 from the Bhagavad Gita

On the morning of Day 29, I awakened in the private hostal at La Virgin del Camino well rested but a bit unnerved about the condition of my right foot and how raw it felt as I eased it into its sock and shoe. As I left the lodging at 8:00am, the day was already hot. Within a few minutes of brisk walking, I spotted a bar and some backpacks resting outside by the open door. It was unusual in my experience to find coffee that early in the day, and I eagerly went in with my backpack and poles, resting them discreetly in a far corner and claiming a table.

I didn't recognize any of the pilgrims, but while ordering a café con leche at the bar, I struck up a conversation with a woman who had already been on the trail that morning for 3 hours. She told me she averaged walking 24-26 miles per day, determined before her return to Denmark, to reach Santiago from St. Jean Pied de Port in 21 days. I was in awe of her determination and stamina, and she was incredulous that I had allotted 52 days to make the walk. Blowing on her coffee non-stop to cool it, she drank it down and was out the door in a flash.

I wandered back to the table. With my first coffee of the day in hand and anticipating an omelet sandwich to be delivered from the kitchen shortly, I sat down to observe the overall scene. The bartender was a pleasant enough fellow to pilgrims, but said nothing nor smiled as he took orders.

Once the bartender understood what was wanted by the customer, he sprang into graceful action like a well-rehearsed dancer responding to familiar music. He energetically whirled around to face his European coffee maker. With one hand he tapped spent coffee grounds out of tiny mesh cups into a wastebasket at his feet, and with a flourish refilled the little mesh cups with fresh, strong smelling coffee powder which he dipped with his other hand out of an enormous sack. He tapped the tiny cup to level it and finally, locked it into place on the machine.

In one flowing action, he added water to hidden compartments, then with great concentration, turned and twisted and adjusted tiny knobs until the great, gleaming coffee machine started simmering and sputtering and spitting, and a black, steaming and fragrant liquid dribbled down, filling about half full the large, wide ceramic cups for the customers. Satisfied that the machine was functioning as designed, he spun around to the refrigerator, and withdrawing a gallon container of 1% cold milk, busied himself pouring it into a pitcher, then steaming it with a small separate machine until the milk in the pitcher frothed to the top and ran down the sides. He took the cup half-filled with coffee and daintily filled it to the top edge with the hot frothy milk before setting his morning masterpiece in front of the customer. He repeated this routine over and over as new customers arrived. I was dazzled with his agility at making coffee.

A well-dressed couple entered the bar, ordered coffee and sat down at a table next to me. Definitely not pilgrims, I thought, but automobile tourists. They began speaking English and I overheard their conversation about the backpacks and poles scattered outdoors and inside, and their curiosity about the pilgrims. At last my omelet sandwich arrived. I handed the waiter my cup and said: "Another coffee, please." He disappeared behind the bar and began his graceful routine to produce coffee for me.

The couple turned to me immediately, eagerly even: "You speak English." "Oh, yes. I'm American, from San Francisco." The woman was thrilled. "We're American too. We're driving through Spain for two weeks from Barcelona and going as far as we can until we have to turn back to fly home to Denver." Her husband continued: "Are you part of this walking group?" "No, I'm a pilgrim walking the Camino alone to Santiago." They looked at me intently, not understanding what that meant.

A stream of questions poured out of the couple. They didn't even wait for answers, but asked many questions about the Camino. What does the word Camino mean? Is Santiago a place in Spain? Why do people go there? Did you say you are a pilgrim walking alone? Why? Is this something religious? Do you walk everyday? Do you walk on the roads and isn't that dangerous? Where do you stay? Do you have reservations ahead of time? Is it safe for a woman to do this alone? What does your family think about this? How did you hear about this?

I smiled at their very good questions. It was my turn to ask them: "Have you heard or read nothing about the Camino to Santiago de Compostela? About the pilgrims who have walked from all over Europe for over a thousand years to the Spanish city of Santiago farther west from here—almost at the Atlantic Ocean?" They shook their heads no.

I munched on my breakfast and considered this very nice couple from Denver, Colorado who sat next to me. They were probably in their late 50's, on a driving holiday, no Spanish and actually didn't know about the Camino and its history, of how the ancient paths wove through little towns and crossed numerous highways. "Why are you making this pilgrimage?" the woman asked, breaking the silence. "Oh, no," I thought. "There's the question again." I smiled at her, but said nothing. I decided to ignore her, and proceeded to wrap the rest of my sandwich and put it in the backpack for lunch. I would not get involved in what would end up being an hour's conversation, nice as these folks were.

I paid for breakfast. Picking up my backpack, I rested it on the edge of the table, eased into it and adjusted its various straps. I turned to the couple to say goodbye. They had positioned their chairs towards me, watching my preparations to leave. We shook hands and exchanged names—looked at each other at first casually, then deeply.

I sat down and began tentatively. "Do you know the story of Jesus and his 12 Apostles?" They nodded, and the woman added, "We're both Christians, but not practicing anything in particular at the moment. We sort of gave up on our Church." We smiled at the matter of fact comment and quieted . . . each of us somehow privately lost in her stark statement.

"O'k," I started, "here's the very old and very imprecise story of the Camino in a nutshell. 1st, a few so-called facts, even those without solid sources, and 2nd, lots of legend and myth, and 3rd, a 1000 year old history of people from all over the world being gripped by the mystique of making a pilgrimage to Santiago to have their sins forgiven. So, what I don't tell you this morning in 30 minutes, you can google when you have the time back in Denver." The woman crossed her legs to get comfortable. The man began to take notes on the back of his airlines envelope.

I continued: "In his 30's, we're told, Jesus selected 12 men to be his disciples, his helpers, his special followers. Two of those men were brothers, James and John, sons of Zebedee, the fisherman. It's James who is the namesake of the city of Santiago, here in Spain. What is fact? What is fiction? Even the Acts of the Apostles record various accounts of events in Christ's life and the years following his death. And is it fact or legend that suggests the 12 Apostles assumed the roles of missionaries to spread out and proselitize the known world?

It is generally believed that James gravitated towards the Iberian Peninsula. I don't get the sense that he was adept at his job of 'spreading the Word.' Some written accounts and legend suggest that he stayed in Spain for several years, but met with little success in his preaching or attracting followers—much less converting people to the Christ's way of life. At any rate, after several years living in what we now call Spain, James returned to Jerusalem with 2-3 followers, but alas! he was promptly beheaded by Herod Agrippa about the year 44 AD. So he is now St. James the Martyr.

The story grows thin and even murky with lots of versions of how St. James landed back in Spain. Generally, most storylines tell of his body and head being secretly placed in a boat, often described as stone, sometimes as wood, and sailing with angels through the Mediterranean Sea and Straits of Gibraltar, up the western coast of Spain and landing roughly at a place called Finisterre—meaning in Latin 'the end of the earth.' Was he alone in that boat, or with angels as legend suggests? Did his followers accompany the body, then bury it inland from the sea? Did it even happen at all? Anyway, fast forward about 800 years to the 9th Century. Literally everybody had forgotten about where St. James lay buried.

I glanced at the clock on the wall of the bar. My 30 minutes were up. "I need to leave," I announced. "Let's just say that finding James' body hundreds of years later was, as you might suspect, shrouded in several versions of myth and fabrication. A popular story says that a shepherd, maybe a hermit, saw stars glittering and beckoning from a hillside and the tomb was discovered. A local bishop became involved and declared the remains that of Santiago the Martyr. Of course, a Catholic church and a monastery were built on the site, the bones were displayed as relics, and it became a powerful magnet as early as the 9th Century for both believers and non-believers to visit as walking pilgrims, and with the hope that their sins would be forgiven once they arrived at the site.

The monastery grew into a village known as Santiago de Compostela, which means Saint James of the Field of Stars, and the little church grew into a very grand Cathedral. That's where I'm headed. All this grew unimaginably in the minds of the population of Europe, and for hundreds of years, from all over the world, not hundreds of thousands, but millions of people have put on pilgrim gear, attached a symbolic shell to their belongings, and trudged across various countries and paths, or Caminos, to visit the Cathedral in Santiago, where you can still see the relics displayed."

I stood to go. The man pulled out a map, circled the city of Santiago, calculated distances and announced to his wife: "Let's not drive to Madrid today. We're not tied to any reservations. We could easily make it to Santiago. I'd like to see this Cathedral." She enthusiastically agreed, and outside we went—they to their destination in a deluxe air-conditioned rental car and I walking with a sore foot in the blazing sun to find the yellow arrows that would guide my day's walk.

This dear couple formally shook hands with me. "Pray for us when you get to Santiago," the man said. "It's a deal," I answered mischievously, "and when you reach Santiago this afternoon, please pray for me that I make it to Santiago." I walked away, and never saw them again.

CAMINO—DAY 30

Centro de Salud Ambulatorio Urgencias

Postcard # 30—May 23, 2010 sent from Astorga, Espana

Dear Elena: I am happy to report that I did not fall out of bed on my head from the upper bunk last night. But upper bunks are for other people, not for me. Today was a long walk & guess what? 3 more bright green lizards & one of them and I looked at each other for a long time. I also saw a frog take a big leap into a canal. All these things make me happy. But I walked too far today—from San Martin del Camino to Astorga was 24.7km or 14.8mi. This brings me up to 321.8 mi walked so far and 180 miles to go. Astorga is beautiful—1 big Plaza after another. People out on Sunday evening having drinks & dinner in outdoor cafes, promenading, kids playing, running, skateboards, scooters, babies, babies, babies everywhere, pilgrims greeting each other, recognition from days back on the Camino. This postcard is what the country looks like here. Grandma's on the Camino and heading towards & over the Mountains of Leon. Hardest days ahead. Love, love, love, love

Journal—Day 30 (Sunday) May 23, 2010—written at Astorga

This am left San Martin at 7:00am—unusually early and delightfully cool. The foot changes—more pain today & bandage slipping off frequently. Climbing up the ladder to the upper bunk last night was really painful on my feet. Still, I walk from place to place. I stopped at Puente de Obriga (13th Century) longest/oldest medieval bridge on the Camino. Weird story of Don Suero de Quinones. Rested today 4 times at bars (coffee or cold drinks) taking off shoes/socks—it's common to do so, but discreetly. The walk to Astorga in extreme heat was too far—24.7km or14.8mi. Extra long ascent into Astorga—so beautiful from the distance up on a hill with medieval walls all around. The Albergue Siervas de Maria is delightful, friendly & with a library & internet. A lovely woman took my backpack & deposited it and me in a small room for 8 women—again I had a lower bunk, and next to a window (heavenly breezes in the hot afternoon) that had a view of distant mountains, close up tiled roofs, and a pond below. The room shares a wall with a tiny Pilgrims Chapel, all hand painted . . . I eased my feet out of the shoes, pure pain. Showered, slept for an hour.

Reflection on Day 30, written back home in San Francisco

"It isn't the road ahead that wears you out—it is the grain of sand in your shoe."

Old Arabian Proverb

Was I ever glad to make an early getaway from the San Martin dormitory where I slept on an upper bunk fitfully through the night. There are reasons why I remained wary of being assigned the top bunk at each day's destination. I am a large woman and it was awkward for me to haul my bulk up the ladder. It was difficult to hoist my backpack up to the mattress due to an old shoulder injury. I was afraid if I fell from the upper bunk at my age that it would be the end of the Camino for me. But most of all I was inordinately afraid of falling at night on trips to the bathroom. San Martin was the only time I was forced into the situation, and it was not a pleasant experience. The several climbs up and down from the bunk in the night actually made my right foot injury worse—the bare foot bearing my weight on several narrow iron rungs of the ladder caused a great soreness to erupt throughout the foot. Day 30's walk from San Martin to Astorga of 14.8 miles was painful every single step, and it took just about all my energy and focus to keep interested in the medieval villages, and the flora and fauna along the way.

I didn't have to act pathetic when I arrived in Astorga at the Albergue Siervas de Maria—I was pathetic. The young women hospitaleras took one look at me and deposited me in a room on a lower bunk next to a window with a breeze. I showered immediately and then slept for an hour. When I awakened, I knew I needed medical attention for my foot.

I limped out in sandals and was caught up in the beauty of the old town where the dormitory was located. I wandered aimlessly through spacious plazas filled with outdoor cafes, shops, hotels and public buildings. Pilgrims, young people, couples, families were promenading or sitting outside, all enjoying the last rays of sun on a Sunday afternoon.

I found an open Farmacia and waited my turn at the counter. There was no one who spoke English and asking them about my foot was relegated to sign language. I took off my shoe and lifted my now badly swollen right foot to a chair. The staff gathered around, sucking in their breath audibly as they looked aghast at my foot's blisters and purple big toe. One ran for a map of Astorga and began to dramatically draw a route for me to immediately visit the Centro de Salud Ambulatorio Urgencias. Another quite beautiful woman pressed into my hand a piece of their pharmacy letterhead paper, on which she had written in enormous letters: URGENT. I mustered a smile of thanks to them. They all ushered me to the door and I had a sense they just wanted my foot off their customer's chair and me headed in the general direction of the medical clinic.

It was a fifteen minute walk to the Centro de Salud, and after a short wait, a woman doctor and a nurse worked on my feet for nearly an hour. My English again was a big barrier, but our mutual efforts for understanding paid off. The doctor illustrated on a sheet of paper what she proposed to do. I understood only too well, but agreed to the ordeal. A special needle on a little electric drill bore into the wobbly big toenail in nine places, with the hope of releasing pressure—but alas, no fresh blood was released. It had hardened!!!!

When the medical staff understood that the big toe injury was now 28 days old, and that I had continued walking all that time, they pantomimed that I should stay in Astorga for a full week to rest the foot. The wonderful women carefully cleaned and wrapped the traumatized toes, and I limped off the examination table to a nearby chair.

The Urgent Clinic staff gathered around—they thought I was very brave, and I thought them very kind. We had had several good laughs throughout the procedures despite the gravity of the situation. When I left they each asked me quite solemnly to say a prayer for them when I got to Santiago. I agreed, but I was solemn too, as I took each of their hands and made little signs of the cross over my feet. It was not in jest. We fully understood that I would need all the help I could get to make it to Santiago.

It was 9:30pm when I left the Centro de Salud and I was starved. I calculated that it had been eleven hours since I'd eaten. More importantly, food was essential in order to take another much-needed Ibuprophen. I stopped at a bar for an ensalada, forgetting that the Albergue closed at 10:00pm.

When I got back at 11:00pm, all was dark and the massive doors were locked tight. What to do? I rang the hanging bell once, startled by how loud it was. I waited and waited, and at last a sleepy young woman, herself the hospitalera, let me in and accompanied me to the second floor. I had to walk through the small chapel to reach the door to my room. Vigil lights flickered on the altar. I could just see the outlines of medieval figures stenciled onto the walls. I sat down in the chapel and reviewed the tensions from the day's walk, the medical procedure and getting into the locked dorm. My breathing became slow and deep. My intent was to sit quietly and make my heart available, to be open to the presence of God and His action within me. I was only occasionally aware of a thought or the flickering lights on the walls of the tiny chapel and became fully aware only as the Cathedral bells chimed midnight. I stood for a few minutes in front of the altar, then slipped into the sleeping area, and so as not to disturb my roommates, I lay down on the bed in my clothes and fell sound asleep.

CAMINO—DAY 31

A Cowboy Bar on the Camino? You're Kidding!!!!!

Postcard # 31—May 24, 2010 sent from El Ganso, Espana

Dearest Elena: Well, I'm lucky—2 more frogs today on my path, and another green lizard! Frogs say hello to me, but the lizards are silent. I spent the morning in Astorga at the fabulous Cathedral & admiring the Gaudi Palace, though I couldn't get in, as it was cerrado on Monday. Then, because my toe is mal, I only walked 15.4km or 9.3mi from Astorga to El Ganso. It's amazing, Elena! El Ganso is crumbled, with only old stone walls standing, roofs caved in—people gone & yet the Camino passes through. I am sitting in the Cowboy Bar talking to a German couple and a Japanese-American father & daughter from Texas (he JP Morgan IT and she a graduate student about to enter medical school). The country today was flat towards the mountains, then suddenly undulating, rolling,—I'm headed into mountains. Call up Grandpa and tell him you got this card and I'm o'k. Grandma

Journal—Day 31 (Monday) May 24, 2010—written at El Ganso

From Astorga to El Ganso, walked 15.4km or 9.3mi . . . I really did pull back after my doctor consultation last evening that lasted one hour. Today, I walked more slowly, more thoughtfully, more carefully. Rested frequently and the foot held up. Village of El Ganso quite amazing—very old, dating to the 12th Century, only a few habitable houses, & dozens of walls standing, roofs caved in, or completely gone—times past. The requisite stork's nest perched precariously on the church steeple with industrious parents feeding! Baby storks? I just can't tell. A few nice renovated houses (maybe 5 or 6) all the rest abandoned ghosts of the centuries past. Weeds high in unkempt gardens, wildflowers growing and blooming in roofless and abandoned bedrooms. Lucky tonight to be in Albergue Gabino and in a tiny downstairs room for 3 people with a tiny bathroom. Passed several hours in the Cowboy Bar, complete with American posters, guns & various other paraphernalia on the walls. Only about twenty pilgrims there tonight, but it grew quite raucous and intense with music, stories, much laughter, lots of dancing to Western cowboy music (not me with my sore toes). People from Brazil (one a Maori), from Holland, Canada, Japanese Americans (Houston) father & daughter, two married men from Holland. Really liked the German couple! Very reserved but they entered into the Spirit of the evening and got up & danced.

Reflection on Day 31, written back home in San Francisco

"I do not need to seek God. God is already here waiting to be found; soaked in my reality. My journey is to be one of recognizing God, always already present, and surfacing that presence in my daily life."

Julian of Norwich

On Day 31, I forced myself to slow down. I felt more confident today after my trip to the Ambulatorio Urgentias last night. The woman doctor had assured me I was not harboring a fatal infection that would cause some drastic measure, like amputation of the big, troubled toe, but that it was simply a slow-healing and very sore bruise requiring time to heal and the growth of a new toenail. Still, her medical assurance did not lessen the discomfort I felt with every step and I continued to hear in my mind last night's high-pitched little drill piercing my loose big toenail until it touched skin. So much for the doctor urging me to stop walking for a week, for in fact I trudged nearly 10 miles today to the tiny village of El Ganso.

I found the Albergue Gabino, which was rumored by the crowd outside as being full, but the man who registered pilgrims looked me over and shuttled me off to a tiny empty side room with one single bed plus a lower and upper bunk. He placed my things at the single bed and grandly pointed out a funny little sink and toilet inside the room separated from the beds by a hanging curtain. I was thrilled. I had an hour alone to unwind from the walk, unpack my backpack and wash some clothes to hang in a sunny courtyard. It was windy and I felt confident that they'd be dry by dark.

I worked on my feet as the doctor instructed me to do, and before finishing this task, I was joined by two more women pilgrims assigned to beds in the room. One was a friendly, sweet soul. She too, felt the narrow little side room was a bit of luxury with only 3 people and a tiny bathroom. The other seemed disapproving of the accommodations. The sweet woman looked at my feet sympathetically, but said nothing. The other woman looked more closely, even lifting one of my feet up and turning it from side to side. She announced: "You need to get your feet looked after, you know. You could get in a lot of trouble out here on the Camino." I smiled at her. "It's not funny," she said crossly. "You shouldn't be walking. It's my guess you're wearing the wrong shoes. And people aren't very careful about what kind of socks they wear". She picked up my shoes, looked them over, and walked out the door with them in hand. "Your shoes need airing. I'll put them in the courtyard," and added for good measure "I don't think you'll make it all the way to Santiago with those feet. You could go back to Astorga and take a bus, you know—let those blisters heal." And she went into the bathroom, closed the meager curtain and was silent for 20 minutes.

I giggled the entire time as I finished wrapping my feet. Just as I was preparing to leave for a walk and dinner, she stuck her head around the curtain and announced to both of us: "I'm going to bed early tonight. I hope neither one of you snore. I'm very tired and need my sleep." I replied cheerily: "Good night. Sleep well. I'm out of here for a big evening at the Cowboy Bar."

There is not a lot to do in El Ganso, but there is one attraction which many pilgrims have come to know by experience, if not by reputation. The Meson Cowboy is by no means a grand edifice, but instead a ramshackle building—the big name over the door is Meson Cowboy, then in smaller letters Terrazo, then The Cowboy Bar. I'd read about the Cowboy Bar, so fixed up a bit and ambled over to have a look. When I arrived and sauntered in about 6:00 in the evening, there was no one there except the bartender. We said "Howdy" to each other and I settled at a table alone, spread out my evening "altar"—family pictures, little felt heart, postcards and journal. I loved being there. It was completely quiet. I ordered a glass of wine. What a luxury—I envisioned that it would be a peaceful evening.

I looked the place over. It reminded me of the saloons in western movies. The room was long and the walls decorated with a hodge-podge of items from the American "Old West" and especially from cowboy movies—posters, guns, some rather nice framed photos, boots, clothing, cowboy hats hanging on the wall, and western paraphernalia of all types—coffee pots, frying pans, and lassoes. I noted a very old juke box against one wall and wondered if it was in working condition. On the other side of the bar were a long bench and a few tables and chairs scattered around. Over the cash register hung enormous horns of a bull, mounted on a piece of wood and flaring out menacingly. The bartender, dressed in black with a long white apron, lounged against one wall and looked quite bored, but I also detected a watchfulness about him. He was definitely a businessman. I could smell food cooking so knew there would be some grub available later in the evening—more substantial than the sandwiches and ice cream and coca-colas advertised on a board at the front door.

I let the incongruity of El Ganso's Cowboy Bar sink in and become familiar to me. Pretty clever, actually, of an owner on the Camino path to situate a bar so different culturally from anything the pilgrims would encounter along the way. All that he might have added for western atmosphere would be a wooden plank sidewalk outside, and some horses hitched near the door.

I began to write the daily postcard to Elena. I wanted her to know that seeing frogs and green lizards today on the path was at least as important as seeing the grand buildings of Astorga. As soon as this first idea was written on the card, I put down my pen and was drawn into the silence of what?—the Cowboy Bar, my mind, my heart, God? My intention was very clear—to be open and unafraid and available to the mystery of my pilgrimage and to the unknown. It is fair to say that I surrendered there alone at the table to the stillness, now and then recognizing an arising thought, and dismissing it, letting it go by gently saying a word embedded in my heart through my practice of Centering Prayer.

Perhaps 10 minutes passed, perhaps a half hour. The juke box began playing a slow dance, a honky-tonk western tune I actually recognized. I opened my eyes, surprised to see several other pilgrims in the bar, sitting singly or looking around at the posters. Several people stood at the door watching the bartender write out the evening menu on a slate board. And the place slowly changed from a silent retreat for me to a busy and somewhat typical bar on the Camino. The scene was like an old hand-cranked phonograph winding up from slow-motion musical notes into the recognizable hum of evening melodies in Camino bars.

I wrote a second sentence on the postcard and two friendly people sat down next to me. Informalities were exchanged and I learned they were a father and daughter from Texas walking the Camino. They shared their simple story, but one of such touching and familial intimacy. She was a graduate student about to enter medical school and her father involved in a busy IT career at JP Morgan. But he was not too busy to walk and support her in this major life transition. We shared many things in common, it seemed, in our Camino experiences, our back home political views, our spiritual and family values.

A dignified, middle-aged German couple entered tentatively, sat down on my other side and we too engaged in conversation. They were curious about the 3 pictures I had on my table, and soon we were sharing stories about back home loved ones. The woman couldn't believe that I was sending a postcard to my grand daughter every day. "Everyday?" she asked several times and we laughed as I kept repeating, "Yes, every single day." The Germans told me about their country's interest in American western history—cowboys in particular, and especially about the events staged in Germany replicating cowboy rodeos.

Brazilians walked in and the place burst into a party. Everybody was kissed and hugged—the juke box was reloaded and turned up full volume. The bartender's family began scurrying around, taking orders for food and drinks. More pilgrims entered and joined the whirlwind Brazilians, and that group danced their way out onto the Terrazo. At that stage, I finished the postcard, ordered dinner and while waiting, turned my attention to the day's journal entry. I recall that as I wrote, I was continually amused by the joyous bursts of laughter that arose from the Terrazo. I wandered out to find the group dancing, and there was another round of hugs and kisses. Although I didn't know them, the Brazilians said they'd been seeing me on the paths over the past few days. They were "watching out for grandmother," they said, and gave me another hug. They pulled me to the dance floor, but I declined, horrified to even think of any one of them stepping on my tortured toes.

The waitress fetched me back to my table for dinner. The Texans had left, and new pilgrims sat at my adjoining table. As I started eating, we said hello, and the two young men introduced themselves as being from Holland. Partners, I sensed. They were thrilled to learn I was from San Francisco and told me about their month's vacation there the previous summer. It was clear to me from their descriptions that they had stayed with their friends only two blocks from where I lived. Such a coincidence, we thought, as they began naming restaurants and landmarks with which we were both familiar. They were so intense in their animation: "Why, we two walked down the street where you live everyday on our way to the Castro."

We lifted our glasses to San Francisco. I asked why they were on the Camino. They looked at each other and then at me thoughtfully. One said, "I think we can tell you. We are just married, and the Camino is our honeymoon." I calculated this startling message for a few moments, then leaned over and took their hands: "Bless you both. And may Saint James bless your marriage." They beamed. All 3 of us recognized this moment of time as a graced Camino gift.

Having finished dinner, I returned again to my journal and finished scribbling down the day's events. I was getting ready to leave when the Brazilians formed a kind of samba line and snaked from the Terrazo into the Cowboy Bar itself. They were excellent dancers and totally uninhibited, changing partners, now dancing alone, then in 3's and 4's, calling out, trilling joyously, gracefully waving their arms, undulating their bodies. They pulled other pilgrims to their feet, and soon the Cowboy Bar was rocking with the dancers' beat.

The Germans watched: "We like to dance, but we couldn't compete with that," the man said. "But remember, when you go home to Germany," I encouraged them, "you can say that you danced at the Cowboy Bar." They looked at each other, smiled in agreement, shrugged and he held back her chair and led her onto the dance floor. Whatever they danced, the foxtrot, I thought, they looked so beautiful moving gracefully, and so very, very happy.

There were now only 3 pilgrims seated in the middle of the whirl. I turned to the two men on my left. They were seated, but clearly grooving and moving to the beat, snapping their fingers. I pointed to the dance floor, then at them, and back to the floor. I could feel the crackling chemistry between them, see it in their eyes, and then they were on their feet in a flash, loving the rock-a-billy beat, loving the Cowboy Bar scene, loving each other.

It was time for me to trace my way back to the Albergue Gabino. I walked down the dark and crumbled empty streets, looking at the stars, thinking about the evening and how it differed from others on the Camino. I continued to hear the music for a couple blocks and I thought how special the memory of the Cowboy Bar would be for me, what a gift I'd been given to have experienced those few precious souls letting their hair down. Actually, maybe my hair was down also.

I entered the Albergue, and stopped to check on my shoes. Sure enough, they were airing in the courtyard and were getting damp with dew. Everything was dark. I found my little pitch black room and entered quietly. I'd left my toothbrush on my pillow before I went out, so picked it up in the dark and started into the bathroom. My foot hit something and I nearly fell. "Careful," a voice whispered, "she's sleeping on the floor. Step around her." This was nearly impossible as the woman's mattress filled almost the entire floor space next to the beds and between me and the bathroom. Nevertheless, I squeezed by her mattress, and teeth brushed, I finally got into bed, and arranged myself comfortably.

I heard the woman roll over. Her snoring started somewhat quietly, little streams of air escaping through her nose and windpipe. "Well, isn't this ironic?" I thought. "Oh well, just go to sleep, Mary. She can't control her mouth, and she can't control her snoring, either." Two little snorts emerged, then long gagging sounds, then an ear shattering snort. This went on for ages. It was impossible to sleep. Oh, dear, Lord. What to do? I sat up in my bed, reached for my hiking poles and gently, gently nudged her with one of them. She quieted, and I went to sleep.

The next morning, she was gone, I thought, when I awakened. I was relieved. The other woman lifted our mouthy room mate's mattress back onto the bed and just shook her head. Neither one of us said anything. I picked up my backpack and headed into the kitchen/dining room. I sat at the long table with several pilgrims who had danced the night away at the Cowboy Bar and poured myself a cup of much needed coffee. The woman appeared out of the restroom. She pointed at me and said to the people assembled at the table: "Oh, here's the woman I told you about" she said loudly. And then to me "do you know that you snored all night long and kept me awake?" I acted surprised. "Really? I snored all night long? Nobody ever told me I snored." She walked towards the door to leave, and fired back: "Well, I'm telling you that you snore." "Buen Camino," I called after her. I fixed my toast and jam, and joined two good-humored German women celebrating a birthday.

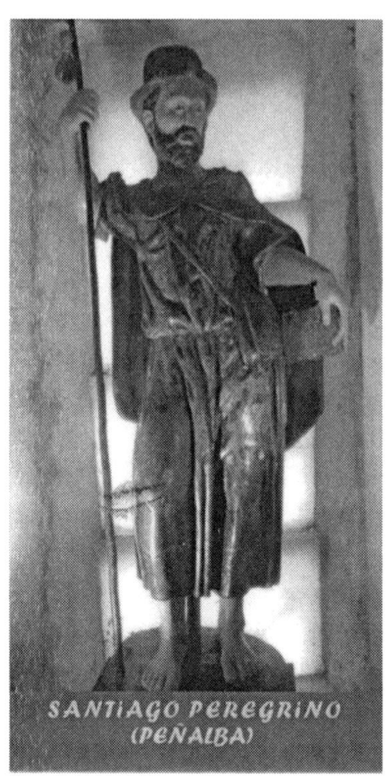

CAMINO—DAY 32

Amazing Grace

Postcard # 32—May 25, 2010 sent from Foncebadon, Espana

Dear Elena: Tonight I am staying in a Pilgrim's Albergue—1 room has 20 people in bunks (I'm on a bottom bunk) and the adjacent room has 26 people sleeping on mattresses on the floor & believe me, every one of us is grateful to have a roof over our heads in this rain. Today, I walked only 13.5km or 8.1mi because the terrain grew very steep as I started up the Leon Mountains, & it began to rain hard. The path was very rocky & full of gullies, which soon flooded with water & mud. Still, I could hear the cuckoos & the changing scenery & vegetation as I climbed was wondrous. Meadows solid wild flowers. I'm so grateful for this time. Full of love. I like this postcard of Santiago the Pilgrim. I think he's just been given the news that he must sleep on an upper bunk. Grandma's on the Camino.

Journal—Day 32 (Tuesday) May 25, 2010—written at Foncebadon

At breakfast this am in El Ganso, I sang Happy Birthday to a German woman whose partner had gone outside & picked her a lovely handful of wildflowers. She was so touched. Then down the steps came the Brazilian woman and sang Happy Birthday again, in the style of Marilyn Monroe to John F. Kennedy (including Happy Birthday, Mr. President) and all accompanied by the sultry voice, slinky dancing with a long flowing scarf and blown kisses)—It was as bizarre a birthday breakfast as can be imagined, but the proper German woman entered into the spontaneous spirit of the event & declared it her best birthday ever. I started walking in slightly overcast, yet sunny weather. The paths were beautiful, and a full spectrum rainbow hung in the skies for over an hour—like heaven and earth kissing each other, and following me, drawing me in until the rains started in Rabanal—quite a mystical experience. Stopped for coffee & croquettes. Some kind of fish . . . a strange but tasty lunch. Serious climbing now & the path was very rough, as it crossed meadows, entered scrub forest, then pine forests, more meadows. White gorse in full bloom. No poppies today, but very much natural lavender, and a new flower—dark purple hibiscus. Gorgeous even in this afternoon's downpour. So glad to stop at Foncebadon. Very tight quarters. Very cold. One Nigerian here. Several Italian men peeled potatoes (4 enormous sacks) & I made a salad with 4 huge heads of lettuce, 2 cans of corn, ½ doz tomatoes, & a dressing of oil, vinegar, parsley, oregano, sel, poivre & lots of garlic. It served 35 Pilgrims as a 1st course and the Potato Chorizo Stew was a big hit. Great Experience for a community of Camino Pilgrims. Today walked 13.5km or 8.1mi.

Reflection on Day 32, written back home in San Francisco

"Be not lax in celebrating. Be not lazy in the festive service of God. Be ablaze with enthusiasm. Let us be an alive, burning offering before the altar of God!"

Hildegard of Bingen

I had planned a much longer walk today, but frankly, the trail was so precarious, the climb so steep (400 meters) in the Leon Mountains, the fog and chill and wind driven rain so insistent that when the sign for the Foncebadon village presented itself, I stepped under a sheltering tree to rethink my destination. I'd read in numerous books that Foncebadon was truly primitive and crumbled, and harbored packs of wild dogs that sniffed and growled at pilgrims as they walked. Nevertheless, the weather was so nasty that I would try to stay here—dogs or no dogs. I checked my trusty Brierley guidebook for Albergues. "Good, three different dormitories add up to nearly 100 beds, and it's still early. I'm sure to get a place."

But, not so fast. I was waved away at the first two places in the village "completo, completo" . . . and by the time I pulled my pitiful and soggy self up onto the porch of the very small Domus Dei parish hostal, my last chance at a room, at least 10 Pilgrims were lined up in front of me to register. Dozens of wet plastic ponchos of every color were drying on the porch and I could see that the inside hummed with activity. The odds were not good with 10 souls ahead of me that there would be a bed, much less a lower bunk for me.

Nevertheless, I put down my backpack and prepared to wait. During the long registration period, in which the queue buzzed about there only being seven beds left, several pilgrims just ahead of me gave up and trudged back into the driving rain. Here, exhaustion masked as perseverance once again worked to my advantage. The very intense middle aged man at the desk by the door registered me and announced with finality—"there is only one bunk left." With no shame at all, I pantomimed that I needed a lower bunk and looking me over, he said "Yes. But of course".

At most Camino Albergues, the hospitaleros volunteering their time to run the places work in teams of 2-3, and after a pilgrim is registered, and paid the small amount for a bed and had his/her credential stamped, one of the colleagues walks the pilgrim to the exact assigned bed, often carrying the backpack. It is considered the hospitality of the Camino and not only has it happened to me over and over, but has welcomed me, comforted me, assured me, centered me for the evening.

But this man in Foncebadon was running the place alone, so the process was more tedious. He had to leave his registration desk to guide me through the kitchen into a dark, damp, cramped back room filled with pilgrims, backpacks and wet clothes and straight to my assigned, supposedly empty, lower bunk. There on my bed, with things spread all around, was a very settled-in, very pretty woman.

The hospitalero was assertive: "This is not your assigned bed". She smiled coyly at him, responding that it didn't matter, she was more comfortable here below her boyfriend, and besides, no problem, there was her old assigned bed untouched and ready for me. The man's volume increased: "No, no. You will move to your assigned upper bed. This lower bunk is reserved for old people," and he stared her down. Pilgrims all around sat up and began to watch intently. Reluctantly, she gathered her things and moved. He was successful in putting us each in our physical places. As I unpacked, I had to smile to myself, for surely, I was put in my psychological place. Lower bunks for <u>old</u> people, indeed!!

As soon as I unpacked and found a place for my rain soaked belongings, I went to the woman's bunk and said: "Hello, my name is Mary. I'm sorry this happened. Are you o'k?" "No, I'm very sick today with an upset stomach." I dug around in my kit, and brought her two tums, which she gratefully gobbled down and seemed to be asleep in 10 minutes.

I began to investigate the place. It was indeed a House of God, a Domus Dei, a tiny desanctified church renovated into a hostel. Beams and old windows showed its original architectural design. I soon saw that I was lucky to have a bed in a room that held about 20 Pilgrims, for the adjacent room had another 26 folks on mattresses on the floor, most of them napping mid afternoon to escape the chill. Everything was cold (no heat), damp and smelled like way too many Pilgrims crammed together. Smelled somewhat of wet socks and sweaty tee-shirts. In another part of the building, I found a dining room with tables. Nobody was there so I sat and began my daily drill of postcard & journal writing.

Soon, several middle aged Italian men wandered in from the sleeping area, all jovial, and began to either read or write. They soon discovered that communicating with me was pretty difficult although we pantomimed and had good laughs over God knows what. One found a CD player, and two CDs, one by Enya and the other a terrific medley by Luciano Pavarotti. They were beside themselves with joy, and sang along with everything. Their good voices and the Irish and Italian music cheered me as well as them.

We were all amazed when the man who ran the place came in about 4:00pm and asked us to sign a list if we would be eating dinner there, as he was going to cook. He thought there would be about 35 people to eat and if anybody wanted to help him, he'd appreciate it. He'd need potato peelers and somebody to make the salad.

I jumped up and grandly announced "Well, I'll make the salad, and these handsome Italian singers will peel the potatoes". They barely blinked, then cheered and agreed. And I went and made cups of tea to fortify us for the job ahead. The men were good sports and peeled and chopped potatoes (four bags full) and I gathered all the salad greens, plus tomatoes, cucumbers, celery, hard boiled eggs, scavenged in the pantry for cans of corn and peas, wondering all the while if the provisions would be salad enough for thirty five people.

Meanwhile, the hospitalero was preparing a 20 inch pot for the Potato-Chorizo Stew, browning a dozen onions in olive oil, and mincing two entire heads of garlic. He put me to slicing 20 lengths of chorizo and for the next 45 minutes, I tended the stew. After the onions and garlic cooked down, I added the chorizo—stirring until all was browned and slightly caramelized. By this time, the man and I were friendly. He dubbed me his sous chef, and I was instructed to add the absolute mountain of large-dice potatoes to the pan, and cover all with water. Oh my goodness!!!!! This was some operation. "What do you think," the man asked, "about salt and pepper, and would I be so kind as to season the stew?" With no hesitation, I added lots of salt and pepper, found a jar of dried basil and with a flick of my wrist, added the entire contents to the bubbling pot.

The weather had cleared some, and the people at the albergue who were sleeping and lounging were lured into the kitchen by the heavenly smells emanating from the pot I was tending. In between stirs, I prepped the salad, and found indeed that it made a mighty amount. Knowing from tasting the stew that it was going to be excellent, I decided to mix a special salad dressing instead of just putting on the table the typical oil & vinegar cruets for folks to season salad to their taste.

Momentum increased as 6:00pm approached. Tables were set for 35 diners. People were shooed out of the kitchen to be seated. Energy and anticipation were palpable. Laughter and good will ruled the day. Great quantities of bread were cut. A bell was rung to call in folks from the porch and the sleeping areas. The chef gave me his final instructions. Oh, I love it when a plan comes together.

When all had gathered, the man said in English, "Before we eat, introductions and a prayer are in order." So each of us stood, saying our names and from where we came. It seemed sacred, for we were from all over the world, meeting by chance in this humble place and preparing to share a meal. Then the man asked who would say a prayer. There was a long awkward pause with no response. And I stood and said, "I will read the poem on the bulletin board next to the front door. It's like a prayer." I unpinned it, and read these beautiful sentiments to the group slowly and distinctly to accommodate those whose first language was not English:

A pilgrim does not demand, A pilgrim is grateful . . .
He leaves what he can, and takes only that which he needs . . .
If you conform with the bare essentials,
then what you don't really need seems a luxury . . .
If you keep stopping, then your progress is slow.
And if you go quickly, you miss what is best . . .
The sun will tell you the time to get up, light your way, so enjoy his company.
A good pilgrim is she who listens and hears the stones talk . . .
A roof to sleep under, a puddle to wash in,
bread to eat, a wine to drink. And a Camino to walk.
If you get blisters, bless them . . .
And perhaps you won't get anything worse. Amen, Amen, Amen.

And indeed everyone Amen'd loudly. I carried the salad in from the kitchen and dressed it with fanfare. Efficient assembly line service doled out 35 plenteous servings, with a bit left over. The parable of Loaves & Fishes came to mind. I looked over the tables and noted that everyone was devouring the salad and talking animatedly with their seatmates, but that our glasses were empty. Feeling a bit like Mary approaching Jesus at the Wedding at Cana, I approached the hospitalero's side and said: "There is no wine. We forgot the wine." He exploded in laughter, "Mary, Mary, we don't have wine here. We forgot water". And it took no time at all to enlist helpful volunteers to fetch pitchers of water and pour our dinner drinks. The stewpot was ceremoniously rolled to the table and the contents proved a huge success. Every bite was eaten, providing 2nd and 3rd servings to many pilgrims.

I did not concern myself with the cleanup, as the pilgrims cleared and washed up with good humor, putting all back in place. A free will offering basket for the dinner was passed around and people appeared to contribute generously.

Very quickly pilgrims headed off to bed. I slipped easily out of my Martha role, and back into that of Mary. The dormitories grew completely quiet by 9:00pm. Only the sound of rainfall on the windows and the occasional barking of dogs roaming outside. I stayed seated alone in the quiet dining room lit by two candles, thinking of the gift this day had been, starting with the charming spontaneous birthday breakfast in El Ganso for the German woman; the vivid rainbow that followed me for an hour all the way to Rabanal; the rainfall that caused me to stop early here at Foncebadon and well short of my day's walking goal.

Sitting there alone, I was flooded with gratefulness for the lower bunk that awaited me, the hospitality of the Foncebadon Domus Dei; the spirited exchanges with the Italian men; the woman who had eaten the tums (coming back for more,) the energy and joy of the food preparation; the evident oneness felt by the pilgrims at the shared meal. Gratefulness for today turned to joy, and I found myself smiling, then laughing out loud with the realization that here at Foncedeban, I had shifted from an interior life easily and spontaneously towards other pilgrims, towards give and take, and the pure fun of being with others. At least for today and yesterday at El Ganso, I had left behind my solo journey and its reserved involvement with the Camino community.

Perhaps this balance of silent walking on the Camino with active pilgrim involvement was exactly the lesson I needed to learn.

With this gentle review of my day, I was ready to fully quiet my mind and body for a session of Centering Prayer.

As I settled into meditation, a gentle male voice said "Good evening, Maree. May I join you?" And there began in the stillness of the darkened dining room one of the most spiritual conversations with which I was blessed on the Camino. My visitor was Nigerian, about 40, the only black Pilgrim I met (or saw) on the Camino. He spoke with a perfect command of English, and he emanated a great spirituality, a great curiosity in what the Camino might offer him and other Pilgrims, and what he himself would bring to Camino encounters. He spoke of his work and interests, of his wife in the Netherlands and his teen-age daughter. I spoke of my life, my retirement interests, my husband, son, daughter, son-in-law and granddaughter back in San Francisco.

We were both solitary souls walking solo on the Camino and spoke about that dynamic. We talked of the complexities of organized religion, of the philosophies of Duality and non-Duality, and I of the Christian meditation practice of Centering Prayer. He wanted to learn about it. I described the simple and gentle steps of Centering Prayer, and we sat in silent practice together for a half-hour. After, he spoke with emotion, thanking me for the conversation, the salad dressing, the prayer I had read at dinner. We shook hands and he disappeared into the room with the mattresses, and I never saw him again.

CAMINO—DAY 33

The Tiny Music Box

Postcard #33—May 26, 2010 sent from Acebo, Espana

Elena: The picture on this postcard is the most famous site on the Camino. Pilgrims bring a stone or a memento (something very special from Home) to leave here at the Cruz de Ferro or Iron Cross. I brought a stone from home I had picked up on the beach years ago & had on my desk at Job Corps. Now here is a little story: About 3 weeks ago in a dorm, I observed an older man in the bunk next to me take out a tiny, hand-operated music box & gently play a tune to his wife. She seemed so appreciative & gave him a little kiss. He put the music box into his backpack, but alas!! when I got up next morning, they had left, & the music box was on the floor. I looked for them. I prayed to find them. I carried the little music box with me all the time, hanging from my backpack. But at the Cruz de Ferro, I knew I must leave it there. So I tied the little plastic bag to the cross with a shoestring. Continued the walk on beautiful misty/foggy roads & could hear bells & music before I came upon a strange little sanctuary called Manjarin with all kinds of flags & decorations out front. I stopped & rested with a coffee, watching other Pilgrims, observing the rituals of hospitality offered by a man named Tomas in a medieval garb. Religious music played. Templar paraphernalia was being sold. I pressed on to Acebo, walking a total today of 11.2km or 6.7mi. Grandma

Journal—Day 33 (Wednesday) May 26, 2010—written at Acebo

Today was a short day for me . . . the hike indescribable with flowers & steep ravines. Rain of course made the steep descents from the Cruz de Ferro into Acebo quite treacherous and when I got there, I just stopped from emotion and exhaustion and checked into a lovely and private Pension del Pelegrinos. Great room, great lunch, then a long several hour reviving nap. Even though I'd walked only 11.2km or 6.7 mi, I needed a break. Got up for a long session on email—letters to Larry & from Larry. Many Pilgrims came for a meal in this family-owned bar/hotel where I am staying. Had a great talk with four beautiful women from South Africa, a family of sisters & female relatives walking together. I'd seen them before on other stages of the Camino, and learned today they had reservations every night pre-arranged by a South African travel agency, and that their baggage was transported by van everyday. They seemed incredulous that I walked alone, without a watch or phone, & with no nightly reservations. This stop is reviving me. Here I can leave the bar restaurant, go up some back steps to my beautiful private room & enter the peace & quiet. Where I stayed in Foncebadon last night at the Domus Dei was so intense, crowded, the bed so creaky that I did not sleep at all, accounting for today's exhaustion.

Reflection on Day 33, written back home in San Francisco

"Do not overlook tiny good actions, thinking they are of no benefit; even tiny drops of water in the end will fill a huge vessel." . . .
Buddha

As I began Day 33, I felt excited at the walk ahead which would take me to a landmark about which every Camino book had a reference—the Iron Cross, or Cruz de Ferro, as it translates. The cross marks the highest point on the Camino, and I knew it would be a steep climb and, I suspected, an emotional experience as well. Like pilgrims over the years, I planned to leave a stone there that I brought from San Francisco and that had special meaning to me. The day was beautiful, and the mountain slopes dazzled the eye with their golden yellow gorse in full bloom. Step after step, rest after rest, then more steps brought me to a level place where I got my first glimpse of the cross. It was a very tall oak pole set deeply into an enormous mound of dirt and rocks, with stones by the hundreds of thousands piled and scattered on the ground and up the entire mound to the base of the pole. The cross on top was very small compared to the scale of the mound and pole. At first glance, I was not impressed.

There were only ½ dozen pilgrims milling around the area and I slipped off my backpack and slowly circled the landmark. What was this all about, that the Cruz de Ferro attracted such attention? I leaned against a nearby fence and watched several of the pilgrims scramble to the top of the mound, then assume kneeling postures or place their heads reverently against the pole. Two were crying when they came down. The others were solemn and didn't speak as they gathered up their packs and headed down the trail.

A group of French high school students approached the mound and with some flurry of activity, took out their stones and placed them either at ground level or high on the mound at the base of the pole. When they returned to their group, the leader, probably a teacher, gathered them together, handed each a paper, and they said a prayer together in French. I went to the group and gestured if I could see the paper . . . a boy handed his to me and turned away. I was delighted to see that the prayer was printed in French, English and Spanish. Here's a translation of what the students prayed: "O Lord, may the stone which I bring to this Holy Place be a sign of my pilgrimage to Santiago. When I reach my final judgment, tip the balance of my life in favor of my good deeds. I lay down this token which I carry from __________. Please forgive my sins and help me carry my burdens in life. Amen." The group's reaction to the prayer and the exercise of leaving a stone was perhaps predictable, given their young ages. While some prayed fervently and respectfully, others seemed embarrassed and uncomfortable, whispering behind their hands or shielding cell phones from their teachers' view. Their ritual completed, the group hastily disappeared down the path.

I fished the stone I'd brought to Spain from my waistpack and held it in my hand. I'd found it on the beach in San Francisco some 20 years ago and kept it on my desk at the Department of Labor, often turning it over in my hand as I conducted business calls. Certainly, it reminded me of a significant time in my life. Yes, I would leave the stone here at the Cruz de Ferro, but I wasn't sure just what it represented in the Camino ritual—what sin, what fear or transgression, what burden should I leave here as part of my pilgrimage?

I looked around, surprised at the quiet. No other pilgrim was on the mound or in the vicinity. I would leave my stone now. Clambering to the top of the mound was far more difficult than I thought it would be—I struggled upwards 30 or 40 feet through a tangle of personal items left by pilgrims and large and small rocks. Footing was difficult. I began to see more clearly the variety of objects that pilgrims left here—a multitude of personal items that included photographs, letters, postcards, money, rosaries, shoes, shoelaces, hats, a belt buckle, a bridal veil, baby booties, stuffed animals and little dolls, St. Jude medals, a small urn of ashes and flowers picked that day along the Camino path. I began to touch the items, look deeply at the pictures, read the single page notes. I felt the experience getting out of hand. There were powerful and deep emotions vibrating here and I couldn't deny the sudden effect the place was having on me. I placed my stone carefully on a little wooden box, and scrambled down the hill.

I sat down on the ground where I'd left my backpack, and let the torrent of silent tears come. There were just too many stories and too much humanity packed into the Cruz de Ferro, and I was overwhelmed. I felt helpless and empty. Some time passed and I was vaguely aware that pilgrims came into and out of the area, leaving items and having their pictures taken. I got out the prayer again I'd received from the student, hoping to find a clue in its words. When I got to the line "I lay down this token which I carry from home" I had a flash of insight, a gripping certainty of something I had to do immediately—and that was place the tiny music box I'd been carrying for 3 weeks here at the foot of the cross.

I turned my backpack over and untied the little plastic bag that was attached to a zippered pocket. I removed the music box from the bag and played the tune by turning the wooden handle. Whose music box was this I'd found by the side of my bed? Why had the couple carried it on the Camino in the first place? And why did it come into my hands 3 weeks ago in a dormitory, its owners nowhere to be found?

This is what happened 3 weeks ago. One evening as I was preparing to get into bed, I observed in the lower bunk just 2 feet from me an older man playing a tiny music box for his wife, who was already in bed in the lower bunk next to him. She seemed so pleased and they exchanged a tender little kiss. He carefully wrapped the music box and placed it into his backpack. There is a story here to the couple carrying a music box, I thought—more than meets the eye, and I got into bed myself and went to sleep.

The next morning I awakened at 7:30 am and the dorm was nearly empty. I hurriedly dressed and as I was leaving, checked around the bed for any belongings I might have dropped. There was the music box on the floor at the edge of the man's bed. I ran to the front desk, then the bathrooms, the kitchen, the area outside in front of the dormitory. I could not find them. I ran to the bar next door, moving from table to table holding up the music box. Many pilgrims were drinking coffee, but my older couple was not there, either. I really wanted them to have the music box back in their possession.

Back at the dorm, I left careful instructions with the hospitalero where I calculated I'd stay that night and gave him the telephone number. I also promised to call him that evening to check if he'd been contacted by the couple. I did call him the next 2 nights, and each time he grew a bit more distant—"No Madame, there are no inquiries here about a music box." And so the little bag swung silently and forlornly from my backpack for nearly 3 weeks until my inspiration to leave it at the Cruz de Ferro.

Once again, I struggled up the mound, this time carrying the music box and the prayer from the French students. And once again, I was alone, standing at the foot of the cross. Where would I place the tiny music box? It needed a special place so that it didn't fall down into the crevices of the larger rocks. I spotted a new shoe string, probably from a hiking boot, tied around the pole tightly, its ends hanging down. With no hesitation, I secured the sturdy plastic sack protecting the music box to the pole, knotting the shoe string twice for good measure.

I tried to remember what the couple looked like, tried to believe that they would want me to leave their treasure at the cross. I said the prayer on the paper out loud, this time altering it for the occasion to include the couple: "O Lord, may the token which I bring to this Holy Place be a sign of our pilgrimage to Santiago. When we reach our final judgment, tip the balance of our lives in favor of our good deeds. I lay down this music box which I carry for my brother and sister who lost it on their way. Please forgive our sins and help us carry our burdens in life. Amen."

CAMINO—DAY 34

Birth on the Camino

Postcard # 34—May 27, 2010 sent from Ponferrado, Espana

Elena: It would be difficult to tell you all my feelings today. This am I came upon a puddle in the road & was flabbergasted to see 100's of tadpoles swimming—gaining energy to become little frogs. Ask your mama about this. She can draw you a picture. Then as I walked down a mountain side I could hear gentle wooden bells before I came upon about 300 goats, all lying down resting, dogs maybe 8, also resting & sleeping by the road. Pilgrims had stopped to observe the scene & as I reached them (& the shepherd), I realized that one female goat, not 10 feet off the road, was giving birth—I saw this wonderful thing—the baby so perfect—the mama so skilled in chewing open the sack & licking the baby dry. After 15 more minutes the shepherd signaled the dogs, the goats were rounded up & almost all came by & nudged the baby. The shepherd picked up the baby & carried it to a truck, the mama bleating frantically, & he gently placed baby, then mama in the truck, nursing. Oh, my. Today walked 18.4km or a bit more than 11miles in all.

Journal—Day 34 (Thursday) May 27, 2010 written at Ponferrado

Sleep so excellent last night in Acebo. The silence of a private room restorative. This am much work on my feet & a good breakfast started me out on a beautiful but rough path. Saw metal structure of a bicycle memorial. More puddles with tadpoles. It took a minute before I realized they would soon wiggle themselves into baby frogs. Most of the 18.4km or 11mi were on extremely rough paths but with most beautiful wild flowers. Stopped still for ½ hour watching a goat give birth, the silence of herd, dogs, shepherd, pilgrims as baby emerged & within a few minutes could stand. Tender to see herdsman pick up baby & mama, putting in back of truck to nurse. Started cold this am in Acebo, but warmed throughout day & amazingly all changed at lower altitudes approaching Ponferrado where roses by the thousands in full bloom in gardens. Honeysuckle also. Young woman from Czech Republic appeared right in front of me on an isolated mountainside, offering to carry my backpack. Her partner, she said, had taken a taxi from their last town to their next stop, & she would be happy to carry my backpack for me. I said no but realized I must have looked pathetic. Pin from eyeglasses lost, but a volunteer hospitalero (from Houston, TX) where I'm staying tonight at Albergue San Nicolas de Flue marched off with my glasses & fixed them perfectly in 30 minutes. After settling into Albergue, took a long walk in Ponferrado. Great menu & dinner in a café looking out on an enormous plaza with hundreds of Spanish folks out promenading, exercising, playing with children. Endlessly interesting to me. Grateful for bed space (bottom bunk) & grateful for birth of baby goat. Adjoining church to the albergue very beautiful & sat there tonight for an hour soaking up the silence. All is remarkable on this trip. All is satisfying.

Reflection on Day 34, written back home in San Francisco

"To offer no resistance to life is to be in a state of grace, ease and lightness. This state is not dependent upon things being a certain way, good or bad. Watch any animal and let it teach you acceptance of what is. Observe its surrender to the Now. Let it teach you Being."

Eckhart Tolle

I remember Day 34 clearly because I started in the morning rested—my senses seemed unusually tuned to the cool and foggy weather, the birdsong and the wildflowers blooming together along the paths and in every field. In retrospect, it was a day on the Camino that burned itself into my memory.

Early in the day's walk, I came upon multiple puddles in the road with virtually thousands of tadpoles frantically struggling in their evolution to become frogs. I slipped off my backpack and sat down on a nearby log to watch the activity in the nearest puddle, about 8 feet wide, and soon found myself crawling forward on the ground to get an even better look. I gently touched the water with my finger and the tadpoles' already rapid swimming became a frenzy of activity. Fascinated with the reaction in the puddle, I touched the water again. This time, as if with one mind, hundreds of tadpoles retreated to the far side of the puddle away from me. As their fear instinct subsided, I smiled and said, "O'k, o'k. You can relax. I won't do it again."

Suddenly, I heard someone running towards me. "Oh, Madame, are you hurt? How did you fall? Let me help you." I stood up on my own awkwardly and brushing off the wet mud on my trouser legs, assured her that I was simply watching the tadpoles. She looked at the puddle, then me, then with her rosary wrapped around her right hand, she made the sign of the cross over me, and off she went at a fast pace. I called after her: "Buen Camino. Thank you. Thank you," but she never turned around to acknowledge me. The entire encounter was so bizarre that I got the giggles. I put on my backpack, then elaborately waved good-bye to all those frenetic little tadpoles, wishing them well as they bloomed into frogs.

Walking the path was beautiful. I assumed a rhythm of caution in the swirls of mist, however, as I descended a long steep hill with a particularly muddy and rocky terrain. I was concentrating on using my poles to leverage safe footing, when I began to sense subtle clacking noises from the terrain below me.

As I approached the bottom of the hill, I observed a large gathering of reclining goats in a large open clearing on the left side of the road.

The misty scene stopped me in my tracks. As it came into focus, I could see three shepherds—one calmly leaning against a truck stopped near the path, and the other two men smoking and chatting on the opposite side of the road from the goats. There were several pilgrims standing stock-still observing the scene. Every goat was lying down. The occasional clacking sound came from wooden bells around the necks of a few goats. Other than that noise, not even birdsong could be heard.

Sheep dogs, maybe 8 or 10, were lying amongst the goats, several appearing to be asleep. I sectioned off a quarter of the visible goats with my eye, then counted the section and estimated about 300 in the herd. I noted a not unpleasant smell in the air, a bit like a freshly opened ripe cheese. Filled with curiosity at the mysterious silence, I joined the pod of pilgrims. Only then did I begin to understand the gentle event. Not ten feet from me lay a female goat giving birth.

I slipped my backpack to the ground, then sat down in the dirt to observe the event at eye level. Even in my calmness, my heart opened in complete wonder at the scene. I was fully aware that this was an unbidden privilege of observing Birth on the Camino. Probably 15 minutes passed as the young female goat struggled to cooperate with contractions that caused her to kneel and rock on both front and back legs. I sensed the birth would occur within minutes. A snippet of Romans 8:18-25 came to me: "The whole of creation is groaning in one great act of giving birth."

As the struggle of the goat to give birth intensified, several pilgrims quietly left the group and walked on. Others began to comment and take pictures. One woman left the road and took her camera right up to the goat and snapped pictures from several angles. I admit I blew my cool, and hissed at her, gesturing for her to leave the goat alone. She retreated, giving me a scowl, but happily reviewed her photos with her partner as they noisily left the scene.

In a matter of a few seconds, and as complete surprise to the remaining observers, the goat dropped and knelt on its front knees, perhaps in adoration, and the torn sack shot out onto the ground. Just as with the birth of my own two children, I watched, breathless, until the life force exerted itself with healthy crying and writhing. The new mama goat stood immediately and began to chew the sack open, freeing four long legs, a perfect little head and body. She licked the baby's entire body, and nudged it into standing position over and over until it could not only stand on its own but take a few wobbly steps.

About 10 minutes after the birth, the most remarkable thing of all occurred. The two shepherds on the right side of the road called the man with the truck on a cell phone. After a bit of conversation they whistled for the dogs and the entire bucolic scene erupted into action. The dogs began racing among the goats in their herding moves, following the whistling and hand movements of the men. The goats all scrambled to their feet and seemed to arrange themselves into a couple dozen formations. I didn't move from my position seated on the path.

At first all seemed chaotic but the most amazing pattern of planned action emerged, and quite rapidly. Formation after formation of goats was moved forward by the dogs towards the new mother and baby. As each goat trotted by the baby, it gave it a sniff and a nudge, then scampered up onto the road, passing within feet (sometimes mere inches) on either side of me seated there on the ground, surrounded by the moving goats and unable to get out of their way. The goats were being herded to greener pastures. I was weakened by my proximity at eye level to the passing hundreds of goats—overcome by their raw smell and dazzled by the adult animals deliberately sniffing and nudging the newborn.

The man with the truck came over and picked up the baby by the front and back feet and proceeded to carry it towards his truck. The mama goat grew frantic with high pitched bleating, and struggled greatly to keep up with the man's pace. I was very interested in the outcome, and proceeded towards the truck. The man was friendly and talked to me in Spanish the whole time he worked with the new family. He arranged sacks in the back of the truck—then covered them with quite worn and used sheep skins. He gently picked up the baby and placed it on the skins. Then, with much effort in spite of his strength, he lifted the mama goat into the truck and arranged them as a nursing pair, actually enabling the baby to nurse for the first time. He closed up the truck, talking non-stop, but alas, I knew no Spanish, and his explanations were lost on me. He drove away in a cloud of dust.

I stepped back into the now empty meadow by the side of the Camino, found a log to sit on and ate my lunch. I pondered how little I understood the events I'd just witnessed. One goat prepared to give birth. The entire flock quieted. The dogs slept. The shepherds waited and watched. Birth occurred. The herd of goats reacted with one mind. I wondered if there was an "egregore" of goats. Was it group mind? Or was it just the nature of goatness? to sniff, to nudge, to bond with the baby and then go about their business of being goats. It was as though they demonstrated "Good job. Well done, mama. Now let's get on to the next pasture." As I fed crumbs from my sandwich to some very pretty blackbirds, complete happiness overtook me. I didn't have to understand what had just occurred with the goats. It was just another day's event, another blessing on the Camino.

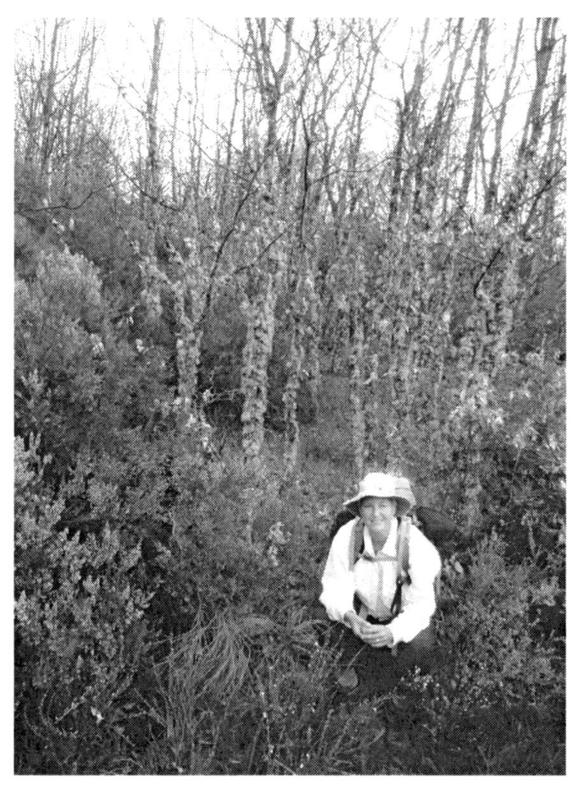

CAMINO—DAY 35

Traveling by Two Feet, Four Feet, Two Wheels, Four Wheels

Postcard #35—May 28, 2010 sent from Cacabelos, Espana

Dear Elena: It was just beauty in nature today—everywhere I looked. Pilgrims were friendly—mainly because the weather is warmer. Today was unexpected in many ways: The valley area I walked through is like a banana "warm" belt & it produced cherry trees laden with (like magic) millions of cherries—ripe and delicious. I bought a bag of sweet and juicy cherries from an old woman wearing many layers of clothes and scarves. Roses, especially climbing ones, are all in full bloom . . . & the air is perfumed. I watched for a long time storks feeding in the nest. When will I see baby storks? Hopefully, before I reach Santiago. Today I walked 19.2km or 11.5mi from Ponferrado to Cacabelos.

Journal—Day35 (Friday) May 28, 2010 written at Cacabelos

Slept so well in Ponferrado last night. The town is old & beautiful & the walk out was amazing, especially the Templars Castle—much renovated & gorgeous. Beautiful medieval bridges. Met up with Australian women pilgrims Jill & Sarah & we all thought the Templars Castle could serve as a movie set. Then walked alone through suburbs in full bloom & finally out into the countryside. Walked only to Cacabelos, a total of 19.2km or 11.5mi. Lucky to get a bed at the Albergue Municipal, a comfortable arrangement of small connected 2-bed housing units in a semi-circle around church grounds. I shared the room with a lovely woman originally from California but now living in Germany. We had real giggles as all the sounds of the adjacent units came through open rafters. Had an excellent meal alone in a randomly selected café. Was pleasantly surprised before dessert to be joined by the wonderful Australian women Jill and Sarah who convinced me to sample their dish of the restaurant specialty, octopus. Delicious.

Reflection on Day 35 written back home in San Francisco

"Do not worry about what others are doing! Each of us should turn the searchlight inward and purify his or her own heart as much as possible."

Gandhi

I am certain that my natural inclination for walking alone, and my dedication to that decision, accounted for much of my good feelings on the pilgrimage. Simply put, walking solo I was a free spirit. I didn't have to accommodate a companion pilgrim's need to push on or stop to rest or eat, to negotiate the when, where and why of each day, to talk through every decision.

While most people on the Camino appeared cordial with their walking companions, still I intuited and observed numerous tense situations arise between people and heard a few heated conversations. I was always amused at the two beautiful sisters walking together whose path I crossed several times. They could be vestiges of charm to the world and each other, but also venomous when out of sorts as walking partners.

Even in the best of times on the Camino, there was a certain degree of stress and difficulty asserting itself on the minds and bodies of pilgrims—the uncertainty of weather, food, accommodations, long distances, tight schedules, blisters, cramps, illness. For many pilgrims, it was the pure drudgery of the day after day grind of walking. These issues alone presented serious topics to occupy travelling partners.

I readily admit there was a truly selfish motivation to my walking solo. Here was a lifetime opportunity to be alone with myself and my soul for extended periods of time. It was a daily and conscious choice to encourage and free my mind to express itself without constant intellectual and conversational influence from another person. To make decisions in silence. To give my mind and soul a chance to hear the silence of the Camino and echo it back to me. A chance to become aware and carefully observe the silence. To taste, smell and feel it. And, of course, to strive to be the silence in the rhythm of the walk. Walking solo was undoubtedly the most important influence shaping my overall Camino experiences. And then there was the issue of prayer—to pray or not to pray, that was the daily question.

But there are many ways that people travel the Camino besides walking solo, or in couples or groups. I observed with enormous curiosity hordes of pilgrims whizzing along by bicycle, or by car or van, or on a bus. Or clip clopping along on a horse or a donkey. Or pulling baggage carts or a child's buggy. And the vast majority of those folks traveled with one to a dozen or more companions, talking non-stop from morning till bedtime. I suspect that that decision radically influenced and shaped their overall Camino experiences.

I only encountered about two dozen horseback pilgrims, and they were sensational looking—what a way to travel to Santiago—listening to the melodious clip-clop of the metal shoes on the horses. One horseman told me that it has become increasingly difficult to take a horse on the Camino due to lack of overnight boarding. But the most attention was given to the several pilgrims who led or rode mules or donkeys. Their animals were quaintly decorated with flowers and ribbons, hats and saddle blankets, and backpacks, as well as buckets for food and water, hung off the saddle.

Pilgrims' cars and buses traveled from city to city on freeways and secondary roads, and especially closer to Santiago, I observed vans that carried backpacks from point to point for walkers who had purchased their transportation services. Pilgrims would leave their well-identified luggage at the dormitory in the morning, and walk backpack free to the next prearranged accommodation. I asked the four beautiful South African women who used this service if they worried about their belongings, and they said "no, it is for us a reliable service, and we walk so much easier without all that weight."

I encountered dozens of bicycle pilgrims on the walking trail everyday from all over Europe and Spain, usually travelling in pairs or small groups. They tried to travel the walking paths exclusively, except when truly rough and rocky paths forced them to take to the highways. The bicyclists were sleek and handsome in their silky, skintight gear (almost all men). They appeared so powerful and muscular to me as I observed them on the road, usually bicycling very fast even on steep inclines. They were universally friendly as they approached and passed me—always raising one arm and shouting out "Buen Camino". I frequently observed them to be deep in conversation as they rode.

Over a week-long period, I encountered numerous times a couple bicycling while pulling their two year old in a kind of 3-wheeled buggy or stroller. Of course they were a sensation on the trail, stopping frequently to let their child run around. I kept reminding myself not to judge their parental decision, but I did think it must have been hard on the toddler, rather than a grand childhood adventure.

I was resting one day at a public water fountain in a village when a group of Romanian bicyclists stopped to refill their water bottles. There was a lot of teasing going on among the group, and suddenly one of them, with a camera mounted on his helmet, came over, adjusted the camera and made a short film of me. Another fellow with fair English grandly announced that they liked to stop and film all the beautiful women on the Camino. There was much laughter among us as I pretended to pat my hair and smooth on some lipstick.

Many times on trails, bicyclists approached me so silently that I only became aware of them as they passed. Once on a narrow walking trail, not knowing that a bicyclist was just behind me, I stepped to the side and was nearly hit straight on from behind—this occurrence rattled both the bicyclist and me, as his handlebar grazed my elbow, and nearly upset both of us. He stopped his bicycle and began apologizing profusely—maybe in German, maybe Italian, but it certainly was Greek to me. I admit I was shaken, but I had to laugh as I watched his face, for he seemed absolutely terrified—horrified even that he had nearly knocked over an older woman. "It's o'k. I'm o'k. You're o'k. All is o'k," I tried to assure him. But he was undone. I finally took him by both shoulders, looked him in the eyes and repeated: "It's o'k. It's o'k." I kissed him on both cheeks, then made the sign of the cross for good measure. He managed a pale smile, then got on his bike and wobbled away. I liked to think that we had both learned a good lesson in that encounter.

Bicycle pilgrims carried the same credentials as those who walked, and could therefore sleep in the dormitories, or albergues, set up to accommodate the pilgrims going to Santiago de Compostela. In the dorms I could observe the bicyclists more carefully. Often when I arrived and located a bunk bed in the late afternoon, they would be in their bunks sound asleep, napping before dinner. They had arrived at their stopping point exhausted from traveling 50-70 miles. The dorms usually provided some sort of enclosed and locked area to secure the bicycles. I also observed that a nap put the bicyclists in excellent form for more physical evening activity, calisthenics, swimming in nearby rivers, often working on their bicycles, and polishing off beer and wine with dinner. They went to bed early, and by 6:00am, bicyclists were usually awake in the dorm, dressing and out the door for the day's adventure.

On the Camino at the town of El Acebo, there is a large dramatic metal sculpture of a bicycle dedicated to a 70 year old pilgrim from Germany who died of a heart attack on that very spot in 1987. I approached the sculpture slowly, joining a half dozen bicyclists respectfully kneeling on the ground in silence in front of the memorial, their helmets off, their reverence palpable. They said a group prayer in Italian. I added out loud in English: "May he rest in peace, Amen." I was sobered. We were both on the Camino at age 70. At the very same spot.

CAMINO—DAY 36

Never Alone on the Camino

Postcard # 36—May 29, 2010 sent from Trabadelo, Espana

Elena: Can you believe I have been on the Camino walking for 36 days? Count with your mama from 1-36. It's a lot of days, and as of today, I have walked 378.8 miles. I want you to look on the front of the card and find the yellow arrows. They point to the 3 highest points a pilgrim climbs on the Camino. Tomorrow am I am going to climb to O Cebriero (from 600 meters to 1300 meters high in 17km. Your mama will explain this to you that it will be very hard work for me. I like climbing up, but coming down I must be very careful not to fall. Today was extra beautiful but I'm out of the valleys again & climbing back up into the mountains. It's very much cooler again . . . Elena, from walking so much, my feet smell kind of bad, but you are still going to have to kiss them when I get home . . . o'k? Today I walked 17.2km or 10.3mi. Love from Grandma. PS—Just kidding about kissing the feet.

Journal—Day 36 (Saturday) May 29, 2010—written at Trabadelo

Slow & easy does it. I am truly a snail now—my right foot is swollen across the top again—not bad but enough to feel it through the shoes. The big toe is just such a strange purplish color. I walked through many fine vineyards today, overcast but didn't rain. Walked through small villages crumbling from neglect but some very "high end" houses. Even though it was only 17.2km or 10.3 miles, I am very tired. I'm having extraordinary memories of my past and the women in my life. Unusual today that I stopped for Menu at 3:00pm so hungry when I still had several miles to go. Great energy afterwards. No wine with lunch. Walking by river gave a nice air to having to walk by a highway. Saw 2 black squirrels—first in Spain. Cannot get over wayside flowers—today foxglove, dogwood, holly hocks—a symphony of birds/ rather a symphony chorus of birds. Walked through a beautiful small town called Villafranca del Bierzo, famous on the Camino for its 12th Century Romanesque Church of Santiago. In medieval times, so many pilgrims became terribly ill or injured and couldn't make it all the way to Santiago. This particular church would grant pilgrims who could only make it this far the absolution they sought in Santiago de Compostela. I found the Church plain yet thrilling. A laser light show—a sword on the floor & almost silent organ music playing chords, then recorded footsteps, like on gravel. Stayed for over an hour, both meditating and resting my feet. Staying tonight in Trabadelo at Albergue Municipal. Lucky to get a lower bunk. Unwrapped my big toe & showered. Wonderful conversation with Samos, a beautiful Iranian woman, and later talked intently to a very gentle Greek man living in Germany & walking the Camino this year for the absolution of his sins. All pilgrims have stories; all are searchers whether they know it or not.

Reflection on Day 36, written back home in San Francisco

"What is this awesome mystery that is taking place within me: I can find no words to express it; my poor hand is unable to capture it in describing the praise and glory that belong to the One who is

above all praise, and who transcends every word . . . My intellect sees what has happened, but it cannot explain it. It can see, and wishes to explain, but can find no word that will suffice; for what it sees is invisible and entirely formless, simple, completely uncompounded, unbounded in its awesome greatness. What I have seen is the totality recapitulated as one, received not in essence but by participation. Just as if you lit a flame from a flame, it is the whole flame you receive."

St. Symeon the New Theologian (949-1022) . . .
a Stephen Mitchell translation

Over the six weeks I spent so far on the Camino, I developed several types of rhythmic mental patterns which seemed, as I walked, to work their way into my unconscious, somewhat like the famous Prayer of the Heart outlined in the Russian book <u>The Way of the Pilgrim</u>. One of my favorite patterns was mentally counting from 1-100 in simple ways—for example, a count with each step and tap of my poles—until I reached 100. These counting patterns, I found, started with deliberation but over the weeks became unconscious. They brought detachment from the painful foot injury, made the time go faster and the distances seem shorter, and often opened a door through which I passed into the mystery of the Camino. Despite being simply an interior mental activity, counting resulted in profound interior silence, where love materialized in all I saw, where I was not separate from, but seemed to pass into the sky, the path, the horizon, flora, fauna, buildings or people I met. I often employed variations on this counting exercise, and without exception, each time the gift of love emerged in my heart.

As I walked, I thought of the story my sister's family told me about the last days leading to her death. She too, had been on a long journey and was nearing her destination. The family observed or heard Jane counting from 1-100, over and over, and sometimes from 100 back to 1. This may not be an uncommon phenomenon of approaching death, but we had never heard of it before. Why would Jane have counted from 1-100, over and over? Maybe she was counting out her breaths, knowing that while she counted numbers, she was o'k. Maybe she sought clarity in some unresolved issue. Maybe she was growing to accept the inevitable ending, passing in and out of that door into the next life. Whatever the case, it comforted me that Jane deliberately counted out loud, for I had been assured she was not agitated, and I think and pray that in some mysterious way, she was calmed by the progression of numbers. And so, like Jane, I counted, too.

I gradually began to understand over the span of time I walked the Camino, that I had taken with me to Spain far more baggage than I carried in my backpack. The heavier of the two loads came from pride, privilege, possessions. After all, I was an intelligent, mature, capable and self sufficient woman, wasn't I? Of course, I didn't need the Camino's answers to anything. I had the answers. I was self-contained. I knew that I knew. What gradually came to me, and was very hard to acknowledge, was that I didn't know, and probably never would know, the questions or the answers unless I changed. My little voice pouted argumentatively: "Maybe a little bit of change is all that I need." I heard another voice: "Maybe radical surgery will be required." I grew weak: "Dear Lord. Why did I ever come on the Camino? It's hard enough just making this walk. I do not want to make any changes in my life at this age."

What I came to understand as I walked one day after another was that I was processing many of my life's questions. I didn't take these questions with me written down in a journal hoping for answers. I didn't even know what the questions were, but they arose from the unconscious and out of the extended periods of time I spent walking alone and in silence. I continued to walk, knowing that something was stirring in me, and seemed to be shifting my perspective.

I looked deliberately at everybody and everything—tried to mentally acknowledge and accept the good, true and the beautiful in the nanosecond that my eyes swept across it. I tried to withhold analyzing, judging or criticizing what I observed. I paused frequently just to observe with my left brain, in order to question, interpret and understand realistically all that I saw in the minute by minute Camino context. This helped me find my way, stay safe and make sound decisions. But my right brain was almost always fully operational, often in overdrive, coaxing my heart, quietly awestruck by the simplest sights, sounds, tastes and the feel of the Camino experience. I had one chance at making this pilgrimage, and while my left brain was there to direct the traffic, my right brain and heart gently guided the agenda.

I experimented with walking meditation, but my training in how to quiet my body and mind was not compatible with walking safely without falling, without missing directional Camino arrows. Traditional 20 minute practice for me was more structured, and always occurred while sitting comfortably, gradually moving into the silence, and with specific intent to be available to the Ultimate Reality—to God. So while not impossible to meditate while walking, it was difficult for me.

It was generally tricky to find the time and space for sitting meditation. But every day, I watched for opportunities to practice Centering Prayer, and indeed they presented themselves, thereby allowing me to slow down, rest the foot and recharge my spiritual batteries. It didn't matter where—I sat and meditated in unlocked churches, graveyards, on benches in plazas or parks, in bars, restaurants, on little stone bridges and only sometimes in quiet dormitories.

A favorite activity of mine while walking on the Camino, and far different from Centering Prayer, was structured self examination. I was aware from the beginning of the walk that the endless sights and sounds of the Camino would distract me from allowing my 70 years of life to surface for examination. I helped the desired process along by compartmentalizing the various stages of my life, and over several weeks, visiting and revisiting these life stages carefully as I walked. For example, one week I coaxed out deeply buried memories of the first 17 years living with my parents on a farm in southern Illinois. Other times, I scanned and dug into university experiences and my teaching career in the 1960's. And other weeks, I tackled stages that included marriage, children, sickness, living abroad, life changes brought about by career and retirement. Thomas Merton said "The monk and the nun leave the world only to listen to the deepest voices they have left behind." I am neither the monk nor nun, but it was my intent to listen deeply to the voices that have waited patiently to be heard, and this time perhaps understood."

I probed these desired memories realistically, but lovingly. Many connections were made that I'd never thought of—some startling and unwanted, some gentle and loving. Long suppressed people, concrete situations and emotions bubbled up into focus. Issues of love and indifference. Light and shadow. Fear and insecurity. Power and control.

Guilt and righteousness. My overall condition in the final analysis no better or worse than the human condition at its best and worst—with the good, the bad and the ugly thrown in. Memories emerged on the Camino because I was willing to pry myself open, not blink, and coax them to accompany me on the walk.

This exercise in actively examining life stages was not an easy one. It required utmost discipline while walking to stay on track while conducting this personal survey with my somewhat erratic memory, to not suppress the resulting dialogue with my soul, to keep level headed and centered when situations and anxieties from the past raised their heads like snakes in the grass, coiled and ready to strike.

Regardless of how I felt about any type of memory—good or bad that surfaced in this activity, I breathed deeply, welcomed it and smiled. Looked that memory in the eye. Stayed with the person or feeling until I became centered. Acknowledged it with this stance "Oh, there you are. I'd forgotten about you. Yes, I remember you well. You were part of my life."

I was amazed at how this welcoming stance neutralized good or unpleasant memories, even enhanced my state of mind. It was as though my mind and soul were reorganizing into a different self, seeing people and situations from throughout my life with new insight—accepting, loving, forgiving, then letting go—emerging into new understanding. Forgetting the old. Repatterning into new life.

One of the most important mental activities in which I engaged while walking was to examine the relationships I've had in life with women. I've personally known hundreds of fine women in my life, socially and professionally. By extension, poets, writers and women religious have also entered and enhanced my life through study, lectures and reading.

Here's an example of the kind of experience I had on the Camino teasing out memories of a woman in my life. Virtually every day of the walk I'd think of Ann, my sister. I knew she was a bit concerned about this walking pilgrimage of 500 miles in Spain where I could not speak the language, but she generally kept her concerns to herself and encouraged me wholeheartedly. She did pepper me with questions. "Do you have sensible shoes? What will you do about underwear? Oh my goodness. You mean you'll be carrying everything in a backpack? Well, this is pretty interesting. I never heard of anything like this before, but I think you'll do fine. You always land on your feet, Mary." Ann has always encouraged me in all endeavors—solid or shaky. We've always stayed best friends. On the Camino, my heart welled up with love for this fine woman whose common sense, fabulous sense of humor and influence I've felt keenly—things for which I'll forever be grateful.

As I played with these memories, I realized my sister Ann O'Hara Swofford is the family glue. After our parents died, she became the conductor of the O'Hara family reunions, finding ways to keep us in touch and pulling us together from Florida, Illinois, Missouri and California. Our family is in awe of the care she takes to keep track of children, grandchildren, and relatives on everybody's sides of the extended families. It all seems so effortless for her, for example, everybody gets a birthday card and hand-written note, every year. But it's real effort to send dozens and dozens of cards every year. Is there someone in need? Annie's "on it" with immediate response, offering resources of time, energy, love, spirit, creativity, generosity and right action. If an illness or a problem emerges, Ann tackles it by making soup and twice-baked potatoes. This woman is well over 80, but remains formidable in body and spirit, interested in everything. She models fidelity to family and the life she's been given. She's my ideal, really, and the rock of her children's lives. I've never seen a more faithful wife anywhere. For 60 years, she's shared a banana with her husband Bill every morning, and a scotch and hors d'ouvres every evening at 5:00pm. "Ah-hhhh" she says, "it's 5:00pm somewhere in the world. Life is good."

For at least 40 years, I have kept a personal list of major women influencers. This list has grown over the years, of course, and once on the list, a woman is on forever, so greatly and loyally do I revere her. The list includes family, friends and colleagues. Almost all intimate relationships. But sometimes interrupted relationships. A few of the women—only acquaintances. How I admire them. Study them. Long to be like them. On the Camino, I reproduced this list in my journal and worked with that list in another structured walking activity that covered many days. I spent considerable time walking and visiting with each of these women whose influences stirred me so deeply to gratefulness and humility, starting with my mother Irene, and ending with grand daughter, Elena.

Irene Hoy O'Hara, Jane O'Hara Carter, Ann O'Hara Swofford, Genevieve O'Hara Brueggeman, Sister Mary Girarda, Yvonne Pautler O'Hara, Lucy O'Hara, Isabel O'Hara, Stella O'Hara Kelly, Nora O'Hara, Mildred Hoy, Clara Ehresmann, Ethel Deterding, Shirley Streckfus, Sr. Mary Bernard, Jet Sullivan, Constance McLaughlin, Joan Phipps, Pam Coughlin, Jean Bottcher, Peggy Wahl Loar Voorsanger, Effie Wyman, Betty Wyman Mitchell, Donna Wyman Crossan, Jane Moody, Betty Drehr, Mikey Cloney, Barbara Shough, Maria Morgan, Gay Haas, Lee Makapagal, Eileen Silverberg, Barbara Pennington, Michele Thompson Cooney, Karin Gebistorf, Mary Lou Nelson, Velma Parness, Sun Mai Jean, Isabel Bernier, Joy Hockman Silverberg, Jackie Roberts, Amelia Wyman Varela, Janet Keyes, Leona Rubinoff, Lise Bolden-Brown, Claudia Schuster, Cathy Cahur SC, Elena Presser, Sally Cahur, Helene Becque, Marie Howard, Jane Ferguson Flout, Cynthia Brix, Sr. Lucy Kurian, Dr. Kiran Martin, Rev. Amber Sturgis, Sr. Marguerite Buchanan, Sr. Suzanne Toolan, Catherine Regan, Mirabai Starr, the Very Rev. Cynthia Bourgeault, Sr. Joan Chittester and Elena Varela.

Was I in fact walking the Camino alone? Or was I being walked? I would suggest that I was never alone. I loved the communion with memories of my life experiences, and with the women influencers. But the richest experiences occurred in quiet times during meditation when I gave myself over and was totally lost in contemplative spaciousness—unaware of my body, passage of time, hunger, thirst, exhaustion—and this gift resulting in light steps, irrepressible joy, lightness of being, God within. Yes, God within. I was a Trinitarian Daughter/Son walking with the Father and the Holy Spirit on the Camino. "In the name of the Father, and of the Daughter/Son and of the Holy Spirit." Oh, dear God. What on earth was happening to me? Was this blasphemy helping my foot to heal? Was I healing into a truer self? Or was I in fact becoming whole?

CAMINO—DAY 37

No Bed at any Price in O'Cebreiro

Postcard # 37—May 30, 2010 sent from Alto do Poio, Espana

Dear Elena: Of all the Mary & Jesus statues I've seen in churches, this is my favorite one from Eunate. They look so happy. Mary is holding ripe wheat—maybe she is tickling her baby. Jesus is waving hello and holding a book although it looks a little like a sequined purse. What does your mama think Jesus is holding? Today, Elena, was a hard day for me. I climbed a mountain O'Cebreiro only to arrive in the beautiful village & learn there absolutely was no room at any price with a bed for me. It was quite chilly & windy, and I was prepared to sleep outside on a bench, but was convinced by two other pilgrims (Australian friends Jill and Sarah) in the same situation to walk to Alto do Poio, another 8.6 km or 5.2 mi farther. I did so, walking on a little used highway, arriving here at 10:30pm. Ate soup prepared by a very kind lady & came back to my reserved hostal room, where I soaked my feet in hot sudsy water. Missing you

Journal—Day 37 (Sunday) May 30, 2010—written at Alto do Poio

Today was an extremely big walking day, due to "Completo, completo" everyplace filled—hostal, albergue, hotel in O'Cebreiro. (oh-thay-bray-air-o) The walk to O'Cebreiro was much anticipated as being among the most strenuous & steepest of the Camino, going from 600 m to 1300m. Going up was not bad but I was beat when I got to the town and no place to stay. Frustrating but I kept extremely calm. Visited the Church. Couldn't stay there although it would have been an enchanting experience to stay the night. Could have stayed in the lobby of the Albergue but hospitalera was very snippy—"absolutely not! No bed. No stay. It's privato, privato." And there appeared on the scene Jill & Sarah from Australia. They too were in need of beds. They felt the only solution was to walk on even though it was 8:30pm. After they phoned to discover that there were beds available in Alto do Poio, about 5 miles away, I set out, much to the consternation of a number of simpatico pilgrims who did have beds & were observing this quiet little drama play itself out. Long story short, I walked an additional 8.6km or 5.2mi farther in the gathering dark to Alto do Poio, arriving at 10:30pm. Terrible cramps & pain in feet & legs. Total walked today was 27.6km or 16.6mi. It was the longest walk in my 37 days on the Camino.

Reflection on Day 37, written back home in San Francisco

"The temporary appearance of happiness or distress, and their disappearance over time, are like the coming and going of winter and summer seasons. They arise from sense perception and one must learn to tolerate them."

—Bhagavad Gita, 2, 14

Day 37, the day I walked from Trabadelo to O'Cebreiro, then on to Alto do Poio, is burned into my memory like no other day on the Camino. All the usual suspects of difficult pilgrimage were there: a day long and difficult steep climb up a mountain, constant pain in my right foot, exhaustion at arrival, no accommodations at any price to be had in the bustling village, day drawing to conclusion with no solution in sight. But let me tell you, Elena, of the varying degrees of hospitality which I did experience in the course of solving my problem of where to spend the night.

There are many rooms to rent in O'Cebriero—in private houses and over bars, in small and large hotels and in one very large and well situated pilgrim albergue. I made my way to the end of the village and up onto a lovely overlook where the impressive albergue was located, but was rudely turned away by the hospitalera with a peremptory "Completo, completo." She was not interested in even answering questions. I walked back into the town, checking my guidebook and also a list of accommodations I found posted on a bulletin board, and proceeded to visit every single one. I was desperate to have a bed. It had turned quite chilly and windy, and I recall thinking: "O'k, tonight I'm willing to spring for a room in a hotel." But not a room could be ferreted out. No room at any inn at any price. By this time, it was 7:00pm. I revisited the main hotel, knowing it was fully booked, but trying my best, I asked if any late arrivals were in question, and when those rooms would be released. The ploy did not work. I was stared out of the hotel.

I stopped in at a very lively bar with Irish bagpipe music. There was a sign "Rooms to Rent" outside and I said a prayer and waited in line at the bar to inquire about availability. I made my case, but the woman behind the bar shook her head with finality and explained that it was a holiday and there were many tourists besides pilgrims up in this part of Galicia. She went on about her business and I turned to go, when two very well dressed gentlemen sitting at the bar, Britishers in their 70's, I guessed, stopped me. "But wait, madame," one dignified gentleman said, "what will you do without a room?" "Good question," I laughed, "I'm not exactly sure." The two men looked at each other thoughtfully and one said, "Well, we're here on holiday, and we have two rooms." I was a bit too eager. "Oh, you mean that you would be willing to share, and I could rent one of your rooms?" And after the men looked at each other, a little too long, I thought, one said, "Oh, we're checked in already. I mean, you could share my room." I let this sink in and thought: "Mary, this is one complication too many for today." I thanked the courtly gentlemen profusely, and left to check out availability of other rooms on the list. But there was not a single room to be found in O'Cebreiro.

I dragged into the beautiful church at the outskirts of the village. The chapel's interior was so calm, so serene, so quiet, even though faint wheezing and whining of the bagpipes from the bar down the street could be heard in the sanctuary. I sat down, slipped off my backpack. I couldn't go another step. In prayer, it came to me that I could stay very comfortably in the church that night. I approached a woman guide and asked to speak to a priest. None available, but how could she help me, she asked. I told her of my plight and she said, "absolutely not, it is forbidden by church law to sleep overnight in the pews." I shouldn't have laughed, but I did. And then I sat down again to calm myself. I looked at the statue of Mary and said: "O'k, Mary, I'm out of possibilities. Please help me find a place to sleep tonight." And very soon, three hearty male souls appeared at my side, led by the woman who had announced I could not sleep in the church overnight. "We have a solution for you," she announced gravely. These men will drive you back to Trabadelo where they know of a room for you. It is not so far for you to walk back tomorrow. They can take you right now." One man reached for my backpack—they were all enthusiastic in having solved a pilgrim's need for a bed. But while grateful for their efforts, I was aghast at driving off into the Spanish countryside with three strangers, even though I'd met them in a church. Equally as sickening was the notion of rewalking the long slog up that mountain again tomorrow. "No, no, I can't go back to Trabadelo. I must press on to Santiago. But thank you, thank you. God bless each of you. And I lifted my backpack onto a pew, slipped it onto my shoulders, and made my way back into the village.

I wended my way forlornly up the long main street, realizing what a jolly evening's celebration was brewing. The streets were full of tourists and pilgrims alike—strolling, shopping, sitting at outside cafes. Restaurants were full. Bars were overflowing with patrons and a kind of Irish folk music played everywhere. Views of the mountains and valleys peeked out from every side street. The village was perfectly charming, but the sun was going down and I had no place to stay. I headed back to the albergue. My mind played out various scenarios. Maybe there will be another hospitalera by now, and she will find a bed for me.

Or what about sleeping on one of the couches in the reception area? That seemed a perfectly logical solution. The same lady was at the desk, and I approached her about sleeping on a couch. She raised her arm and pointed to the door, and raised her voice as well: "Completo, completo—not allowed. Do you understand English?"

I sat down on a bench outside the door. I considered that if I slept on this bench I'd be outside but at least would be out of the wind. Would that be so bad? Pilgrims were coming and going from the albergue, a few I recognized from encounters on the trail. Several very kind souls became interested in my plight. A group of four determined to get permission for me to sleep on the couch in the entryway. They were soundly rebuffed by management. Another woman said: "Look, I'll sneak you in a back door and give you my mattress on the floor. I'll sleep on the bare bunk in my sleeping bag. She'll never know." Another woman said, "I have friends who have a room in town. I'll run and ask them if you can sleep on a couch there." This buzz of activity and pity for me arose from the kindness of their hearts, but it made me nervous that my predicament was turning into their mini-drama on the doorsteps of the albergue.

I looked up and there were Jill and Sarah, the Australian women I'd run into numerous times on the trail. "Worst luck, Mary. We can't find a single room in this town either so we're walking on to Alto do Poio. It's about 9 kilometers." I did the easy math in my head: about 9 km was more than 5 miles. How could these women, much younger than I, possibly walk another 5 miles at this time of day? They sat down to use Jill's cellphone, dialing a number listed in their guide. After a bit of conversation I heard "Yes, yes, we'll take it, and hold the room. We're walking from O'Cebreiro." Jill touched my arm: "Mary, they have rooms. Do you want to come too?" My mind recoiled at the idea, but a steely reserve came over me. I would walk on. My head nodded and a room was secured for me.

We needed to leave immediately. There was no time to eat dinner. It was nearly 8:30pm, but surprisingly light outside at the end of May. Several pilgrims urged us to take a taxi. One pilgrim cautioned us to walk on the highway to Alto do Poio because we would at least have auto headlights. But Jill and Sarah determined to use the Camino path which headed up into the wooded hills. This was serious business. I studied the pattern of traffic on the two-lane highway out of town. I made my choice to walk on the highway and waved goodbye to the women as they started up the Camino path.

Once on the highway, there was no turning back. The road was extremely curvy and I remembered hoping that it was 5 miles measuring the curvy road and not 5 miles from one town to the other as one might estimate looking on a map. While there were a few flat and straight stretches of road on which it was easy to walk, a good deal of the distance sloped uphill and required concentrated effort. An extraordinary burst of energy animated me as I began the walk. I knew I could do this but it was essential that I be permeated with alertness for any eventuality in the gathering dusk—from automobile or truck, from animal or human.

And remember, Elena, that the Spanish mystic John of the Cross said: "If a man wishes to be sure of the road he treads on, he must close his eyes and walk in the dark." But I didn't dare close my eyes. I walked facing traffic and when cars approached, usually at high speed, I stepped over the barrier to the side and let them pass, then immediately stepped back onto the freeway. Carefully. Very, very carefully. A friend of mine recently reminded me of a sign she'd seen on a Himalayan mountain road: "It is better to reach your destination 10 minutes late than to arrive in heaven early." And so it went mile after mile. Despite my attention to the road, I could not help but furtively glance at the gorgeous hills in the gathering dusk. Light mist gathered in the valleys below. Stars and planets became visible. A slice of moon appeared. It was almost dark. Still, to my amazement, an evening glow played from hill to hill—enough for me to see.

When I arrived in the village of Alto do Poio at 10:30pm, it was dark. At last—the safety and comfort of a hotel. I went inside and my heart sank. A dingy bar. No food. The woman at the bar demanded payment, but would not show me a room. When I asked a second time, she shrugged and said: "I don't show rooms. Take it or leave it." And she walked back to her boyfriend. A man came in and went behind the bar.

I approached him and asked to see a room. He led me upstairs without a word, down a long, forbidding hall and opened a door. As I tried to walk in, he announced "No Entry" and barred the way. In the dim overhead light, I could see a bed, and a chair, and a bathroom. "I'll take it" I said, and followed him downstairs to register. He took my money but kept no record of my stay. He had no stamp to mark my credential and just laughed at me when I showed it to him. When I asked about food, he pointed to the clock and made a sign like a key locking a door, then pointed across the way to what looked like a restaurant.

I paid him, grabbed the key to my room, and still wearing my backpack, trudged across the highway. The door to the restaurant was locked, but the lights were on and several people were inside cleaning up. It was worth a try. I knocked. They looked up and waved me away. I knocked again insistently. They let me in. All stared at me as I made motions towards the menu and shamelessly clutched my stomach. The men seemed intent on turning me away, but a very old woman mopping the floors put her mop in the bucket, approached me wiping her hands on her skirt, and led me to a table, talking all the while. The men went back to their business. She brought a chalkboard to the table and squinting at the menu, pointed to the word "lentils". This was progress. I agreed to lentils and pointed at two more items, salad and pork cutlets. She shook her head from side to side. Lifting up a dishtowel tucked into her apron belt, she vigorously erased everything on the menu except the word lentils. I smiled in agreement, and the old woman scurried into a side room where I could see her withdraw a heavy iron pot from an industrial refrigerator, dole out two large scoops of lentils into a soup bowl and stick it in the microwave.

I washed up, and walking back to the table, stumbled and nearly fainted from the evening's exertion and hunger. One of the men helped me to the chair as the old woman set the steaming bowl of lentils and two slices of bread with butter at my place. Another man rushed to bring me a glass of wine and stood thumping his chest, insisting I drink. I suppose he thought it would revive me enough to eat the lentils and leave so that they could lock up for the night. And it did revive me—both the wine and the lentils. But the day would have its toll on me. My muscles were tight. I continued to shake from the extended exertions. My foot ached terribly. My legs were cramping. I hoped I could make it across the street to my room. I ate every bite, then paid my bill, the man refusing to take money for the wine. I slipped the tired old woman a generous tip, and shouldered my backpack, just as Jill and Sarah arrived, knocking at the door. They too were admitted. They looked harried. "We took the Camino trail as far as we could, but it grew too dark in the woods. We were afraid we'd get lost, so we turned around to O'Cebreiro, and walked on the highway like you did." "Well, thank God we're all here safe", I said, and left them to negotiate the menu with the old lady, who looked resigned to more customers as she placed her mop back in the bucket and reached for her little chalkboard. Bless her hospitality and kindness to three exhausted pilgrims.

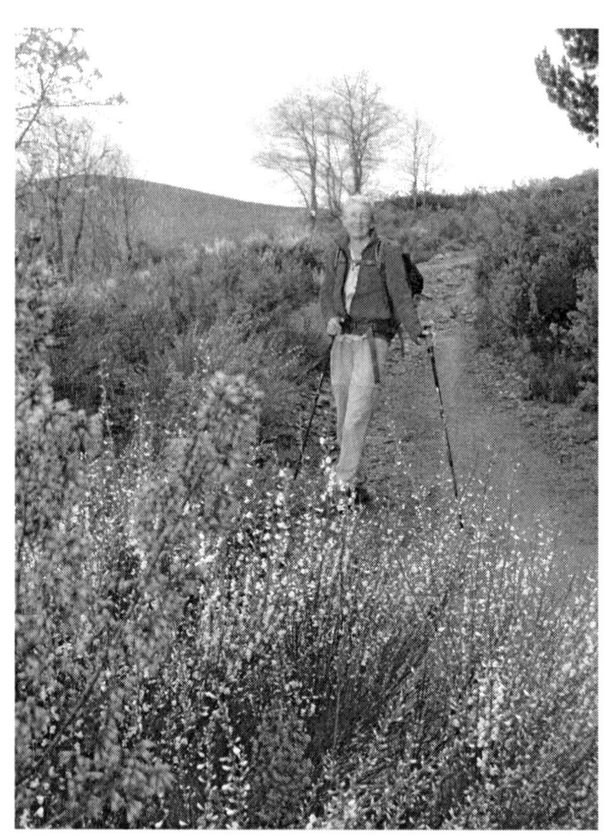

Camino—Day 38

The Snail's Pace

Postcard # 38—May 31, 2010 sent from Triacastela, Espana

Dear Elena: This am when I left Alto do Poio, it was amazing fog & clouds in the sky where I walked. I was strong in spite of cramps in my legs through the night. I am tremendously happy today. Flowers absolutely everywhere. There was a long detour I didn't exactly understand down a steep mountainside but I didn't mind. I passed a snail today & stopped to watch it cross the road. I realized that I am like a snail, carrying a pack on my back, and the snail's two antenna are like my hiking poles. They use antenna to see and feel their way & I use my poles to feel my way. I move very slowly like a snail also. That is a good Pilgrim. Love from Grandma on the Camino

Journal—Day 38 (Monday) May 31, 2010—written at Triacastela

Awakened this am feeling good despite the leg cramps resulting from too much walking yesterday. Left the crummy hostal & began the walk to Triacastela—started in amazing fog & it was very steep going down, and then grew hot, but truly beautiful views of the surrounding mountains. I really took it slow and my poles were the critical factor in being able to walk at all. Walked through villages today where animals lived side by side houses. Passed a sobering chicken-processing plant with enormous trucks lined up to back in and deliver their loads of live chickens. Now and then, a sleek, refrigerated truck would zip out of the driveway and head for the freeway. Finally into Triacastela having walked 15.7km or 9.4mi. I've cumulated to 404.8mi. Had nice emails from sisters Ann & Genny. Sent email back to family. Woman hospitalera washed/dried/folded my clothes. Walked around town, ate a pilgrim's Menu & in general passed the afternoon & evening. Spent extended time in chapel meditating. Tonight in Triacastela, many pilgrims I didn't recognize asked me about the long walk yesterday & where I stayed last night. They envisioned me passed out on the highway or sleeping under a tree in the chill night air. No doubt about it. One observes, and one is observed.

Reflection on Day 38, written back home in San Francisco

"O snail, Climb Mount Fuji . . . But slowly, slowly."
Issa

When I awakened on the morning of Day 38, a particular calm surrounded me, not only interiorly, but exteriorly as I gazed out the grimy window of my hotel at the Galician ground fog. I'd been awakened in the night with intense leg cramps, a result of the additional 5 mile walk late in the evening, but in the morning—I was captured by calmness that bordered on happiness. The foot required serious attention, but breakfast and an Ibuprophen helped me start and I was soon on my way out into the peasoup fog.

No more highway walking for me. I proceeded onto a wide path which I would follow confidently for several hours. The morning's mystery enclosed me—white billowy fog blanketed the path, the surrounding hills and woods. It shadowed the farmhouses and barns, fencerows and animals, occasionally swirled and danced towards me, thickening here, lifting there, playing mischievously. Not an early morning birdcall could be heard, but as I walked I did hear the horses and cows, the farm dogs barking and herding sheep, now and then a farmer call out to the animals, or a tractor's grinding startup echoing from an equipment shed. The air was cool and the wind carried a country kind of perfume, now from tangled honeysuckle along fencerows, and then from fresh mown hay, and all mingled intermittently with animal smells. This was Galicia at its best.

I slowed my pace to match the fog. My feet were slow, and my mind slowed to a crawl. My brain could barely process the beauty that surrounded me. My heart engaged. Why hurry, I thought, I have nothing but time, nothing but beauty to see. And right on the edge of the road, I spotted what looked like a kitchen chair. How odd to be out here. Perhaps it was waiting for a pilgrim who needed to rest. It was clean and sturdy, so I slipped off my backpack and positioned myself comfortably on the chair just off the path. I sensed the fog lifting after a bit and I began a period of Centering Prayer. After perhaps 20 or so minutes, I opened my eyes and was surprised to see that the fog had retreated and I could distinctly see the surrounding countryside.

As my eyes adjusted, I caught a glimpse of what first looked like a large walnut on the path. Soon the walnut began to move, taking on the distinct nautilus shape of a large shelled snail, slowly winding its way across the path, leaving a slimy and silvery trail behind it. How stately and deliberately its progress across the track of the road towards me. This required a good look.

I positioned my chair to observe this creature from a closer vantage point. It was making progress faster than I would have suspected—gliding along with wavelike contractions on what appeared to be a layer of mucous. I got a bit closer in order to examine its set of surprisingly long antennae. Eyes at the end, I thought. I wondered if my snail was watching me watch its every move. It seemed a complicated creature with organs all contained within its shell, no distinct feet, googley eyes and its voracious appetite. I knew it had another pair of smaller antennae that it used for smelling and searching for food and water, but I couldn't see them. What puzzled me about this snail was its being out in the daytime. "I thought you guys only came out at night in order to munch your way through my geraniums," I said out loud. I didn't know if snails had ears. I would have to Google that.

With great effort, the snail hoisted its bulky shell onto the weedy area between the two tracks of the path and proceeded to feed on a sturdy leafed plant which swayed under its weight. A snack, I thought, did seem appropriate at this time of day. I dug around in my backpack and unearthed a bag of dried apricots and munched a handful while I watched. Soon the snail was on the move again. It maneuvered through the weeds growing in the grassy center of the path and started across the track, this time heading towards me. How vulnerable my snail looked on the path despite its hard shell. I couldn't resist picking up a stick and giving the snail a very gentle poke. In a flash the antennae disappeared and the snail seemed to lock itself up tight in the shell. But spirit was strong in my little friend, and I was patient. It had not been deterred. Soon, the antennae raised and the wavy contractions commenced that undulated the snail only two feet past me and it disappeared into a cluster of weeds. I felt sheer relief to witness the snail off the path.

It was time for me to go. I picked up my backpack and put it on the chair by the side of the road. As I slid it onto my shoulders and closed the straps across my waist and chest, I thought of how like a snail a pilgrim is carrying her possessions on her back. I picked up my walking poles and compared them to the snail's antennae—each critical guides to our safety and progress. Who could guess the distance my little snail would ultimately travel from its patch of weeds to its destination, if it even had one? But I, the human pilgrim, knew I was only 4/5 of the way to my destination. I still had 100 miles to go carrying pack and poles before I reached Santiago.

MONASTERIO DE SAMOS

Camino—Day 39

The Less Travelled Road to Samos—and to God

Postcard # 39—June 1, 2010 sent from Samos, Espana

Dear Elena: Today instead of staying on the Camino "proper" I detoured on beautiful paths through woods, meadows & through tiny villages with cow-dung everywhere on the streets. The goal was the Monasterio de Samos founded in the 7th Century. I took a tour, ate lunch, napped in the Albergue Monasterio de Samos where I have a lower bunk & tonight attended Vespers sung in Gregorian chant by the Benedictine monks. Attended Mass. It was a special day for me. I must admit I feel tired (but very content) & today I realized I fly home in 2 weeks. On June 16, Elena, when you wake up, you can come across the street, creep up the stairs & wake me up before you go to school, for I will be home that morning. Good idea? I can't wait to see you & I think you will be a little bigger than when I left. And maybe Grandma will be a little smaller. Grandma's on the Camino.

Journal—Day 39 (Tuesday) June 1, 2010—written at Samos

Today I walked 11.1km or 6.6mi (a sort of a detour) because Samos was of great interest to me as one of the oldest Benedictine monasteries in Europe. Upon arrival, I lined up my backpack at the locked front door of the Albergue Monasterio & went off to the Bookstore to sign up for a tour. It was in Spanish but I got a lot out of it & was especially interested in the renovation features of highlighted murals & current paintings created after the major fire in early 1950's caused by an explosion in the distillery. Lucky to meet a man who translated the tour for me. Had a great menu, checked into the Monastery Albergue (bottom bunk). Studied the amazing & engaging medieval-like murals on the walls of pilgrims, horses, angels and sea serpents. Had a good sleep, then a walk around town. A 1000 year old Cypress tree by a tiny stone Pilgrim Church with Mozarabic features in the door & the great height of the ceiling. Sat in a park talking to a man about Centering Prayer. Attended Vespers with monks singing. Maybe ten—all old except one. Finished the evening writing cards until Dorm closing time at 10:30pm. Feeling happy, centered, so grateful to be on the Camino.

Reflection on Day 39, written back home in San Francisco

"Two roads diverged in a yellow woods
And sorry I could not travel both
And be one traveler, long I stood
And looked down one as far as I could
To where it bent in the undergrowth.

I shall be telling this with a sigh
Somewhere ages and ages hence:
Two roads diverged in a wood, and I
I took the one less travelled by
And that has made all the difference."

—Robert Frost from The Road Not Taken

I've known the poem I've just quoted by Robert Frost since I was a little girl because my sister Jane recited it to me many times. The poem stayed with me through the years, aided by high school, university and graduate studies in American literature, and as I matured, I began to realize the poem's finer nuances about life's decisions. Let me tell you, Elena, how I came to a fork in the Camino on Day 39, and chose the less travelled path to Samos.

On the morning when I left Triacastela, pilgrims at breakfast in the bar across the street buzzed about whether to press on to Santiago by the shorter path, or to take the longer alternate route to the Monasterio de Samos. I was familiar with references to this monastery for many years so wanted to visit even though it was several miles out of the way from the direct path to Santiago. My mind was made up. At the point where the paths diverged, I would choose the route to Samos.

The morning was beautiful. Sunshine and a warm breeze lifted the spirits of the land. The rural ambiance of Galicia was charming as I walked mile after mile along a river separating bucolic fields of green grain and pasturage. Colonies of little lizards chased each other on the path. Tiny brown birds I couldn't name flittered and twittered and alighted in great numbers in the clumps of bushes by the river. Jet-black ravens soared in the air and several black birds with red beaks squawked endlessly as I rested a bit on a concrete bridge. Three stately cormorants poised and preened in Galician wetlands along a pond area adjacent to the river.

I walked into and through wooded areas, across meadows, into and out of tiny Galician villages—think simple but sturdy old, old stone barns and occupied houses. Think abandoned and crumbling buildings. Elderly men dressed in black trousers, white shirts and suspenders slowly and arthritically tended to chores. Old women wearing shapeless black dresses, shawls pulled around their shoulders, sat on porches, engaged in some kind of handiwork or another. Sturdy middle aged farmers and housewives moved with mechanical resignation through chores in the barnyards—cows and cow dung everywhere on the roads and streets, chickens scratching and geese honking and grazing, beautiful old grain storage bins on stilts to keep out rats, and now and then, ancient farm equipment that should have been displayed in museums could be seen hanging from rafters in open sided barns.

The day's leisurely walk to Samos was only 6.6 miles. Despite the sunny weather, puddles created muddy conditions. I made each step slowly and deliberately, observing the countryside carefully, and anticipating extended prayer time that afternoon in the monastery's church. Rounding an enormous bend in the road on the crest of a low hill, I could make out the tiny village of Samos down below, tucked and snugged close to its heartbeat, the 6th Century Benedictine Monasterio de Samos. The overall scene emanated peacefulness. Closer up, I could see beautifully tended gardens and crops planted right up to the monastery walls, animals grazing nearby. Traffic was sparse and nearly invisible. I might have been a pilgrim approaching Samos anytime over the past 1500 years.

The Samos complex had design elements typical of large European monasteries—four long multi-storied grey stone buildings were connected to form a cloistered square around a large central garden area. Grandly arched interior walkways allowed access to the inner courtyards, with beautifully cultivated flowers and blooming bushes, impressive fountains bubbling—perhaps those fountains had been bubbling for centuries. Four smaller buildings formed a second square built and angled directly into one of the walls of the large building

Leaving my backpack in the monastery albergue, I rushed off to take a tour of the massive complex. No tour was available in English, and the day's guide spoke only Spanish. A dozen of us proceeded into the monastery. Furnishings were sparse, but well-crafted. Walls were adorned with very old secular paintings and religious icons, and also with many mid 20th Century murals. Libraries and enormous meeting rooms were numerous and it seemed to me, largely unused.

The massive church built into the complex was truly beautiful. The tour group was allowed access to the sanctuary to see its ornateness up close and also examine the side altars. I stopped to study one of the horrifying statues depicting St. James on horseback brandishing a sword with which he had just sliced off an infidel's head and sent it rolling, as though it were merely a chicken's head. The bloodied plaster head had landed close to the horse's hooves—for emphasis, I thought. So much for the Christian messages from the Sermon on the Mount.

The tour guide kept a tight schedule and ushered us from the church, turning the key in the lock. She emphasized by pointing to the sign on the door that the church was only unlocked for tours and evening Vespers. I would not be spending extra time in the church.

As the tour was dispersing, a middle-aged pilgrim approached me and asked the time. Neither of us carried a watch and we chatted about that dynamic. I had observed this man during the tour taking voluminous notes as the guide spoke. I remarked to the man that I didn't understand very much from the tour, not speaking Spanish. He answered with intensity, "Please allow me to translate my notes for you. It gives me good exercise in English." We exchanged names and where we lived and Robert from Switzerland was "off and running," fluently giving me the particulars of the monastery tour as he had written them down. He was researching a scholarly article on European monasteries along the various Camino paths and this was one of his major stops.

We strolled in the monastery gardens, and the history of Samos came alive with Robert's astounding information and insights. He described the historical development of Christian religious communities in Spain, their founders, how politically aligned to royalty they tended to be and their allegiance to the papacy in Rome. Robert talked of how monasteries were designed, built, sustained, protected and their vulnerability in wartime. And he talked of their interwoven history with the Camino. He was an engaging historian, and I an eager listener.

"And you, Mary, you are alone on the Camino?" We began casual pilgrim chit-chat as we made our way outside and walked around the exterior of the monastery. I wanted to see the gardens and tilled fields. As we strolled, the conversation quickly turned to our personal religious affiliations—both of us Catholic, neither actively practicing. Robert said: "But I go to church at Christmas and Easter with my family. That counts, doesn't it?" We laughed. "The truth is, Mary, I lived as a monk for 3 years. The monastery pulled me in, but the magnet of the world had a stronger pull and here I am, no longer a monk, no longer an active Catholic, and teaching World Religions in a University." I perked up. "World Religions, is it? What would I learn if I were to take your class?" And again, Robert grew animated, as though he were in front of students, or an audience of 1000, and spoke eloquently about his survey course which emphasized Christianity, Judaism, Buddhism, Hinduism, Islam. "Is this a required course for graduation?" I asked? "No, not required. But it is filled every semester by the seekers. They register for my class because the world has grown so small and the misunderstandings so large about religious beliefs of our international neighbors . . . they come for specific knowledge and insight into the wide variety of beliefs and practices in world faiths.

"Robert, I am curious about what you say, and encouraged, actually, that such a class is taught in a secular university. What is the main message you want all your students to grasp about the world religions?" Now Robert was really enthusiastic. He told me about the syllabus for his class that lays out the basic history, structure, dogmas and traditions of each religion. He invites a panel of speakers representing the world religions to discuss The Messengers and the Messages. Students plot the religions geographically and in overlapping timeframes. They tackle the distinct doctrinal differences, similarities and nuances that can be coaxed from the texts.

These points were only the tip of the iceberg, Robert explained. He wanted students to understand that all religions are intrinsically good, but that it's some practitioners in virtually all religions whose actions are extremist and exclusionary and cause the problems. Fundamentalists. Extremists. Students say in the end of class evaluations: "I was raised in a vacuum. Why doesn't my religion teach about other religions? I never heard this when I was growing up." "Why are people belonging to one religious tradition so negative and fearful about others' spiritual beliefs?" "It seems so backward that one religion would claim superiority over all others, including exclusionary policies based on gender and sexual preferences."

"Robert, I can tell you have an extraordinary love of your subject, but you haven't told me what your core message is you want your students to grasp." Robert was thoughtful. "I want students to know and to reinforce for them that in each major world religion there are ancient teachings that humans are not separate from other humans, nor the rest of creation, nor are they separate from God. We've lost sight of that principle. The problem occurs when people see themselves as separate beings. Then they build up insular or dualistic ideas of superiority to the other. Exclusion of the other. They lose sight of the infinite flow of creation with all human, animate and inanimate creatures. Think of the implications of this, Mary, if all religions taught unity and equality of all so that their followers could at least understand and respect the physical as well as the spiritual interconnectedness among all beings."

Robert caught his breath. "Every religion has some form of the Golden Rule. This is a commonly held religious teaching, but where do we see this in action? In churches? schools? corporations? governments? What if, for example, world religions modeled those principles in all religious decisions, acting out of understanding the other as oneself. No more dualistic thinking: "I" separate from "you", or "we" separate from "they", winner vs. loser. It's astounding to see my students awaken to the implications of these ideas. I encourage them to debate this in class, how true tolerance and compassion among religions might act as the world's moral compass, might influence how people and families treat each other, how we parent our children, how corporations conduct business at home and internationally, how earth's precious resources and environment might be protected. Just think how leaders and industrial powers might cooperate to sustain and protect the world's resources. Think how different it would be for underpaid and exploited workers in 3rd world countries if international business owners were not so focused on the profit margin. Think how this might deter government's unleashing military power when conflict arises." Robert was hyper-ventilating. He caught his breath, then continued.

"I will never forget one woman student who said in class: 'I understand this as we speak about it today, but I don't see many examples of religions, corporations, even individuals promoting this as the moral compass by which to operate. Let's be clear. I'll forget about this by tomorrow and go about important concerns of graduation, getting a job, making money. I won't survive professionally or personally if I don't watch others 'dually' through competitive eyes. I must live as though I'm number one.' "Oh it was explosive, Mary, the discussions that followed her remarks, how my class was divided in support or rejection of her argument. Students were deeply energized and deeply divided about how the practice of non-dual, Golden Rule thinking and action could change the world."

We stopped to watch a mother cat carry her kittens from under some bushes into a nearby equipment shed. One by one, she gripped a kitten by the neck, transported it gently across the garden area and deposited it in the dark and hopefully safe recesses of the shed. Back and forth, back and forth, until her kittens were safe.

Robert was not finished. "It was the best class I ever taught. All any professor can do in a class like mine is present the practices and beliefs of the world's great religions and whether or not over the centuries they have held true to the original messengers and messages. My hope is, of course, that students will be attracted to non-dual thinking and action that can become a habit in their personal and professional lives. Understand this principle of non-duality, I tell my students. It must go from the mind as you understand this intellectually into heart knowledge from which your actions are influenced. Be knowledgable. Follow your conscience." And Robert sat down on a low rock wall, deep in thought.

My own head was swimming. "Robert, I have observed in every world religion, in my limited way, some leaders who have distorted and weakened, sometimes lost altogether the truth and depth of their faith's deepest messages, given way to power and greed in order to exercise control over people. For example, our own Catholic Church, which I still love deeply, fails in many ways to return to the basics taught to us by our messenger Jesus. Too much hierarchical gender bias and control has emerged over women religious. Too much exclusion of people of different persuasions—for example, non Catholics and divorced people at the communion table. Homosexual practice as a mortal sin. Iron-fisted control over theologians. No marriage for priests. No marriage for same sex couples. No ordination for women." I sat down next to Robert. I was exhausted from the walk, and probably from the talk as well.

We shook hands and said good-bye, and after a lunch and rest, I walked around Samos. The village is quite small. I visited a tiny pilgrim chapel, then sat on a bench in the next door park, soaking up the late afternoon sun, actually sinking into a period of Centering Prayer. When I opened my eyes after a half hour or so, there was Robert, resting on the bench next to me. We smiled but didn't speak, sitting contentedly watching pilgrims come and go from the monastery albergue. It was always interesting for me to watch pilgrims arrive at a dormitory in the late afternoon, suited up in their walking clothes and boots, leaning forward slightly from heavy backpacks on their shoulders, looking dusty and droopy from the day's walk. Then after a bit of rest and a clean-up, pilgrims walked out in sandals with renewed energy to see the town, or do a bit of grocery shopping, or stop in a café for a drink before dinner. Everybody had an evening routine on the Camino.

Robert turned to me. "Mary, you were meditating just now. What is your practice?" "I have a Christian meditation practice called Centering Prayer. Have you heard of it? "Oh yes, I know a bit about it from articles on Cistercian monks in the United States. But tell me what you do and what is required?" I wanted nothing more than to have a quiet evening before going to Vespers in the church. But I figured I could just tell Robert the particulars and he would be satisfied.

"Centering Prayer sounds simple when I describe it. I want to clarify that while it is called meditation, it's nothing like Eastern traditions of meditation, nor are any elements borrowed from the East. Centering Prayer is a contemporary distillation of monastic practices dating back to 4th Century Desert Mothers and Fathers. Those women and men withdrew from active life to seek solitude in the desert to deepen their prayer lives. But Robert, it goes farther back than that. Jesus sought solitude and silence frequently in order to commune with God the Father. Jesus prayed in the desert, and in his active life, often withdrew from others to pray.

Remember the Biblical recounting in Mathew 6:6—where he reminds us how Jesus tells people to pray: 'When you want to pray, go into your secret room and close the door. Pray to your Father in secret. And your Father who sees in secret, will reward you.' Of course, we both know that Jesus spoke in metaphor. People didn't have big houses and secret rooms. Instead, he suggested they seek a quiet place, so that they could quiet their minds, emotions and hearts and rest in God.

So to start with, Centering Prayer is not a prayer with words that I could teach a person to say out loud. It's a prayer of intent to be open and available to God within. It takes place in the mind and heart without words. Some call it prayer in secret. So it's very different than prayers we learned in childhood—like prayers with words to a God outside of us or in heaven, or prayers of praise, or petition, thanksgiving or the Rosary.

Centering Prayer is prayer in silence, as silent as you can make your mind. Of course, the mind is programmed to be unpredictable in its commentaries that arise from nowhere. The mind can't be stopped, but when practicing Centering Prayer, there is a method which slows down the thought process, helps the practitioner gently detach from the thoughts and let them go, whether they are ordinary or filled with emotion or drama. This method helps the practitioner return to the original intent to be available to God within. So, that's what Centering Prayer is: quieting the mind, using a method to dissolve thoughts and let them go, and maintaining the gentle intent to be open to God's presence and love within one's heart for a specific period of time." Robert was a sincere seeker, bursting with questions during this preliminary information. I continued.

"Here are the guidelines, Robert, which sound so simple in theory, but require practice and discipline to follow. The first thing you do in Centering Prayer is choose a special and very simple word to use as part of the method. A word that you like, for example, "Abba" or "Peace." This word we personally choose is called the Sacred Word. Think of it as a symbol. The Sacred Word you choose symbolizes your intent to consent to God's presence and action during the prayer.

The second step is to start the prayer in silence. Sit comfortably, settle briefly, close your eyes and silently introduce the Sacred Word just once in your mind and heart. These two steps work together—sitting comfortably allows you to give 20 minutes to the practice, and introducing the Sacred Word symbolizes and anchors your intent to consent to God's presence and action within. Of course, Robert, this all rests on the practitioner's grounded belief that God permeates every bit of all creation, and especially permeates our own human being." More questions from Robert about the mystery of Divine Indwelling.

I continued. "The third part of the method involves dealing with the inevitable thoughts that come and go and are part of the human condition. When the practitioner becomes engaged with thoughts, memories or rising emotions, or hears distracting sounds or feels physical discomfort, then she returns ever so gently to the Sacred Word. Saying the Sacred Word gently symbolizes one's intent to return to the Silence. This is the part that one often finds difficult, because thoughts are unpredictable and attractive and so tied to the ego and emotions. Still, as attractive or disruptive as the thoughts may be, this is the integral step: when engaged with thoughts, return to the Sacred Word. This reactivates and anchors one's intent to be totally available to God. And this action just lets the pesky thought go. There will be more thoughts. You'll have lots of practice in returning to the Sacred Word.

And the last part of the prayer, or the closure, is the simplest of all: remain seated in silence for a couple minutes to reorient you to your surroundings and transition you to your daily activities." Of course these four steps in Centering Prayer were interrupted by probing questions from Robert. But I insisted going off to the monks' evening prayer or Vespers. "Why don't you come along and try the prayer with me in church when Vespers are over?" Robert gathered his notebooks and we joined the stream of our fellow pilgrims attending evening prayer. I was so grateful to be on the road less traveled.

About 100 pilgrims gathered for Vespers, and the monks filed into the church and took their places, settling into choir stalls situated between the pilgrims and the front altar. It did not look as though many local residents were in attendance. Lights were low. Fewer than a dozen monks remain at Samos—and they began their evening chants. Their voices were softened by age and diminished by the sheer size of the vaulted ceilings and tiny side chapels. I listened to the rise and fall of their voices as their ages-old prayers were sung on one side of the aisle and echoed from the other side. My heart joined the cadence of the prayers—their words from a language I couldn't name.

This very evening scene at Samos had been repeating itself for centuries, whether pilgrims filled the pews or not. The chant's repetitions seemed the essence to me of the monastic life. Prayer and chant and work. Ora et Labora. Never ending. These men, like their guests, were pilgrims journeying to a final destination. But as monks they were at their destination—confined but very willing prisoners in the Samos Monastery—locked up with God yet freer than any pilgrim could fathom the concept of freedom. They worked and prayed and obeyed their earthly Abbot at Samos, would be buried here at Samos, their bodies no longer of consequence, and their souls subsumed into God's eternal love. Would that we pilgrims gathered at evening prayer with the monks had such clarity about our places in life or death.

Vespers drew to a close. Some pilgrims lingered in silent prayer, or milled about watching the candles being extinguished, checking out the headless infidel at the foot of St. James' horse, or quietly whispering with friends about details of the monastic architecture. Elderly monks shuffled towards off limits corridors and probably straight to bed. A few others tended to chores around the altar and the choir stalls, or began their gentle task of hospitably clearing the church of pilgrims.

Robert was at my side as we reached the massive doors of the church. "Mary, I have a question for you. When we talked earlier today, you called Centering Prayer 'meditation', didn't you? I'm curious about this. On what things do you meditate? We were on the monastery steps now, and a decidedly cooler outside air had descended on Samos, its freshness a distinct relief from the smell of incense and musty interiors. "Actually, Robert, I don't meditate on any particular thing, certainly not on the words of a prayer or an important event in Christ's life, or on something I'd like to have happen. I use the word meditation because that's a commonly used word for entering into and maintaining a deep silence. The whole purpose of Centering Prayer is to set aside a period of time each day to be silent, fully receptive and fully available to God within and not to engage during that set time with my own worries or personal agenda. Of course, thoughts arise over and over in every prayer period I have, but my only job is to say my Sacred Word which symbolizes my intent to be available to God." I find that saying the Word releases thoughts, lets them go."

Robert was curious. "Mary, this concept is so different from other Christian prayers. It must be very hard to teach this method of prayer. How did you learn about it?" "About 20 years ago I went to a workshop, learned the method and was deeply attracted to it. Ever since, I've been meeting weekly with a Centering Prayer group at a local Catholic parish in San Francisco. For me, this prayer required study and daily practice until it embedded or lodged in my heart. There are dozens of books written about Centering Prayer that will explain this to you clearly, but the best ones to teach the method are by Father *Thomas* Keating called Open Mind, Open Heart, and the other by Episcopal priest, Cynthia Bourgeault called Centering Prayer and Inner Awakening. These books are easily available through an organization that supports Centering Prayer, called Contemplative Outreach. Easy to google.

"So, Mary, you meditate with a group, have a daily practice and read books. Is that all you do?" "Oh no. This is a driving force in my life. Besides meeting weekly with a group. I teach Centering Prayer. I write about it. Watch speakers on YouTube. Attend 2-3 Centering Prayer retreats each year. It is an endlessly compelling part of my life." Robert looked me straight in the eye. "How could this be, Mary? You are not an actively practicing Catholic, and yet you are devoted to this Christian meditative practice. Why?" "Because, Robert, Centering Prayer has fundamentally changed my life. But not just my life. Practitioners point to many kinds of beneficial changes they perceive in themselves through this practice. For example, some speak of living more in the moment, rather than interiorly rehashing the past or planning the future. They often speak of becoming more tolerant and accepting of situations and people whose views are not their own. In other words, they believe they become more loving, attentive and gentle in relationships. More forgiving, more giving, more grounded, more spiritual. They speak of losing life-long fixed attitudes and fears, resentments, sarcasm, letting go of rigid behaviors and responses.

Of course, all these benefits are good. But here's the best one. Thomas Keating suggests in Open Mind Open Heart, that when we experience difficult and painful memories and emotions accessed from the subconscious, it's like an "archeological dig." We are accessing thoughts from throughout the whole past range of our lives—not only from the hidden ground of our wounded experiences but also from the ground of our successes and happiest periods. Consistent letting go of all these thoughts and feelings and returning gently and lovingly to your intent to be available to God—weakens the drama or pain of the thoughts, increases trust in God's love and forgiveness, dismantles the brittle and false self, and allows a healed true self to emerge . . . Keating calls this long process "Divine Therapy".

There was nothing else to say. We two pilgrims looked at each other a long time. Robert took my hand and we said Good Night. I never saw him again.

CAMINO—DAY 40

Baby Storks in Nests

Postcard # 40—June 2, 2010 sent from Sarria, Espana

Elena: Today was beautiful but a long walk without stops for coffee—it was from Samos to Sarria—a distance of 16.3km or 9.8mi. The paths are truly in rural Spain, (the area is called Galicia) covered with sheep & cow dung—villages nearly deserted. I like to see really old men & women. They just look at me & point the way as they have for generations of pilgrims. Today I saw a snake but it was squished on the road. I looked at it for a long time & marveled at its colors & patterns. One thing I liked about today's paths was walking by running water, rivers, streams & creeks. But what was best—baby storks in nests. Grandma's on the Camino & sends kisses to go around for the family. How many would that be?

Journal—Day 40 (Wednesday) June 2, 2010—written at Sarria

What a walk from the Monastery Samos to Sarria—16.3km or 9.8miles. How could it be 40 days since Larry kissed me goodbye, I turned around & headed through the Porte d'Espagne & up into the Pyranees? Anyway, bloody hot today. Was startled to see first baby storks in nests. Mostly just fuzzy heads bobbing—so the question is—how long have the eggs been hatched? Maybe it takes time for the babies to be seen at all. I wasn't the only one interested. Many old people were watching the nest activity. Nests seem more precarious than ever now that the babies plus parents are moving around. Curious about safety of babies, predators, ample food delicacies. Despite excitement over hatched storks, I was very tired on walk today. Foot and big toe absolutely not healing.

Reflection on Day 40, written back in San Francisco

"Take time to inspect the sky and the grass, to watch the creatures that are our neighbors on earth and to reflect that we come this way only briefly and that what each of us does to the ecosystem will endure long after our footprints disappear."

William Woo, past Editor, St. Louis Post Dispatch

It had been about four weeks since I'd first seen nesting stork mates. The nests and majestic birds had given me great pleasure in the almost daily sightings, but I'd nearly forgotten about their business at hand—hatching the eggs. And then, on Day 40, I saw two parents balancing precariously on the edges of a giant nest, and movement of two tiny bald heads. My heart quickened. Had the babies hatched as expected, or did another stork deliver them wrapped securely and carried in a blanket? It was difficult not to be silly about this spectacular event. Was that a tiny, tiny squawking I heard? How does that nest hold together with the parents rocking back and forth, I wondered. How old are these two chicks? Did all the eggs hatch? What indeed is going on deep within that haystack of a nest? All these were questions which would remain unanswered for me during the walk

In the remaining week on the Camino, I would see only a few more nests with baby storks before reaching Santiago. With each sighting, I stopped and watched the parental behavior, and thought that the birds seemed totally concentrated on the interior of the nest, lifting and landing, leaning in with bobbing head movements. I could only imagine the pressure on the male provider to hunt for food for the chicks. Now and then, I saw old people sitting out on benches watching the activity in the nests and wondered if they found the yearly stork cycle of migration to northern Spain and return to Africa, nest rebuilding, egg laying and hatching, as mysterious and sacred as a pilgrim might. People watching the birds seemed so happy, constantly smiling and pointing at the nests. Each time I met an old person watching a nest, I longed to talk to them about the birds, but found no one with English to tell me how long before the baby birds could fly, or whether they have predators that could rob the nests. Did the babies ever fall to the ground? Were they ever abandoned? How long before they could fly safely? and how long before the migration period back to Spain?

I knew how lucky I was to stop and observe the storks and nests while walking the Camino. Nature was taking its course here in northern Spain, and I was part of that mystery. It took a long time for a baby stork to develop inside an egg and have the strength to peck through the shell and emerge. And indeed, it had taken a long time on the Camino for me to develop into a pilgrim and emerge from my shell of back-home security. What startling changes the embryo underwent as it morphed into a stork. It would only remain to be seen how the gestation of a solo pilgrimage would encourage my growth and development back home in San Francisco.

CAMINO—DAY 41

A Simple Mattress on the Floor

Postcard # 41—June 3, 2010 sent from Mirallos, Espana

Dear Elena: I was so happy to find this card today because I walked on several of these amazing paths—kind of like our raised stone path in your backyard. I was very, very careful to not fall into the water. Today I walked for some distance with men on horseback also going to Santiago. The horses were wearing horseshoes. (Your mama will explain this to you.) It was extremely hot as I walked so I stopped about every 2 miles to rest a bit & am sleeping tonight in an old barn-like building on a mattress on the floor. I love it. A cool breeze through the windows. Mirallos is only 2 houses, a church & a restaurant—rural Espana. I walked 14.6km or 8.8mi. I'm about 65 miles from Santiago. Have you & Uncle Nathan taken Betty & Ryans lemons or something good to eat lately? Grandma's on the Camino.

Journal—Day 41 (Thursday) June 3, 2010—written at Mirallos

What a wonderful sleep last night. I still have trouble with my big toe, therefore, had to stop in Sarria & purchase more foot medicine & wrappings—fixed it up at an outdoor café & then was able to walk from Sarria to Mirallos 14.6km or 8.8mi. It was over 30 degrees C (or 86 degrees F) today—extremely hot walking so rested every 2-3 miles. Wonderful trails, a new kind today with large rocks used as stepping stones. Deeply shaded trails made walking mostly tolerable. Fields walled in by stone fences/walls. Paths sometimes packed earth, or rough with stones/rocks. Sometimes paved, or rocked or black-topped—always different. Walked for a ½ hour with horses/horsemen on their way to Santiago. One fell. Saw a woman pilgrim with a 2 yr old in a carriage behind her bicycle. I can't even imagine that it's anything but misery for the baby. Staying now in a barn-building, mattress on the floor, and a very good menu in the adjacent restaurant.

Reflection on Day 41, written back home in San Francisco

"Oh God, my God. How utterly your presence fills all the earth! The stars sing your glory back and forth across the night sky. When I look up at the vast heavens, at the stars you fashioned with your fingers and set spinning through endless space and time, I stand in wonder of you."

Psalm 8: 1, 3

The memory evoked back home in San Francisco of Day 41 is clear and strong. Throughout the 9 mile walk from Sarria to Mirallos, I knew I had well under 70 miles remaining to walk before reaching Santiago. A growing feeling of happiness and confidence permeated my attitude, despite my foot injury. My feet were not healing. I was still plagued with blisters and the big toe on the right foot continued to be dark and stormy blue. The right foot was swollen and tender every morning and painful by every afternoon. I tried numerous times to remove the wobbly toenail, but I was not willing to wrench it from the nailbed and risk an open infection. Still, barring something totally unforeseen, I would make it to Santiago.

The day's walk was through beautiful countryside—still rural Galicia—but there were now far more people on the trail. Walking with a dozen horsemen this morning out of Sarria, I watched in fascination as they rode down a paved path out of the city. They and their four-footed transportation were smartly suited up for the pilgrimage to Santiago—the men dressed in colorful shirts and denim trousers, leather belts and boots, and of course, wide-brimmed hats. The horses had been groomed to perfection, hair and tails combed, here and there bright ribbons and on some of the animals, discreet bells jingled. Saddles and saddle bags were beautifully tooled Spanish leather. The men were quite aware of what dashing figures they presented, as all the pilgrims who passed by were excited to see them and took many pictures.

I kept up with their pace for awhile because I loved the hollow clip-clop of the horses' shoes on the concrete pavement. When we reached a precipitously steep part of the roadway, the horses began to struggle and slip, and the riders had great difficulty controlling the animals. Most of the riders dismounted and led their horses to safety. One struggling rider stayed mounted, and in a moment, I was horrified to see his horse slip to its front knees and the rider pitched off to the side. What a lot of commotion occurred at that point. Neither horse nor horseman was injured, and I was not eager to stay close to the riders and the skittish horses, so headed off alone, freed from my temporary distraction.

The day became very hot. How grateful I was for the wide brimmed hat I wore everyday. The drape hanging down the back, while not very attractive, had shielded me throughout the rains and cold, and now protected my neck from the sun. I had not walked a single day on the Camino without long sleeves, and wore them even in hot weather to protect my arms from sunburn. I had not exercised care to apply sunscreen to the backs of my hands, and they were deeply tanned from the repeated exposure to sun. Day 41's temperature soared to nearly 90 degrees Farenheit, and regardless of how much water I drank, I felt parched. The heat took its toll, and I planned to have an early stop in the village of Ferrerios. But no luck. Pilgrims were all wearing out in the heat. All the beds were taken, and I was waved back onto the boiling path.

In less than one mile I came to Mirallos—two houses, a church and a restaurant. Wonderful, I thought, and headed for the restaurant to get out of the heat. It was about 3:00pm, I saw by the bar's clock, and lunch was still being served. On my way to be seated, two pilgrims with whom I had a passing acquaintance greeted me and asked if I was staying the night. I'd seen no indication of sleeping quarters, but one helped me out of my backpack and led me out a back door, across a narrow kind of open space with chairs and a line for drying clothes, and into an enormous unfinished room—it must have once been a barn, or perhaps a dance hall, but now converted to a primitive albergue with dozens of mattresses on the floor. Just a few people were there lounging about or sleeping. My eyes swept the place and I turned to the pilgrim and said: "It's deluxe. I'll take it." He led me back to the bar where I registered, paid 5 Euros, retrieved my backpack and returned alone to the room to select my very own mattress for the night. I located the cleanest, plumpest mattress I could find and dragged it to an aisle close to the funny little bathroom. I positioned the mattress from where, I calculated, a bit of evening breeze could reach me from a nearby window. I was both amused and pleased with my efforts. I was set up for the night.

I went back to the restaurant for my main meal of the day. The men who helped me were eating, and I sent them over glasses of wine as a kind of 'finder's fee' for steering me to this albergue. I settled into a corner table for the routine of postcard and journal writing. The middle-aged waitress spoke excellent English. She was a talkative soul, full of banter as she scurried back and forth among her now dwindling patrons. As I finished my delicious and ample meal, she was busy resetting the dining room for the evening. She was curious about me walking alone, and absolutely incredulous that I would be sleeping on a mattress. "How can you do that at your age? I couldn't do it, sleeping with all those people on the floor, listening to that snoring at night . . . I wouldn't walk the Camino unless I had the money to stay in hotels where I had my own bathroom and could lock my door at night. Why do people want to do this on the cheap, in this day and age?

There was a time earlier on my pilgrimage when I might have engaged this nice woman in a discussion about the Camino, and the motivations and purposes of doing a walking pilgrimage, but it was after 5:00pm. I was very tired and happy, content with my meal and the accommodations which awaited me. I needed some silence. And I wanted to pray. I paid for the meal and told the woman good-bye. It came as no surprise that she asked me to pray for her when I reached Santiago.

I walked out into the sweltering late afternoon. More pilgrims were registering for beds. As I passed through the bar, patrons were watching TV news with anchors wearing low-cut dresses. The juke box shuddered with indefinable music. I proceeded to the church which of course was locked. In every village I passed on the Camino, I trudged up the steps of the church only to find about 95% of the buildings locked tight. I could understand completely the need to protect property from theft and vandalism, but wished it could be different on the Camino, at least. I wandered into the adjacent cemetery. Typical in design, it had a rock wall surrounding it, and was beautifully laid out. Some graves were in the ground covered with monuments. There were walls of burial niches. I wandered around looking at names, dates and the ornateness of memorial carvings. Fresh flower bouquets as well as many tired and faded plastic arrangements marked gravesites.

On one cemetery path, I observed a young woman in her 20's, I thought, sitting on a folding chair next to a grave completely covered with fresh flowers. She looked utterly exhausted and red-eyed from grief and wilted from the heat. After awhile, she approached the grave and methodically tidied the flowers, pinching out the wilted ones. Hers was fresh and raw grief. As she left, she carried the chair to the side wall and placed it in the shade of a tree. I heard her car drive away.

Once I was seated on the woman's chair in the shade, a tiny bit of breeze came up and steadied me. It was peaceful there and I treasured the country silence. The cemetery silence. Interior silence. The Sacred Word that grounds my meditation practice welled up unbidden, triggering an intent to be present to God Within. Relaxing my body. Relaxing into the intent to let go of bodily sensations, to let go of fluid thoughts when I became engaged with them. Saying the Sacred Word as symbol of the intent to be fully available to God within. Thoughts arose here and there. Distant pilgrim voices. A bit of music. Cars passing and dogs barking. A little river of pain in my foot. No matter. Let it all go. An arising thought about the young woman at the gravesite. Who was she and who was buried in the fresh grave? I became aware of engaging with this passing thought, and my sacred word prayed itself from deep within my mind . . . symbolizing the intent to let go of the thought and be available to God. Over and over. Letting go of inevitable thoughts by returning to the Sacred Word. Being beckoned from the other side, and following deeper and deeper into silence. Becoming completely unaware of my surroundings. After sitting in prayer, I left the cemetery, feeling deeply rested.

I passed the evening on the mattress propped against my backpack. The albergue filled with people who spent considerable time and effort getting comfortable in the heat. By 9:00pm, as the shadows gathered in the big room, pilgrims were settling quietly onto their mattresses for the night. Long lines formed at the bathrooms for showers and brushing teeth. At 9:45, the lights went out. I began to doze when about six mattresses from me, a man began to shout loudly and angrily. I sat up to watch, as he singled out two men across the aisle from him and went berserk—yelling, gesturing. They didn't know him, and tried to placate him. All around in bunks, people became watchful, and some left for the safety of the entryway. Tension was high, and the two men did what was probably the best move—they lay down on their mattresses and turned to the wall, pretending to sleep. The man raged at this, and pacing back and forth, genuinely frightened his neighbors before storming out, leaving his things spread out on his bed. The two men got up, consulted with each other, and readied their packs for leaving, if necessary. However, they stayed and lay back down for the night.

We all settled in. The dorm grew very quiet, and as I lay on my mattress, I discovered with delight that I could see the moon through the window and framing the upper outline of the church. As well, a speck of a planet began to glow. Gentle snoring began. And then, because the dinner hour was drawing to a close in the restaurant, the juke box in the bar cranked up and began blasting at full volume. With every window open in the large room, there was no getting away from the intrusive music. Not only was the music unbearable, but the pilgrims could hear the voices from the bar—of course extra loud to be heard over the music.

After an hour, I knew there was no sleeping. I got up, groped in the dark for my sandals and headed for the bar. I was amazed at the scene. It was filled with people—pilgrims and locals alike, some dancing, every table full, standing room only and spilling out onto the sidewalk. The din was incredible. I stepped to one end of the long bar and awaited the bartender's attention. No English. I smiled and gestured about the music, pantomimed about the sleeping pilgrims next door and pointed to the jukebox, lowering my hands to indicate volume. To my surprise, the bartender smiled also, went over to some volume controls and immediately the music lessened by half. Patrons did not even look up, much less object, and I noticed an immediate side effect of patrons becoming quieter also.

Instead of going back to the dormitory, I stepped out into the night and walked down the middle of the quiet country road to get away from the lights and look at the sky. Stars overwhelmed the senses—the moon glowed and cast shadows all around me. Dogs barked in the distance, and best of all, there was a cooling breeze. I walked to the cemetery where I'd spent time only hours before. The gate was unlocked, and unafraid, I walked through the faintly moonlit rows of memorial graves, and took the seat under the tree. Complete peace enveloped me. Complete gratefulness for being on the Camino permeated my mind and heart. I could smell flowers all around me. I thought of the people buried in the cemetery in whose memory so many flowers filled so many vases. I especially thought of the woman mourning at the fresh grave. And I thought of an ossuary my family and I visited about 30 years ago in northern Spain. There was a plaque engraved in Latin that translated, means: "What you are, I once was. What I am now, you will become." I pondered these words until the sounds of the music died down. Car doors slammed, engines started and tires drove off into the night.

I hurried back into the bar as the place was being swept of the evening's detritus. The pilgrims who had been partying in the bar were now tiptoeing into the bathrooms and settling onto their mattresses. As

I passed by the place where the madman had ranted, I saw that his mattress was empty and his things gone. I lay down on my deluxe little mattress and traced with my finger the outline of the church steeple against the moon. Wasn't it Rumi who said: "We come whirling out of nothingness, scattering stars like dust. The stars make a circle, and in the midst, we dance." I drifted off to sleep.

CAMINO—DAY 42

Expanding the List of Influencers

Postcard # 42—June 4, 2010 sent from Portomarin, Espana

Elena: I haven't talked to you very much about the food I'm eating in Spain. It is delicious!!! The Spanish are good cooks—and the pilgrims are grateful and hearty eaters. Pork, rice, salad, chicken, fish & octopus (Pulpas). Ask your mama about octopus. Every time there is "lentil sopa" on the menu I order it—Yummy with little sausages of various types. I have an "ensalada mixta" everyday with tuna. Only olive oil & vinegar are offered as dressing. I especially like the way fish is served "en plancha". And I am tired of French fries with every entrée, so now I say "no potatoes" & ask for sliced tomatoes. Oh yes, & Judias or flat geen beans. Wonderful cooked w potatoes & served as premier plato. And desserts always come with the Menu del Dia & are yummy. Especially almond cake. Grandma

Journal—Day 42 (Friday) June 4, 2010—written at Portomarin

Today was very special, prayerful & peaceful. Not a great sleep last night in Mirallos because of partying & late arrivals, but tolerable. Leaving Mirallos today, I walked only 9.3km or 5.6mi. Glorious paths (full of cowplop) & some paths quite rough. At one point I was wedged into a country lane by huge farm machinery. Retreated to a side road & was fascinated by the maneuvering of modern farm equipment on medieval paths. Watched entire process as a farmer used one small motorized piece of machinery (on wheels that he could push and roll easily) to lift hayrolls onto another piece of equipment attached to an enormous tractor. Then hay roll was rotated by tractor power & shrink-wrapped until every inch was twice-wrapped in plastic . . . amazing process. Met really charming father & son bicyclists from Lithuenia—photographed them & they me—promised to email me. Touching tribute by son to father. My Albergue in Portomarin has full view of beautiful lake (for 10 Euros). Short walk today of 5.6mi but determined of need for a day of rest. On the path today, saw many "horreos" or graneries—long & narrow structures built several feet high on stilts or stacked rocks to store grain and keep rats out. Beautiful structures in various sizes & designs, as old as the hills.

Reflection on Day 42, written back in San Francisco

"Oh, only for so short a while
Have you loaned us to each other.
Because we take form in your act of drawing us,
And we breathe in your singing us.
But only for a short while
Have you loaned us to each other.
Because even a drawing cut in
Crystalline obsidian fades,
And the green feathers, the crown feathers,
Of the Quetzal bird lose their color,

And even the sounds of the waterfall
Die out in the dry season.
So, we too, because only for a short while
Have you loaned us to each other."
—Aztec Prayer to God

As I walked on Day 42, I came upon a beautiful new café/bar out in the country. I nearly passed it by but the courtyard was so inviting with its beautiful stone walls, patio chairs and tables, and classical music playing, that I decided to enter. I slipped off my backpack and parked it at an outside table. I strolled into the bar and ordered a café con leche which a waitress brought me with an unexpected slice of cake. "We're just opening," she said, "and you're one of our first customers." I sat back, pleased, slipped off my shoes and relaxed in the sun.

After a bit, I heard laughter and looked up to see two men enter the courtyard with bicycles. They walked their bikes to a table, and proceeded to adjust some mechanism on the older man's bicycle. I was stunned to see how much the older man looked like my husband, Larry. What was so interesting about these two men was their camaraderie, how animated with each other they were in conversation, how much they laughed. They spoke in a language I couldn't even guess. I went back to my coffee, but now and then was amused by some eruption of laughter from their table. As I prepared to leave, they proceeded to take each other's picture. I stepped to the table and pantomimed that I'd photograph them together.

Their English was wonderful, and they were father and son from Lithuenia, biking the Camino to fulfill a long time family dream. We talked for half an hour, sharing Camino stories and adventures, bits of our lives and having many good laughs. The father was the same age as I and the son was 38. I asked the father what it was like to keep up to such an energetic son and his joking response was "Oh, I have to stop over and over to give my son rest during the day. I accommodate him completely."

And to the son I posed this question: "Tell me, how will you remember this Camino pilgrimage with your father?" The younger man grew very serious and thoughtful. "It would not be possible to tell you from my head what this means to me. It can only be known in the heart. My father has always been my father, but much more—he is my close friend, and I feel his influence in everything I do. He is the best man I know." And they looked deeply at each other with love, and without embarrassment, stood and embraced. It was an unexpected tender moment of filial piety on the Camino, and as we said good-bye, there were tears in both their eyes. But the three of us left in good spirits, and as they pulled ahead on their bicycles and left me far behind, I could hear their good-natured calls to each other far down the path.

This encounter left me thoughtful. The son had spoken from the heart and freely named his father's influence in his life, named him as his close friend, the best man he knew. What a spontaneous accolade for the father to carry away in his heart. More than an accolade, it would be, I suspected, the highlight of the father's Camino experience. And even beyond that, the fulfillment of a parenting role.

There was that word "influence" again, interjecting itself into my walking self-examinations. Why was this encounter with the father and son of consequence to me? I wrestled back and forth with this idea until it was clear . . . the question of who really were the male influencers in my life? Who could I name? I had never thought of men as influencing me in the same important way that I revered the influence of women. Several names came immediately to mind—my father, my brother, my husband, my son and my son-in-law. But those were the easy answers. Many other men as well had entered my life over a 70 year span and been influencers on my growth and development. I stopped under the shade of a tree, got out my journal and started a list in the back. "Good. 15 names. That about does it." I spent the rest of the time walking to Portomarin remembering as many details as possible about the 15 men who made it onto the first of several lists.

Portomarin was a beautiful little town situated above a river and what appeared to be a lake and reservoir. I checked into a small albergue facing the water with a view restaurant on the top floor. The afternoon meal was excellent and I then spent several hours out on a deck gently poring over my list of male influencers and expanding it. To start, family and relatives dominated the list as I concentrated on the first 18 years of my life. These were the brothers and in-laws of my parents and I'd seen all of them frequently over my youth. These were the rock solid men in my childhood in the 1940's and 50's. They were the way I thought men should be in life. And then, one by one, they died, and were virtually forgotten by me until I walked the Camino.

Little stories were coaxed to mind. Family legends—two uncles had been gold prospectors for many years in Montana. Two others made fortunes in Detroit in the early days of the automobile industry. I laughed out loud remembering oddities and little personality quirks, like the time my Uncle Arch announced one evening at the dinner table, in one of his typical malapropisms: "I've sure got a good crop of bikinis growing in my garden this year." My family and I were polite about his confusion of bikinis with zucchinis, but the humor remained, begging to be remembered by me. All these men were kind, and probably never gave a thought in the world, nor had even a glimmer of insight, that their very way of being—peaceful, honest, friendly, loyal and generous—would have the influencing effects of generating the same to those with whom they interacted.

But at the end of Day 42, I realized that many other men had personally influenced me, and must be added to the list. Before going to bed, out came the journal and the list in the back began to grow—priests in elementary and high school, university Jesuits, my sisters' husbands, a string of boyfriends and older gentlemen friends, supervisors. I went to bed that night knowing that my exercise had taken a more complicated turn. The next morning I settled onto the view deck of the albergue's O Mirador restaurant. I knew that pursuing my next set of names from the late 1950's and 1960's would result in increased inner turmoil. I had, for example, to navigate the tricky avenues of dealing with Catholic priests and Jesuits. From childhood, it was understood that religious men were to be treated with awe and respect. In many ways, I feared them. They were apart from the world. Their word was God's Law. They could say Mass, turn wine and bread into the blood and body of Christ. They could hear confessions and forgive us our sins. There was no end to their skill sets and ordained responsibilities.

I will say unequivocally that I was treated respectfully and kindly by all these revered men, but it took many years of being in their company and gradually trusting my own intellectual capacities before I could comfortably present or argue alternate views. And it took a few more years after that, before I could dismiss from my life and practice, much of the teachings to which they had devoted their religious careers. But the individual men themselves I can never forget, for there was not a one amongst them who did not influence me and give me feedback—challenge me to be more, to read and think and write more. All would have wanted and expected me to stay a good woman.

And then on the lists, I ferretted out the boyfriends and older gentlemen friends—a major category of influencer with which I had to reckon. Things have changed radically over the years in the cultural mores of dating and marriage. When I was a young woman, the code was in concrete: the boy or man had control. He initiated the social contact, set the date and time, picked the woman up at her home, took her out, paid for everything. These expectations on both sides would continue with the man controlling the marriage proposal, earning a living and providing housing for a family. This relationship model was rigidly adhered to in the movies and television, in books, novels and womens' magazines. That pattern was what I knew, and what occurred in my fully engaged social life late 1950's and 1960's.

But changes came fast and furious mid 60's as feminist activists and writers raised the consciousness of Americans to shift away from many rigid borders surrounding the sexes. Women, the feminist movement demanded, must be empowered by law to have equal rights as men. There were many complexities to institutionalizing this, and enormous opposition from political and religious fronts, but basically, I was drawn in and fully supported the backbone of the movement: to ensure by law fair and equal wages for women and to ensure by law freedom to plan families or not have children at all. This new thinking, I soon found, had both positive and negative ramifications for relationships with men. I gradually but easily changed from being docile to assertive—because I wanted to change, and believed that becoming more independent, more liberated, more equal was the only way to survival in a lasting relationship with an enlightened man.

As I walked the Camino and encouraged memories of old boyfriends, the stories emerged powerfully, the good times, the stormy times, infatuation, love, drama, despair, separation. Feelings, I found, were not generally benign, and it took real discipline to keep level headed with the memories, to welcome them, stay with them, acknowledge them with the stance: "Oh there you are. I'd forgotten about you. Yes, I remember you well. You were part of my life." I thought of each old boyfriend, reviewed his memories with my heart, and felt relief in fully accepting him, loving, forgiving, then letting him go again—emerging into new understanding of who I became because of him.

I added names of male supervisors to the influencer list. Every one of these men were stars in my life. I was a straight arrow at work, always engaged, energetic, efficient and eager to learn. My supervisors entrusted challenging work and assignments to me, gave me clear and helpful unsolicited feedback, and allowed me to innovate. Their memories evoked pure gratefulness in me for their support of my personal and career growth.

And then I met Larry Wyman. Our relationship was unique in my experience. Dear Elena, we were deeply devoted platonic friends before we became engaged. The defining characteristic for me was intellectual companionship. Compatibility. Trust. Loyalty. Filial piety to his parents. Love and marriage and children followed. How strongly I kept my husband in my heart on the Camino.

I remember thinking during several days of walking: "Will this list of men never end?" I reviewed the important men I met after marriage. These were men who my husband and I considered intimate friends of our family—men who rejoiced in the births of our children, men with whom we met regularly for picnics and dinners and celebrations of important yearly holidays, men with whom we took vacations, confidants in times of trouble or anxiety. They are like family. They are family.

And I thought deeply about my son, Nathan. Everyday on the Camino, Nathan was in my consciousness and my heart, walking with me, seeing nature and people with me. I had no regrets about not walking for six weeks with my son. Unlike the father and son bicyclists, the Camino was not a shared dream between me and Nathan. However, he was proud of me I knew, and called this venture "Mary's Epic Quest." Even though we're extremely close, I could only imagine realistically and with humor the stress of a shared walk with my son—different energy levels, different sleeping and eating patterns, getting lost from each other every single day—in general getting on each other's nerves.

Love filled my heart for my son every single day. If ever a person fit a quote, it is Nathan with Henry David Thoreau's famous line: "If a man does not keep pace with his companions, perhaps it is because he hears a different drummer. Let him step to the music which he hears, however measured or far away." I knew that Nathan would enjoy the freedom of the Camino on his own, would love the countryside, the cities, the art along the way. He could endure any hardship to be borne on pilgrimage and would strengthen from such a personal "epic quest" wherever, whatever and whenever he was ready.

Finally, the list took a distinctly different turn. How could it be possible that priests and monks, brothers and religious leaders would enter my life in the last 20 years? From what depth of the well did spiritual water begin to flow? What parched desert region began to flower under the direct tutelage and writings of contemporary spiritual teachers? Why the magnetic pull to the Source? How mysterious to be drawn into depth of study of the Great Messengers of the ancient world religions.

Name the influencers, Mary. The men you have known intimately, and the ones you have never met. Thank them and bless them, if for no other reason than to have clarity in who you were, and who you have become.

William O'Hara, Patrick O'Hara, Henry O'Hara, James O'Hara, Maurice Kelly, John Hoy, Pat Hoy, Arch Deterding, PG Ehresmann, William Swofford, Franklin Carter, Fr. Leo Miller, Monsignor Fred Witte, Fr. Motherway, Fr. Knapp, Walter Peach, Charles King, Jake McCarthy, Richard Miller, Al Androlewicz, Armando Quiroz, husband Larry Wyman, Michael Learned, Michael Shough, Phil Morgan, Robert Barry, Richard Hutson, Steve Wahl, Jack von Dornum, son

Nathan Wyman, Art Douglas, Jack Silverberg, Harvey Budget, Ramesh Mizra, Jim Mathews, Tom Ozaki, Jorge Presser, Tom Olzewski, Vincent Pizzuto, son-in-law Francisco Varela, Philip Meier, Fr. Terry Ryan, Fr. Bill Sheehan, Thomas Keating OCSO, William Meninger OCSO, Basil Pennington OCSO, Micah Schoenberger OCSO, Richard Rohr OFM, Brother David Steindl-Rast, Thomas Merton, Goenka, the Dalai Lama, Jesus Christ, the Buddha, Muhammad, Lao-Tzu. Who have I forgotten from my past? Who will be remembered in my future?

CAMINO—DAY 43

Many Pilgrims on My Path

Postcard # 43—June 5, 2010 sent from Palas de Rei, Espana

Elena: Take a good look at this card & the path where I walked today. So beautiful, but very rough on my feet. I had to watch every single step for several miles—up, up, up, then down, and up again . . . Because every dorm was filled, I continued to walk from town to town—& ended walking 26.1km or 15.7mi. Tonight I am wiped out, but feeling good. I am getting closer to Santiago, and am now only 43 miles. Very exciting. Grandma's on the Camino, but soon coming home to San Francisco. I miss Grandpa, Nathan, Amelia, Elena & Francisco, Betty & Wilma & Bill. There will be so many things to talk about. Like, how does your garden grow? I think a little raised garden planted with lettuces & snowpeas and marigolds must be very pretty in the Japanese garden. Do we still have a lemon crop? I am bringing home some special Spanish pumpkin seeds for you to plant.

Journal—Day 43 (Saturday) June 5, 2010—written at Palas de Rei

Long, long walking day at 26.1km or 15.7mi. Again, the length of the walk determined by availability of beds in dorms. "Completo" the word today & indeed there were a lot of people on the Camino vying for beds. I stopped frequently to rest every 3-4 miles, once fresh squeezed orange juice, once a salad, so rested my feet & it was not a bad walking day at all. The countryside changes, looks more like rolling Ozark Mountains in Missouri, lots of woods like in southern Illinois. Hay being cut & rolled everywhere. Many farmers, wives (even a very little girl) out in the fields hoeing potatoes, planting tomatoes. Startled to hear church bells ring the Angelus for noon and see another family stop in the fields—I think to pray as my mother and father always did. Villages as old as the hills. As I walked through one of them, a walking funeral procession was just arriving at a prepared gravesite in a cemetery. I watched from behind a wall as mourners gathered around and the priest conducted the final ceremony. Many memories . . . Would be lost w/o yellow arrows guiding me. Also lost w/o the bars that revive a soul w. café con leches & aseos (bathrooms) & simple rest for the feet. I really like the Albergue Os Chacotes where I stay tonight—very modern. Funny issue over dinner. I was sitting in a bar late this afternoon adjoining a nearby very nice restaurant, having a drink & writing my postcards & journal. At 7:00pm I was fading due to the long walk today, & hoped to have a bite to eat before retiring. But the waiter said good naturedly "You must wait until 8:00pm for dinner. The time will go fast." "Well, I am too tired to wait until 8:00pm. Could I at least get some soup?" I asked. "No". But in this case "no" meant "yes", because soon the waiter set my table in the bar, winked at me, and before I knew it, I had my premier plato, then secundo plato, then dessert, with many cranky people looking on from the bar and lounge. The waiter said soto voce "They can all wait until 8:00pm. You need your rest. And I'm serving you extra good wine tonight."

Reflection on Day 43, written back home in San Francisco

"Soon the child's clear eye is clouded over by ideas and opinions, preconceptions and abstractions. Simple free being becomes encrusted with the burdensome armor of the ego. Not until years later does an instinct come that a vital sense of mystery has been withdrawn. The sun glints through the pines, and the heart is pierced in a moment of beauty and strange pain, like a memory of paradise. After that day, we become seekers."

Peter Matthiessen

On Day 43, I began to see many more pilgrims on the trail, due, I thought, to the fact that I was approaching Santiago. In order to gain a Compostela, or Certificate of Completion, a pilgrim must walk at least the last 100 km, or 60 miles into the city. Two days ago in Sarria, I reached that marker on the path, and found the albergues and bars were crowded with a great bustling of eager and energetic walkers new to the trail. I determined to continue my slow pace, but was aware that accommodations would probably be harder to find in the late afternoons.

The lay of the land in Galicia at this stage looked very much like southern Illinois in the summertime. Hay was being cut and baled. Corn was "as high as an elephant's eye," and in one place I watched several men harvesting a small woods for timber. This was pure happiness to be walking in open countryside. My path seemed to cut freely through farms. Of particular interest to me were the vegetable gardens which were a standard part of each farm and situated close to the house.

The gardens were beautiful, row after row of lettuces, potatoes, tomatoes, radishes, onions, cucumbers—all tended meticulously, it seemed to me, without a single weed. Flowers often bordered the entire gardens. Some gardens had watering systems, but frequently I saw farmers watering by hose or (as I'd seen my mother water in the 1940's,) by dipping cupsful of water from a bucket carried from the cistern. I often stopped on the path to look unobtrusively at the gardens and the gardeners. Occasionally, I came across a cultivated garden far away from the house, often with cantaloupe and watermelon plants, what my parents used to call a "truck patch."

I wondered what the people who lived on the route of the Camino thought about the steady stream of pilgrims passing through their farmsteads, year after year. Were they amused? Or dismissive of our determination to reach Santiago by foot? Had they ever made the pilgrimage to the Cathedral either by walking or by public transportation? Perhaps on horseback? More likely, I thought, the foot traffic on the Camino was so much a part of their lives that they simply paid no attention to us at all. After all, farming is serious business. They didn't need additional distractions.

On Day 43, I saw several scenes that were particularly poignant for me. In one, I watched a family in their garden hoeing potatoes and planting tomatoes. Mother, father and very little girl, I thought about 4 years old. The garden plot was well tended, and it was obvious that the couple delighted in the little girl's presence. I watched them encourage her to bring cups of water to the tomato plants being tamped into the prepared dirt. This scene seemed familiar, intimate, sacred even, full of blessings just to watch the family work together. It would take a lot of faith, hope, love, nurturance, cooperation and rain to produce food for their table.

And this memory came full-blown to me. As a youngster, I watched my parents as farmers bless the potato eyes they planted each March in the garden, bless the corn and soybean and wheat seeds for the fields, bless their children with holy water as they went off to school each morning, bless the baby chicks arriving in the spring, and my mother always told me that she and my father prayed to calm the animals that had to be butchered each winter to feed the family. It was a simpler way of life. Here is a poem I wrote some years ago—Potatoes for Everyone.

"I stood in the garden, aged 2, 3, 4 and 5
Next to parents planting cut potatoes.
Each piece contained an eye for sprouting.
Serious Business, this March activity
To feed a farmer's family in the 1940's.

Silently we said a hopeful prayer—
And sprinkled Holy Water on the eyes
I helped drop the pieces into waiting rows—
Daddy protected hopes with crumbled hills of dirt
Mama let me pour a cup of water over each.

Oh, inherited hope-filled ritual! I stand now at kitchen sink
And cut potatoes from earth free supermarket bins,
And breathe a silent prayer of love and hope,
Reliving my mother's dying words . . .
"Are there potatoes enough for everyone?"

The Camino path continued through farmlands much of the day. Whenever I saw a farmer out haying or plowing, I stopped to watch. The sunshine gave me a boost in spirits, but I knew that the old adage—"make hay while the sun shines," was a universal warning to farmers to take advantage of good weather. I came across a family far out in the fields baling hay. A man driving a large tractor and its attached machinery had stopped under a tree in the field. A boy, I thought about 15, drove another tractor pulling two wagons across the field, coming out from the barn. And then a car passed me on the path and drove out right across the hay stubble and stopped under the tree by the equipment. Out piled two young girls, maybe 7 and 10, in high spirits and began to run towards their father. Meanwhile, the woman driver set up a card table and placed dishes of food on it along with a large thermos bottle of drink. I watched from the path, and then we all heard distant church bells ringing, slowly at first, then with more insistency. The Angelus. The family stopped their conversation and stood in prayerful attention for the duration of the bells. I was stunned to see this religious ritual from my childhood replayed on the Camino in 2010.

Here is a picture etched into my memory forever. Until I was seven years old and could walk to the one room school a mile away (over the creek and through the woods), I spent all my time with my parents, often in the garden, sometimes out in the fields. Everyday exactly at noon the church bells rang some distance away—3 bells—a pause—3 bells—another pause—3 bells—a final pause—then 9 consecutive bells. Everything stopped, even my heart. Tasks were immediately set aside. The horse and wagon stopped and my parents and I prayed the Angelus out loud, an ancient prayer recalling the Annunciation of the angel to Mary the Virgin that she would bear a Child.

My little voice earnestly intoned this prayer with my parents: "The angel of the Lord declared to Mary . . . And she conceived of the Holy Spirit . . . Pour forth, we beseech thee, O Lord, thy grace into our hearts, that we, to whom the Incarnation of Christ, thy Son, was made known by the message of an angel, may by his passion and cross be brought to the glory of His Resurrection, through the same Christ, Our Lord. Amen." And we would bless ourselves with the sign of the cross and return to the tasks at hand.

With a formative experience like this, Elena, can you see that I would fall in love with God? I was not lukewarm about this. I can tell you from an open mind and an open heart, and unashamedly, as a child, I fell in love with mystery, with nature, with the story of Mary and Jesus, and though I couldn't have ever known it at the time, I fell in love with God. In the field that day on the Camino path, seeing the family bow their heads and pray was like a thunderbolt to my conscience and memory. What had happened over the years to that jet-like flame burning in my child's heart?

Late in the afternoon on Day 43, I heard bells again, this time tolling from the bell tower of a village church. As I passed the church cemetery, I could see a funeral procession gathering around a casket, and hear a priest intoning final prayers and blessing. I stood by the gate to watch, but two official looking men dressed in black and smoking cigarettes waved me away with a harsh look.

While walking that day, I thought of funerals I'd attended over my lifetime. When I was a child in grade school and also in high school, I attended Mass every day of the school year. This included dozens of funeral masses—not only those of family, but neighbors and people whom we didn't know who asked to be buried at St. Patrick's parish. My family also attended every wake of people we knew—always held in the funeral home of one of the local towns. Always the same procedure. At 7:00pm, we went to "pay our respects," as my parents called the outing.

With ceremony we entered the funeral home, signed the guest book, went to the casket as a family, knelt and said a prayer, and then, it seemed to me, stood and admired the corpse. At no time do I remember feelings of revulsion or fear or even sadness. Fascination, yes, with just about every aspect of the body: who fixed up this person, combed the hair, put on the visible make-up, arranged the rosary through the stiffened hands, dressed the body and placed it in the ruched and ruffled silk lining of the casket? And why was the lower half of the body enclosed? Maybe the person wasn't wearing shoes.

My parents didn't seem concerned with these issues. My mother inevitably comforted the mourners with how natural the body looked, asked about how the last hours of the person's life had ended, and how the family was faring. She always promised an angel food cake for lunch the day of the funeral. We moved on to make way for the next visitors and took our places in some open spot where we would kneel for the rosary. At 7:30pm sharp, the funeral home director rang a bell, everybody would kneel, and the rosary would be recited for the "repose of the soul of the dearly departed." I clearly remember even as a very young child, scoping out a place to kneel where I could lean for support—a wall, a chair, or my mother or father.

After the rosary, visiting started in earnest. The men gravitated to the side room and in passing through, I'd hear talk of the need for rain, too much rain, price of crops, politics, whatever. Women sat in groups in the large room with the corpse, and visited, often moving from group to group. School, babies, crops, canning, how to help the grieving family. The children played, if there were other children, or sat with their mothers and fathers and learned the ropes of being human. And so it was with me as I learned to live with death as I lived with life.

When I was little, I knew about cremation, but that idea was horrifying to me—not in the experience of my family, church or Midwest culture. People, we thought, were meant by God to be embalmed and buried in the ground. How importantly the changes over the years culturally, dogmatically and ecologically. This poem, Elena, captures my hopes and wishes for Grandpa Larry, you, your mama Amelia and Uncle Nathan, and your papa Francisco to remember when I'm gone.

Last Will and Testament by Mary O'Hara Wyman

Ruma, Illinois—there I settled at birth
For 18 years, and turned with moon and earth.
Turned with moon, and turned with earth.
Up and boldly left the farm and bloomed,
Bloomed where ever I was planted.

So here's the plan for you and me.
When I die, you smile and say good-bye
I'll flame in adoration of the life I've led.
Flame in adoration of the newer life I live.
Fly my ashes back to Ruma.
Back to the cemetery at St. Pat's . . .
Close by the farm, close by the one-room school,
So close the farm, the one-room school . . .
And closer still to Irene and Bill.

Don't bury me. Gently lay the ashy residue,
Lay the residue at my parents' graves.
I'll resettle at the Source.
Birds will call me, call me in the morning.
Coyotes howl for me at night—
They'll howl at night and deer will wander by
And winds will stir and sigh.
Winds will stir, and sigh, and stir and sigh.
Take me home, give me back.
Place no marker. Nor a nameplate.
We'll make the circle whole.
Amen.

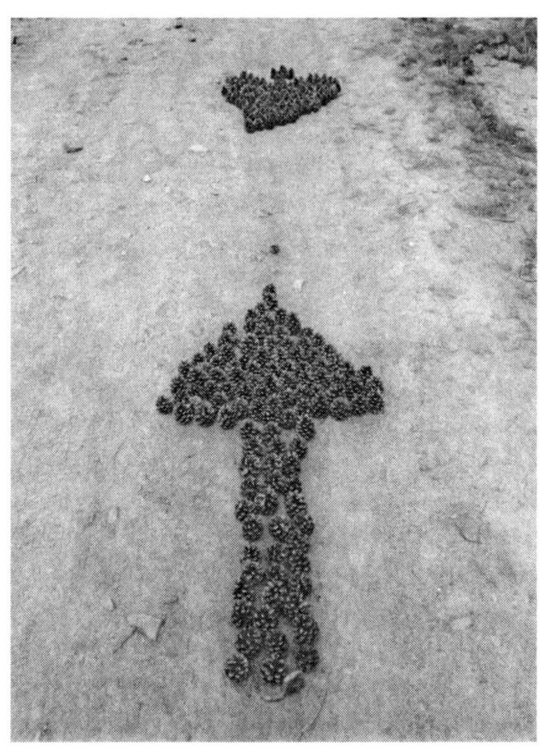

CAMINO—DAY 44

Galicia, the Land of One Million Cows

Postcard # 44—June 6, 2010 written at Melide, Espana

Today I walked 15.3km or 9.2mi to Melide. My calculations show I have walked 461mi. For 2 miles, I walked on a lovely woodlands path behind 19 cows & believe me, I was watchful where I stepped. They were milk cows—no bulls. Ask your mama to explain about milk cows and bulls. And Elena: several times today I came across mysterious symbols placed on paths, like this arrow and heart formed from pinecones. Rock symbols, flower symbols, leaves, etc. We pilgrims are getting closer to Santiago. Oh yes & today in a small village, the women strew the streets leading to the Church with flowers in honor of the Feast Day of Corpus Christi. Very beautiful. Very mysterious. Elena, I see a lot of things everyday that I don't understand, but that touch my heart. Believe me, I will be glad to see Grandpa, Nathan, Amelia, Elena & Francisco.

Journal—Day 44 (Sunday) June 6, 2010—written at Melide

Gorgeous weather, cool, clear, walked 15.3km or 9.2mi. I have walked from my calculations 461miles, leaving only about 35 mi according to book by John Brierley. I am tired, although I felt the best today. My feet are definitely better but still require at least 30 minutes each am. I have begun putting Vaseline on my feet in the am before socks. Helps. Walking along minding my own business this am realized that on other side of Eucalyptus trees cows were walking only feet from me. Then, my luck, 19 cows stumbled thru an opening in the trees & down the bank onto the road . . . right exactly in front of me. There was no getting around the cows. They ambled and stumbled and rambled. Walked an hour behind them—listening to their lowing and mooing and cow plop splatting all over the road . . . Amusing!!!! In Lobreiro, a tiny village, the women had strewn the streets with flowers in honor of feastday Corpus Christi. In front of a stone cross, they set up an altar with replica of Baby Jesus & flower petals everywhere in casual but elegant arrangement. Very naif. Tonight I am staying in the Regional Sports Complex & am quite comfortable in this enormous gym . . . it's partitioned off with about 20 pilgrims in each subdivision. Bathrooms very clean & satisfactory. Cost 5 Euros. Went out for Pulpas (octopus) this evening . . . Very, very good. Fabulous to watch the pulpas cooking routine, mostly on the street.

Reflection on Day 44, written back home in San Francisco

"Though we travel the world to find the beautiful, we must carry it with us or we find it not."

Ralph Waldo Emerson

The last major area of Spain that pilgrims walk through to Santiago is called Galicia, which is situated in the northwest of the country—with Portugal to its southern border, the Atlantic Ocean to the west, the Bay of Biscay to the north and to the east the large area known as Castilla and Leon. Galicia has a quaint and unlikely nickname of "The Land of One Million Cows." While the pilgrim trails did not present one million cows, I would venture a guess that for the week I walked there, I saw cows by the thousands, at least.

Galicia—I loved the way the locals pronounced the name Ga-lith-ia, in a kind of fluid lisp. The area is quite beautiful, with its hilly landscapes, low mountain ranges, and many rivers and lakes. Guidebooks for Galicia have a second descriptor: "The Country of 1000 Rivers." All these various water sources in the northwest of Spain have plentifully supplied jobs for the fishing and hydroelectric industries. And also helped shape the cuisine of the area, with its famous shellfish and octopus (pulpas) dishes.

For the Santiago pilgrim walking through Galicia, however, the overriding impression of the area is rural landscapes for pasturage and grazing, vineyards and frequent, if not daily, rain and fog with mild to very cool temperatures. Population is sparse in Galicia, due to the overall scarcity of jobs inland and the young people shifting away from agrarian and fishing lifestyles. For this reason, many thousands of Galicians have immigrated into European countries, and to South America—especially Uruguay and Argentina, looking for work. This accounts for the many near deserted villages with crumbling houses, few people and cars in evidence.

I came out of a bar in a tiny Galician village one morning having finished my coffee, but still feeling a bit sleepy. Before starting my walk, I stood in the middle of the completely empty street, devoid of people and cars, consulting my guidebook. In a matter of one minute, an enormous flock of sheep came up a side street, rounded the corner and headed full steam straight for me. I could see that the sheep were herded tightly by dogs and four shepherds, and my being in the middle of the road made not the least bit of difference to their plan of action.

I wanted nothing more than to be back in the bar and observing this from behind the tattered lace curtains, but I was literally surrounded by the first wave of sheep before I could move to the sidewalk. I dug my poles in and faced the oncoming army, hoping there was no errant billygoat amongst them intent on headbutting me as he passed. There was such raw energy in the movement of the flock of more than 300 sheep. As the solid mass of sheep approached me in wave after wave, the ones in the middle seemed to look up surprised at a human barrier, then slow down, stopping even, to lower their heads and scamper around me. This repeated for the ten minutes it took for the flock to pass. The smell was indescribable, but not unpleasant. It smelled like raw, wet wool matted with mud. The sounds were magical: the various pitches and intensity of the bleating of the sheep, wooden and metal bells around their necks clacking and jingling, the whistles of the shepherds signaling their dogs, the very noise that the hooves made on the street, plus the rapid fire beating of my heart.

When the flock had passed on and I could only hear echoes, I just had to laugh at the leftovers—such an amazing amount of sheep droppings everywhere around me on the street. Healthy sheep just being healthy sheep on the streets of a village. This experience was funny to me, energizing, made me feel involved in daily Galician life—it was all a pure gift to me on the Camino.

In Galicia, the cows were out and about every day. As a walking pilgrim, I decidedly preferred to encounter cows safely grazing in fields surrounded by sturdy fences. Now and then, however, I would become aware of cows, bulls and horses grazing freely on open lands. One needs to be cautious in those cases, and proceed directly ahead on the path without stopping and freezing in fear, or stepping up close to take pictures, or bolting hysterically in the direction from which one came.

In Galicia, with some frequency, I encountered farmers moving small herds of cows directly on the paths or farm trails or even through the villages where I walked. Cows would lumber along at a snail's pace, stopping to munch grasses along the path, splatting and peeing every 5 minutes, mooing at each other. Was it an inconvenience to be slowed down by cows, to be walking in the rain and mud with them and their owner, or was it the deepest communion with the pilgrimage experience? I met women and men who expressed surprise that the farm animals were so frequently grazing openly in fields without fences and also roaming freely in nearly deserted villages. I often heard women say that encountering animals without human supervision was the one thing that discomforted them on the Camino. And yet, as pilgrims, they continued walking determinably to their goal of the Cathedral in Santiago, and managed somehow, to get through the many herds of cows, horses and sheep.

As I walked the Camino paths week after week after week, I decided I probably had an advantage over the pilgrims who were from large cities all over the world. The wide-open Spanish countryside with all its crops, open grazing land, farm equipment, haystacks and animals was like home to me in southern Illinois. Familiar. Even comfortable in its bucolic simplicity. Not that I ever was involved directly in farming the land during the 17 years I lived with my parents, or the feeding and watering of the farm animals. But I was around animals, day after day, watching from the safe side of the fence, interested in them far more than they were interested in the two-legged creatures who fed and pastured them.

When I glimpsed from the Camino paths very young calves or colts or lambs, I just couldn't hold back smiling at the sweet childhood memories of my father coming into the house in the morning and announcing "We have a new baby calf born last night. Do you want to see it before you go to school?" How enchanting to be led safely by the hand through the feed lot and into the barn to see the new baby. How sweet of my father to take the time to do this with me . . . and to be excited himself at this stir in his heart, this unnamed reverence for new life and the mystery of it.

The mystery of it all on a farm, yes, indeed. But there was drudgery on a farm, whether in Galicia or in southern Illinois. Only a fool or a dreamer would romanticize the overall life of a farmer and his family—especially the farms of 70 years ago. The sheer struggle of day after day survival, striving to keep a few animals to butcher and animals to sell, animals to reproduce, crops to plant, gardens to feed the family, fresh drinking and cooking water, fruit trees for canning a winter's supply, all a struggle to keep a small stream of income possible and food on the table. All done without electricity, furnace heating, or indoor bath rooms. Endless tangles of juggling income from cash crops and investment of newer equipment.

And yet, there was balance in our lives where happiness could seep through and permeate our family. Here is a memory which presents from age three with clarity. The postman in his little 1940's car drove up to our farmhouse each spring and delivered across the fence to my father two enormous flat boxes of baby chicks. The boxes were carried ceremoniously to the brooder house fitted out with a kerosene heater that warmed an area under a tin umbrella about six feet in diameter. I was allowed to go watch, if I would sit on a tiny milk stool and be very, very quiet as my father gently scooped the just-hatched chicks from the box and placed them under the warmth of the tin umbrella. Each of the 8 dozen chicks was the size of a chicken egg, and covered with pale yellow fuzzy down. I was in awe of the tiny orange beaks and little black beady eyes, and legs and claws like toothpicks. My father always lifted one tiny chick and placed it in my cupped hands, guiding me to be gentle with this fragile bundle of new life. It was all the joy I could take in, maybe in a lifetime. And this once a year event led to our steady supply of eggs for consumption and sale, and meat for the table.

Elena, my dearest, listen carefully to this. All my younger years, I remember my mother saving and cleaning eggs carefully to put together a case of fresh hen eggs. We would take them to the nearby town of Ruma to exchange the 13 dozen eggs for 2 cents per egg, or $3.12 cash to send by mail to my sister Jane for monthly spending money during her college years in St. Louis. My mother's attitude was to give and give, because she saw plenitude in everything. Her innate gratefulness for the bounty of eggs from the hen house, the bounty of vegetables from the garden, resulted in her unending streams of gifts to whoever might be needy. If a neighbor stopped by on a bit of business, a relative dropped by to visit or a travelling salesman drove up to sell home products, my mother sprung into action. "You must come see the garden. Mary, run and bring us a basket. I have way too many strawberries, tomatoes, peppers, peas, beans, zucchinis, onions. We can't use it all." Whatever was maturing at the moment, was picked and lovingly offered and off our visitors went loaded with the produce, and many, many times with a dozen eggs as well.

And one of the dearest memories I cherish of my mother was her generosity in feeding people who dropped in to see us, usually in the morning. We didn't have a telephone, and so people just drove up to the house, and usually honked the horn. This might be relatives from long distances, local cousins or friends of friends. "Oh, you must stay for dinner at noon. We have plenty of everything. I'll just get started now. Mary, you come help me. Billy, you stay and visit." And with that, my father would be helpless, but happy to have some conversation time with the visitors and a respite from the morning's farm work.

No amount of visitor protest would stay my mother's hand. She swung into action with all the energy and skill of a chef being televised in a big competition. I tagged along as a little sous-chef, helping where I could. Even as little as age 4, I was at her side, and she always had some simple job for me to do. She stopped for a moment to put on her old-fashioned country apron with its wide bib and tie in the back, then slipped another apron over my head and tied it.

If it was spring, summer, fall or winter, we stopped in the kitchen to stoke up the fire in the wood stove and put on an enormous teakettle plus two other pots of water to boil. I clearly remember her itemizing in the kitchen out loud what she would serve according to the season. A winter menu might include smoked ham slices which she would cut in the smokehouse, or fried sausages which she would dig out of 20 gallon jars of home rendered lard and kept cool on the basement concrete floor. Whatever the main course, it would be served up with potatoes from cold storage and canned vegetables and homemade bread and dessert. Or in spring and summertime when the garden was ready to harvest, the menu might include mashed potatoes, fresh green beans, sliced tomatoes and cucumbers, a little lettuce salad, home baked bread, butter, jam, apple butter, and fried chicken. If the menu required an ingredient from the garden, she would run to pick it fresh, then prepare it for last minute cooking.

These were just the preliminaries . . . I was the table setter. "Mary, do a good job. They can see from the living room we're getting ready. Set out the good plates and the knives and forks. The good glasses from the china cabinet. And napkins. You always do a good job setting the table." And she whirled me into this activity with not a hesitation or a question on my part.

By this time, the wood stove was crackling with red hot heat and the water pots were beginning to simmer. It was time to run down and butcher the hapless hens who were about to meet their fate. My mother set her jaw and marched into the chicken yard that adjoined our small orchard to set the stage for her massacre. This was serious work. At the woodpile, she placed a stout log on one end. She positioned a razor-honed axe at the base of the log. With no hesitation, she picked up a long thick wire with a loop on one end and proceeded to calmly and shrewdly move among the chickens. She was assessing age, plumpness, meatiness. At this point the poor chickens suspected nothing. The roosters strutted and preened. The hens contentedly clucked and scratched at the dirt. They never seemed to learn.

Like a cobra striking at a prey, out flashed my mother's long wire with the loop. Chicken #1 was caught on the first try. All hell broke loose. The lassoed chicken went berserk in its horrible squawking, hens and roosters were obscured in the rising dust and flew in every direction, and at this stage I braced to the inevitable scene that I watched play out hundreds of times. My mother was fearless. She walked to the woodpile with her prize, untangling the loop from the neck or leg of the crazed and frantic chicken. In one balletic move, she grasped the chicken's legs tightly with her left hand, and with her right hand cradled its head into position on the upended log. Her left foot lifted delicately to hold the chicken's head in place, freeing her right hand to grasp the ax handle. Down came the blade with precision, and the whacked off head dropped to the dirt. Blood spurted. The convulsive headless body was thrust into the woodpile and held down with two or three sturdy logs until the blood drained and the pulsing life ebbed.

With renewed energy and determination, my mother marched back into the chicken yard. The task was only half done. Now the chickens were more wary, some clustered in corners, some perched up in trees, some retreated into the hen house, and some ranged warily out into the orchard. This would require a new strategy. She made a run into a gaggle of hens, her wire loop flashing scarily back and forth at the chickens which scattered frantically in every direction. Missed. Missed again. Now another run made towards some hens huddled under a fruit tree. Bearing down, chaos erupted, chickens exploding in every direction, and finally, my mother, singularly eyeballing one in particular, ran it down in the orchard, around the apricot trees, over to the cherry trees—she, gaining speed and thrusting her wire back and forth, aiming for leg or neck, missing broadly or missing narrowly with feathers flying . . . and then the chicken was caught and carried back to the woodpile for the slaughter.

With two headless chickens being bled in the woodpile, my mother set me as the watcher—"in case they flapped away" and she ran for the house and a bucket of boiling hot water to submerge them, the first step in softening and plucking the feathers. My breathing was unsteady. The smell, the sight, the very idea of guillotining these poor unsuspecting chickens all settled as a burden on my little shoulders as I went along with this ordinary farm activity. Thankfully, I was never left to chase down a headless chicken that escaped from the woodpile, but occasionally I saw a particularly feisty headless chicken escape from my mother's hands and flop about on the ground in a most horrifying manner until she could scoop it up and anchor it into place back under a sturdy log.

I always knew I would never perform these gruesome tasks on my own. I would look curiously at my gentle and loving and religious mama . . . but none of it—the butchering, the blood and guts seemed to bother her . . . she had folks in her living room waiting to be fed. Waiting to be nurtured. If it took the sacrifice of two chicken's lives to nurture someone, then so be it. Amen for those chickens.

I stood at my mother's side in the kitchen as she added kindling and a log to the woodstove, and singed off the pin feathers in the crackling fire. She was a marvel at multi-tasking. With a flourish, she sliced open the plucked and singed hens, skillfully separated out hearts, livers and kidneys and threw the slimy intestines and innards out the back door as a feast to the cats and kittens. So quickly the dirty deeds were hidden, and in a large pan of cool water rested the pristine and thoroughly washed and cut-up pieces of raw chicken, soon to be dried and dipped in egg and seasoned flour, then immersed into iron skillets sizzling with melted lard. As she slid the battered pieces of chicken into the hot lard, the distinctive sizzle and smell filled the air. She put peeled potatoes and beans which I snapped into bubbling cooking pots.

We had about twenty minutes of cooking time to finalize the dinner plan. I was instructed to pour water at the table, and pick two mint leaves for each glass. Cut the loaf of bread. Pull the bucket up from the well and put fresh-churned butter in a clean dish. Prepare small bowls of apple butter and strawberry jam. Find chairs enough for the guests. Ask who needed to wash up, or use the toilet, (which was outdoors.) "And Mary, run and pick a few zinnias for a little centerpiece. It will only take a minute." The chicken frying in two large iron skillets was tended with my mother's Third Eye. She knew, and I knew also, the allure of a country meal, the smell of battered chicken sizzling in lard, the vegetables rounding out aromas that suggested to guests the groaning board of love about to be bestowed by my mama. Everybody's mama, really.

How I loved it as it all came together. Potatoes were mashed with a flourish and mounded into a bowl, then sprinkled lightly with paprika. Green beans were cooked to mushy softness, then flavored with crumbled bacon. Freshly picked tomatoes and cucumbers were sliced onto a platter and dashed with vinegar, salt and black pepper and a hint of sugar. Our largest platter, my mother's pride and joy, was warming on the open oven door as my mother lifted the fried chicken from the skillets and arranged the pieces artfully on the platter, then garnished the edges with parsley. My mother eyed each dish as it was carried to the dining room table, wiping a spill here, arranging a dish there, until she was satisfied that all was ready. Meanwhile, the guests were being seated by my father as my mother and I quickly stepped to the back porch to change into clean aprons. She ran a comb through her hair and smoothed on some lipstick.

The seated guests were salivating. All expressed disbelief that such a bountiful table could appear in an hour and 20 minutes. My father quieted himself, and all followed suit. "Mary, please say grace for this meal your mother cooked. And loud enough for us all to hear." And my little voice responded in rote: "Bless us, O Lord, and these thy Gifts, which we are about to receive from thy Bounty, through Christ, Our Lord, Amen." And the noon feast began. The platter of fried chicken was passed from the head of the table where my father presided, down one side of guests to the opposite end where my mother and I sat. I watched what pieces everyone took from the platter, hoping that a thigh or leg would be left for me. My mother lifted a piece of chicken onto my plate, passed the platter on, and always whispered to me: "I hope it's good. Thank you for helping. We got dinner on the table in no time, didn't we?"

Cada encuentro, es un encuentro contigo mismo
Camino de Santiago
Jede Begegnung, ist eine Begegnung mit sich selbst
Toute rencontre, est une rencontre avec soi-même
Every encounter, is an encounter with yourself

CAMINO—DAY 45

Nature—Pressed Down and Flowing Over

Postcard #45—June 7, 2010 sent from Arzua, Espana

I was very excited today, Elena, to see a man & woman walking to Santiago with a donkey carrying their things. The donkey looked just like this one but was decorated w. ribbons. I walked (and I guess the donkey walked also) 17.1km or 10.3miles today & it was up & down a lot—but through magnificent eucalyptus forests & old, old villages. Beautiful churches. Weather cool. Saw frogs in a pool, heads up above the water, doing what frogs do to pass the time away!!!! I am closer to my goal of Santiago. Just 25 more miles. It's like a dream . . . Just put one foot in front of another and go, go, go. Grandma's on the Camino

Journal—Day 45 (Monday) June 7, 2010—written at Arzua

Today I walked 17.1km or 10.3mi from Melide to Arzua & loved every minute of it. Overcast, so it was cooler in the hot weather. Went into several remarkable churches. Saw residue at a number of villages of Corpus Christi flowers strewn on the ground yesterday. Walked in fragrant eucalyptus groves. There are fewer wildflowers now, but June summerish green in the weeds, grasses, wheat, new mown hay, and gardens with full families out howing away on potatoes, onions, tomatoes, sweet peas, corn & the roses—bajillion bushes & bazillion flowers in every color & every sweet scent. Saw holly hocks today. Saw cows in lanes passing me by; saw frogs in a pool, little heads poking up & frogging amazingly. Stopped as I approached. Staying in a very nice place in Arzua, the Albergue Santiago Apostol. Great pilgrims menu in its restaurant. Investigated website train reservations from Santiago to Madrid—I'm that close to the end of the Camino.

Reflection on Day 45, written back home in San Francisco

"Don't try to force anything. Let life be a deep let-go.
See [God/Spirit/All that Is]
Opening millions of flowers everyday, without forcing the buds."
—Bhagwan Shree Rayneesh

More than a year after completing the Camino walk, I continue to feel the effects of the non-stop beauty of the Spanish countryside. Every sense I possess was teased into action every single day it took me to complete the walk. I admit that a certain amount of personal interest and attentiveness was in play regarding all my daily adventures and encounters, but what I'm less able to explain was the awe and astonishment I felt over the simplest things that appeared on the walk. I came to question why encountering something on the Camino provoked the string of predictable and similar reactions time after time, day after day . . . I saw the simplest things, I was awed, then flooded with joy. I grew deeply curious about this pattern.

Let me place the idea of a pattern, Elena, in the context of the flowers and crops I observed along the Camino. A Pilgrim walks 500 miles across northern Spain in late spring and early summer, and sees wildflowers and cultivated gardens, crops and vineyards. Yes, it's all pretty, and pretty simple. For many, it's predictable, and somewhat boring. But consider first the phenomena of the wildflowers that appear every single day on the Camino in unexpected locations, barren landscapes, lush woods and little travelled paths, alongside streams and in animal pastures. Sometimes one or two or three random little blossoms. Or sometimes wildflowers by the millions—filling pasture after pasture, blooming in impossible combinations of colors across interminable hills and valleys. Heart-stopping colors—think acres of wild, fiery-red poppies. Think pastures of yellow mustard blooms interspersed with waves of purple heather. Think miles of wild, white gorse interspersed with sweet smelling lavender and yellow buttercups lining rocky paths and splaying across boulder-filled mountain meadows.

I was endlessly delighted by the variety of wildflowers that I catalogued in a special area of my journal. There were flowers I'd never seen before, so cannot name them. And often on the Camino paths, I'd come across flowers in the wild that I knew only as garden cultivated. I was astonished in the countryside, far from any homes, to see roses, hydrangeas, daisies, pansies, honeysuckle, trumpet vines, iris, morning glories, rhododendrons and azaleas, alstromeria, primroses, calla lilies, hollyhocks, ivy, foxglove, bridal wreath, clivia, heleborus, blueberries and purple grasses with tiny, delicate blooms. Everyday, Elena, while walking the Camino, I studied the wildflowers and was astonished—and joy and gratefulness emerged as state of being. "There's a new one," I would say, and scribble its name in the back of my journal.

As the weeks of late May and early June dwindled, seeing wildflowers in the country was gradually replaced by the profuse blooms of early summer cultivated flowers in the private gardens and parks that I passed in villages and big cities. Again, I just had to stop and take in every well-tended little garden tucked up close to the private homes of farmers and city-dwellers. I often observed a gardener hoeing and weeding a small plot of flowers and vegetables with meticulous care and love. Sometimes the gardener looked up, waved to me in a subdued, yet friendly way, and I thought: "We appreciate each other, that gardener and this pilgrim."

And once, in a farm garden open to the road, I smiled at a skinny little girl about 7 or 8 who was picking hollyhock blossoms of several colors. It was a sweet scene and reminded me of my childhood. She was dressed in overalls and her hair pulled back in a ponytail. A very old and shaggy dog stayed close by her side, and 3 little kittens straggled behind her. Geese were grazing in a fenced area adjacent to a tractor shed. An elderly woman, perhaps her grandmother, sat in a lawn chair nearby the garden. The little girl looked me over, deciding what to do, then shyly approached the road where I walked and handed me a fully opened hollyhock blossom. She said nothing to me, and did not respond to my greeting. She rapidly retreated several yards away, her dog lumbering arthritically to her side. A bit of eye contact. I smiled again. She was solemn, and began sucking her thumb.

I admired the blossom, then turned it over and set it upside down on a nearby wagon-bed, so that it resembled a long, bouffant skirt. Taking a toothpick from my waistpack, I carefully inserted one end into the base of the flower, with about an inch sticking up. The little girl's eyes were big. I motioned her to the hollyhock stalks and pointed to a bud that had not fully bloomed, but had opened enough to show the color of the petals. I smiled again, gestured to the plump and about to bloom bud and the little girl quickly picked and thrust it into my hand, then backed away, cautious but very curious. I proceeded to slowly and carefully turn the bud's green leafs back to fully expose the color of the unopened flower, then gently inserted the bud's base onto the toothpick sticking up from the skirt. I'd made a two-part hollyhock doll—the bud forming the upper body above the skirt.

The little girl inched forward, squinting only at the flower doll, then seemed to understand what it was. She walked backwards all the way to the old woman, then took her by the hand and brought her over to see. The old woman picked up my creation, admired it, then without a word, set it back on the wagon bed. I dug out another toothpick from my pack and handed it to the little girl, gesturing that she should create another flower doll. With each step in the process, she looked at me for confirmation, and soon there were two hollyhock dolls side by side.

I was delighted, and so was the little girl. She scooped up her kittens and brought them closer for a look. She hugged her grandmother around the knees, then tore around the hollyhocks three times. The old dog barked and wagged its tail appreciatively. The geese began to squawk and waddle towards the fence. It was time for me to walk on . . . I picked up my poles. The little girl was guarding her hollyhock dolls, thumb in mouth. We looked at each other, and from her solemn face there was only a hint of a smile in her eyes. Not a word had been exchanged, but as I walked on, a deep and abiding sense of joy filled my heart. I would never forget the little farm girl who sucked her thumb.

As the days passed and the weather turned warmer, deep red and bright pink geraniums lifted their little crooked necks and bloomed, it seemed, in every window box and from every balcony and doorstep. They waved hello and good-by as I passed. Summer was stretching and yawning and waking up fully. I delighted in recognizing cultivated garden flowers and trees that grow in California—yellow and red and pink and white climbing roses, rose bushes that perfumed the air as I walked by, buddleia that attracted hovering butterflies, daphne and hyacinths, batchelor's buttons, Rose of Sharon, forsythia, peonies, lilacs, airy tamarix, purple and white wisteria, mosses and ferns. How beautiful the trees were setting fruit—the figs, apples, cherries, apricots and olives. And the decorative trees in extravagant full bloom—the dogwood, the red bud, the magnolia and hibiscus, the Japanese maples. How could one look at these marvels of evolution, propagation and cultivation and not be struck dumb with astonishment, not be overrun with joy? Persian poet Hafez said: "How did the rose ever open its heart and give to the world all its beauty? It felt the encouragement of light against its being. Otherwise, we all remain too frightened. Slowly blooms the rose within." As I walked, I wondered if pilgrims don't also bloom in the encouraging light of the Camino.

Over a Saturday, Sunday and Monday in early June, I observed a lovely practice in the small villages through which I walked in Galicia. For the Feast of Corpus Christi, women and men decorated the streets and little plazas leading to the Catholic Churches with flowers in highly decorative designs. I had heard that all over Spain, this feastday was widely celebrated with street parades, all featuring floats and a platform holding the consecrated Host . . . the Body of Christ for public viewing. And of course, the celebrations are not only religious, but have taken on the aura of carnival, with dances, plays performed outdoors, large groups of people gathering to take part in the festivities with food and family parties. While the Sacred Host is central to these carnival-like parades, a sinister character appears also—thought to be the devil, weaving in and out among the participants and audience, representing evil and playing tricks. I did not see these Corpus Christi parades or the devils, but many pilgrims were able to observe the festivities over the course of the long weekend. I did, however, see things far more mysterious and delightful to me as I walked through tiny villages—the Corpus Christi "flower carpets." In front of small churches and in plazas, I was astonished to come across extraordinary flower displays—elaborate designs created with flowers meticulously laid out on the ground in perfect patterns, hence the name flower carpets.

It was startling to leave a country path, enter a small village, and come across these carpets leading to the plaza in front of a church. A statue or crucifix brought outside from the church generally served as a central focus of the flower carpet. And there the creativity began. Artistic designs (think Oriental carpets) were laid down primarily with flowers blooming at the time, the colors startling to the eye. But as I studied the patterns, marvelous subtlety of design had been executed by adding aromatic herbs, salt, woodchips, even sawdust. I was in awe. I knew what I saw, but I knew that I didn't understand these ancient and symbolic practices so "religiously" followed in contemporary times.

On the Saturday before the feastday, I observed in one of the villages a Corpus Christi flower carpet under construction. About a dozen women and a few men were laying out the spectacular border and interior design of a flower carpet on the plaza floor facing the church. Even though I didn't understand what was happening, I began to think about the havoc that wind or rain would cause in this project. I scanned the skies—good weather seemed promising, and I settled myself comfortably on a nearby bench, well out of the way, and lowered my backpack to the ground. I discreetly peeled a banana. This was worth watching. One woman was clearly in charge, moving amiably among the pairs and trios laying flowers down to form geometric outlines of the carpet. Now and then she consulted a drawing, or template, and guided small color changes or angles of design.

An ancient truck rumbled up to the plaza, then turned and backed in as closely as possible. It was piled high with thousands of fronds from fern plants. Several men took armloads of the fronds and began lining both sides of the four streets leading into the plaza. The effect was beautiful. More flowers were arriving all the time. Local people brought armloads of flowers from their gardens, I thought, and often of just one type or color and turned them over to the people creating the designs. I loved the camaraderie evident in all these collaborators. I watched one very pregnant middle aged woman arrive walking with four small children in tow and carrying an enormous bundle across her shoulder. She was greeted warmly by the woman directing the project and led ceremoniously to a certain area of the emerging flower carpet. The women creating that section rushed to help her untie her pack, laughing with delight as they unleashed hundreds of lilac blooms that spilled to the ground and heaped into a fragrant, waist-high mound. I couldn't stop smiling. I could tell the lilacs were a very big deal in the design being created.

I checked the angle of the sun. It was time to go. I shouldered my pack and stepped into the church. There was activity there as men were mounting and securing statues on movable platforms for the next day's religious procession. Women bustled about at the various altars, arranging flowers and replacing votives and tapered candles in front of statues. A teenager pushed a vacuum cleaner around the high altar while a man on a precarious and wobbly ladder replaced bulbs in a hanging chandelier.

In a kind of a side chapel, I observed an old priest sitting quietly in prayer. "Good," I thought, "this is the way the church should operate—the priest in prayer and the people . . . the real Church . . . deeply involved in the community of active worship." I lit a candle before leaving. What, I wondered, should I pray for? I decided to pray for this community of beautiful people creating a flower carpet, to pray that this Corpus Christi tradition could be kept alive through future generations, and that the old priest would continue to lead his little flock from a place of deep and silent prayer.

As I walked out of the Church and my eyes adjusted to the sunlight, I was bedazzled by the way the flower carpet was taking shape. From the steps of the church I got a new and fuller perspective of what the finished carpet would reveal. Whole areas of colors were emerging with flowers filling in angled and rounded outlines. With a very happy heart, I oriented myself to the yellow arrows and followed the Camino path out of town, walking down the middle of the fern-lined street and on to the next village. More than a happy heart, really. Every cell in my body was content with the day.

There was that pattern again, Elena. I saw simple things and activities. The simplicity awed me. And joy emerged. Again I asked myself: "Are you being foolish and sentimental in your 70th year? Miss Goody-Grandma Two Shoes? Or are you changing, shifting perspectives on what you see and feel, what your reactions mean? Was I even meandering through northern Spain quite alone? When I stopped to look at the passing scene, was I being led, perhaps even pursued by The Other—dare I say God? Maybe like in the poem The Hound of Heaven by Francis Thompson:

"Up vistaed hopes I sped; And shot, precipitated, Adown titanic glooms of chasmed fears, From those strong Feet that followed, followed after. For, though I knew His love Who followed, Yet was I sore adread—Lest having Him I must have naught beside. Still with unhurrying chase, And unperturbed pace, Deliberated speed, majestic instancy, Came on the following feet, And a Voice above their beat—Naught shelters thee, who wilt not shelter Me."

At any rate, I began to see and feel things as saturated by the Divine. I often brushed these transforming ideas aside with a bit of embarrassment, then marveled at how strongly they presented the next day. Another eye was opening. It was not the mind alone that was processing my Camino—the heart was learning a new way of seeing and loving and being. The heart was asserting truth through beauty and goodness. And yes, asserting Divine Companionship and Oneness with all.

Camino—Day 46

The English Lesson

Postcard # 46—June 8, 2010 sent from Santa Irene, Espana

Elena: Oh my, did it rain today. Grandma walked in villages & lanes & woods in pouring rain. Cows walked with me for awhile & you can't even imagine how it smelled in the rain. I am so happy, for I walked to the village of Santa Irene & got the last bed in a beautiful little Albergue where I am all dried out, showered, waiting for dinner—Elena—I wanted to stay here in this village because my mother's name was Irene. I went to see Iglesia Santa Irene but alas!!! could not get in. Still Elena—I'm here & remembering amazing details about my mother. Your mama knew my mama. Ask her about my mama & what she remembers of childhood visits to Ruma, Illinois. Today I walked 18.4km or 11mi. A pilgrim here from the Philippines wants to write you a note: ***Elena: tu as une grandma formidable. C'est une chance quand on est une petite fille. Bernard***

Journal—Day 46 (Tuesday) June 8, 2010—written at Santa Irene

Today I hoped (and hoped again) to stay in Santa Irene but with only a small number of beds in two Albergues, & with the weather terribly rainy & quite cool, I was unsure, but lucky. I arrived very wet to the last bed. The day was excellent for me in spite of rain. My thoughts of my mother Irene came easily, accurately I think, as I imagined my mother through adolescence, teaching school from age 16 until marrying my father in her mid-20's, raising 5 babies in the depression on a farm with no indoor plumbing or electricity, but really today, delving into my relationship with my mother—I a late baby born when she was 40, much loved & beloved, a perfect childhood on the farm in Illinois & I'm very aware of my mother's decision to go back to teaching when she was 55 (hard for her) to pay for things for me & give me opportunity to go to St. Louis University. That was her dream. Today walked 18.4km or 11.mi. I'm very near to Santiago. During and after dinner, spoke to Bernard from the Philippines about youth programs—Job Corps in USA and Verlanie in the Philippines, then Maher and Asha in India.

Reflection on Day 46, written back home in San Francisco

"The transformative power of a Jesuit education is often realized later in one's life."

Lawrence Biondi, SJ—President, St. Louis University

Because my mother Irene so frequently came to mind as I walked the Camino, it is not surprising that she surfaced strongly during Day 46 as I walked in the pouring rain to the village of Santa Irene. I stopped briefly under the portico of the church only to find the door locked. Disappointed, I pressed on through the village, finally dragging into a charming little albergue about 5:00pm, delighted to be given the very last bed in the dormitory part of the building.

As I was led to the dorm sleeping area, I realized my assigned single bed was on a raised platform separate from the bunkbeds, but completely visible to all the bunks. This is odd, I thought, as I put my backpack down and shed my waterlogged shoes, socks and raingear. Looking around, I became aware that the dormitory space had grown completely quiet from the bustle and conversation that was evident when I entered. My eyes adjusted to the late afternoon light. There were many faces and pairs of eyes staring at me from the adjoining bunks. I immediately recognized the group as high school students whom I'd seen several times during the past two weeks. I waved at them and smiled, but their response to me was weak. I then turned attention to drying wet clothes and preparing for the next day's walk. The students began to talk again in subdued tones back and forth between the beds. I felt like a Mother Superior dampening the evening spirits of the group.

Gathering my writing gear and journal, I made my way from the dormitory into the spacious main dining and sitting room. A lovely woman manager/cook approached and very businesslike, convinced me to take dinner in the dining room with the group of students—and she assured me, there would be several gentlemen who were older like I was, and would make suitable dinner companions. I signed up with her and she announced "Dinner at 7:00pm." and pointed to the clock for emphasis. I ordered a glass of wine and sat alone at a table in the sitting room. A fire was blazing and warmed the room and my cold feet as I proceeded with my evening routine of writing a postcard to Elena and the day's journal entry.

Two men entered and sat on the couch talking. I turned and saw their reflection in a mirror. "They are only about 40, nowhere near my age," I thought, remembering the manager's description of dinner companions. Another man joined them as I finished up my tasks with still another half hour until dinner. I stood and turned to face the men, introducing myself as Mary, from San Francisco. They all stood and gave their names and ushered me into a comfortable chair by the fire. Conversation was awkward, but friendly. After a bit of time I announced: "I'm going to have another glass of wine. Is anyone interested?" It was hard to read their reactions. "Maybe I'll wait until dinner" one said. Another asked how much a glass of wine cost. The third man didn't appear to understand the question.

I walked back to the kitchen where three women were bustling to ready the evening meal for 24 guests. Beckoning the head cook over, I ordered four glasses of vino tinto and asked her to bring them to the sitting room. She raised her eyebrows sharply at me as she collected the money. "Oh dear, she thinks they are all for me." By the time I arrived back in the living room, she was steaming towards my chair with four glasses of wine on a tray. I pointed for her to serve the men first. Another quizzical look from the woman. The men were delighted. Conversation grew far more amiable. By the time we were summoned to the meal, our little gang of 4 had covered the usual Camino informalities: Where are you from? Why did you come on the Camino? Are you walking alone? What is your profession back home? Although we were from three different countries—the United States, the Philippines and Belgium, English was our common language.

As the 3 men and I entered the dining room at 7:00pm, 18 students and 2 very young chaperones exploded from the dormitory in a kind of subdued commotion, as they bumped and jockeyed for seats next to favored companions at the two long dining tables—pushing for any seat, actually, away from us. They were quiet enough, but I could tell that right under the surface their energy was bubbling over, if not sizzling, and they were hungry. Eight of the students were forced to sit with us and we all determined to make the best of it, at least through the premier plato.

I was immediately curious if any of the students knew English. I tried the simplest conversation: "Hello, my name is Mary. What is your name?" I smiled and waited, nodding my head in encouragement at each of the 8 students at our table. Smiles, but deer in the headlight stares. I tried again, a bit more distinctly and a bit louder, even thinking how much I probably sounded like a Mother Superior interrogating them after a ruckus in a study hall, or an Ugly American expecting to be understood in a restaurant. What is your name?" I asked the young man seated next to me. His prolonged silence pained all the observers, and turning red with embarrassment, my young seatmate bolted to the end of the table, picked up an enormous pitcher, and began pouring water in all the water glasses.

I was taken aback, but couldn't stop myself. I tapped my spoon three times on a glass for attention and started again, this time with elaborate gestures and very, very slowly. "Hello. I am Mary . . . Maria." I repeated my name in Spanish two more times and thumped my chest for emphasis. "I am from the United States. I live in California, in the city of San Francisco." Suddenly, tentative smiles from the students. Pokes. Eye contact. One girl began. "I am Teresa. I live in Seville." And from me and the 3 men: "Hello, Teresa." The ice was broken. With the encouragement of the adults, I coaxed the pattern of name and city from each student. The table erupted in excitement. This was getting lively. The students seemed to want more conversation. After another silence, I started again: "I walk to Santiago. Where are you walking? This question was a bit ambitious, if not ridiculous, although one girl managed "I walking to Santiago."

As the meal began, I ran through several questions in my head—subject, verb and object—that I might pose to the group. I eyed them as they tackled big bowls of potato soup with floating hunks of sausages that they pushed into their soup spoons with hearty chunks of bread. But, I wondered as I watched them eat, should I continue with English conversation and run the risk of alienating these lovely young teenagers? Or embarrassing them to tears? Or worst of all, just grossing them out when all they want is their dinner and to go to bed. We all finished our first course in silence. Plates were cleared by the kitchen staff, and another quiet time emerged where we all looked at each other and smiled in harmony.

I started my English lesson again, loudly and clearly. I was out of control. "Hello, my name is Maria. I am from San Francisco, California." Serious looks around the table as though to say: "Uh, oh, here she goes again." But heads began to bob slowly in acknowledgment as they put the words together. Encouraged, I continued: "I am 70 years old. How old are you?" Long thoughtful stares. Whispers in Spanish. Two youngsters held out their hands and traced numbers on their palms. Were they trying to translate the number seventy from English to Spanish or were they incredulous that anyone that old could be on the Camino?

I repeated the pattern. "My name is Maria. I am 70 years old. How old are you?" and I gestured to the boy on my left. He cowered against his classmate who put his arm protectively around his shoulders. I coaxed him to follow the pattern "My name is—. I am—years old. How old are you?" A girl across the table rescued him by standing up and saying haltingly: "I am Isabella. I am 16 years old. How old you are." I clapped my hands in delight at her transposition of words and repeated the pattern and motioned her to ask a classmate to her right. These youngsters were precious as they got up the nerve to try this little bit of English with a stranger. I suspect they dreaded their turn to speak, and I am reminded of Anais Nin, who said, "And the day came when the risk to remain tight in a bud was more painful than the risk it took to blossom." All 8 students at our table blossomed as they told their names and ages in English, and asked their seatmate's age. Some required a bit of coaching but that was gracefully accomplished by their fellow students. The boy at my left finished triumphantly, punching the air with his fists, just as the trays of steaming hot food arrived for our second course.

Spirits were high but before we dug into our food, I noticed that the students bowed their heads and silently said a little prayer. As they finished, I gestured and enunciated carefully: "Bless us O Lord and these your gifts of food and friendship, which we are about to receive, through Christ our Lord. Bless these students from Seville and their pilgrimage to Santiago. Amen." As I watched them tuck into dinner, I thought the students glowed. What they really made of it, I'll never know. How much they understood, I'll never know. If they'd giggle later at the encounter with the silly old lady from San Francisco, I'd never know that either.

It didn't matter. To me, our little encounter had been so simple, so sweet, and the spirit and energy that emerged seemed to me to be empowering to them, and certainly to me. I was aware during dessert that one student from our table slipped over to the other table of 10 students and their chaperones and started the pattern over there: "Hello. I am James. I am sixteen years old. How old are you?" From the corner of my eye, I watched the little exercise proceed with glee and energy. At exactly 8:30pm, the chaperones signaled the students that it was time to go back to the dormitory. I stood with the students and when I got their attention I said: "Good Night. Sweet Dreams. I will see you in Santiago." Each student shook hands with me. "Good Night, Maria. Sweet Dreams. I will see you in Santiago" and they disappeared down the hall and into the dormitory.

The three men and I continued to sit at our table and talk. "Mary, what did you think of those students this evening?" the man from the Philippines asked me. I thought for awhile before answering. "All of them are beautiful. Each a child of God, exactly at the developmental stage they are destined to be. Each one alert, bright, complicated, advantaged certainly, self-conscious, a little awkward, growing in grace, maturing in understanding life." We mulled this over. The man from the Philippines added: "They are very young to be on a pilgrimage to Santiago. Probably not at all because of their own personal quests, but instead, I might guess, cooperating with some school project. It is a very good opportunity for them to experience this walk to Santiago." I sensed in him a particular affinity with the youth. After this discussion, the two men from Belgium yawned and bid us good night and Buen Camino.

The third man and I stood and he handed me a business card. I looked at Bernard Leveaux's business card featuring the name Virlanie with a tag line that said: Giving back the smile to street children. Thinking from his card that he might be a dentist, I asked "Bernard, what do you do back in the Philippines?" "We settled in comfortable seats by the fire and began to talk. He told me about Virlanie, a youth program where he worked in Administration for a number of years and for which he was now on the Board of Directors. He described Virlanie, an acronym for the tongue twisting "Vitalizing Responsible Living Adulthood through Nurturance Industry and Education." I blinked at the long string of words in its title—but the concept of Virlanie and its youth oriented mission was immediately intriguing to me as Bernard described the extent of poverty in his country and that effect on the younger generation. I slipped out a pen and journal and began to take notes.

"At least 5 million children are living in slums in the Philippines, and the documentation of child abuse is substantial in this population. Poverty for street children takes every possible form, for example, homelessness, neglect, hunger, sickness, disease, illiteracy, abandonment, exploitation through prostitution and pornography in the sex trade—Virlanie is structured to identify children and young adults in need of special protection and special developmental services so that individuals we serve can grow strong physically and psychologically. These youngsters have tremendous need to heal from abuse, and to become self-reliant and independent individuals—the goal is really to reintegrate street children into normal community life—to put smiles back on their faces, like my business card says." I asked Bernard a dozen questions about the structure of the program, its outreach and admissions policies, its local community and governmental support, its funding, how it measures personal and programmatic success, and its statistical outcomes in retention and education.

"Virlanie is about 20 years old and operates as a non-governmental organization set up to offer advocacy, training and formal education. Virlanie is small considering the need, but we have served about 15,000 street children in Manila and Makati City in substantial and sustained ways. We serve identified at risk youngsters in three residential types of homes—for babies and very young children, for young adults and also in special needs homes. Our philosophy is to nurture and love street children taken into these group homes, so that healing from whatever form of abuse can take place. The highest goal is family reunification and if that can't happen, then eventually independent living. Homes are set up in a family structure, with a surrogate mother and father, and aunt and uncle staffmembers who provide nurturance and stability, discipline and social skills."

Bernard asked: "Mary, are you a teacher?" "No, I'm retired now. I was a teacher at Roosevelt High School in St. Louis in the early1960's, but switched to a program called Job Corps which really was a turning point in my teaching career. Bernard was immediately attentive. "I'd like to learn more about the Job Corps. I know its international reputation as an alternative vocational school provided by your American government for low income families. How did it appeal to you?"

The question about Job Corps appeal unleashed a flood of memories. Poor Bernard, he was in for it. I told him about the earliest days of the Job Corps program, begun by President Lyndon Johnson about 1965 as part of his federal initiatives to end poverty and illiteracy nationwide in the United States. Peace Corps, Head Start, VISTA, the School Lunch program—all these were designed at that time to give education and social opportunity to a wide range of children and adults living in poverty conditions. And also importantly, I added, it was opportunity to American adults to contribute and give back to society at large in a meaningful way. People of all ages continued to be inspired by President John F. Kennedy's famous inaugural address: "Ask not what your country can do for you, but ask what you can do for your country." In the early 1960's, that statement thrilled me, inspired me to look more at social issues and know I could play a role in solutions. I gravitated from the St. Louis public school system in 1966 to the Job Corps Center for Women, a federally sponsored program where 350 young disadvantaged women ages 16-25 came to live and study from all over the United States.

I began as a reading teacher in Job Corps. As I learned about the complicated dynamics of the total program encompassing basic education, vocational training, and all accomplished within a residential setting, I realized that the early start-up efforts of a new national program like this would either die out quickly from failure—or potentially be a tremendous success for dropouts from traditional education. Actually, it was a rocky start all around in the beginning—for the federal government, for the teachers struggling to design curriculum for the academic and vocational classes, for the counselors and residential advisors who helped young women students from all parts of the United States adjust to dormitory living. Social skills and confidence levels were minimal among the young women, many who had left young children at home. Many had abysmal reading and math scores hovering between 2nd and 5th grade levels. Few had high school diplomas, and all had little or no work experience. All were thrust into this very foreign way of life—a highly disciplined framework of living fulltime at the school, and studying 8 hours per day in basic education and vocational classes.

I loved teaching in the program from the beginning, but it required fundamental changes in me as a teacher—and frankly, changes in who I was as a person. I'd never been around students struggling so in their classes. Every woman student had to have an individualized program designed for her, based on her current math and reading scores. Then each day in class, the student worked on specific materials collected for her functional level. This is where I came in. These students were not generally eager learners. Each had to be coaxed to engage with their individualized lessons, and to cooperate with tutoring, had to be acknowledged and motivated in ways I had not learned how to do in any of my university education classes or seen modeled in the public high schools. This was hard work—setting up a classroom where I was not in front of the class teaching a group lesson, but moving from student to student listening, individualizing each lesson, teaching, coaching and constantly acknowledging and motivating.

I was beginning to learn that classroom discipline was very different here than I'd experienced in other situations. In experimenting with teaching styles, I soon learned that these adult young women, many of them mothers, and some as old as I, responded far better to coaching lessons when I sat down next to them, asked them how they were today, turned attention to the lesson in front of us in a gentle and friendly way, with lots of eye contact, acknowledgement and encouragement. I put away my efficient and brisk manner. I toned down my flashy dress and makeup. This was serious business, and here, I was not the center of attention standing as a focus in the front of students as I had been in the public schools. In Job Corps, each student had to be the center of my attention.

A most particular gift was given to me by the Job Corps, and one which I could not have realized at the time would have such a long range effect on me as a person. The Job Corps Center Director decided to cross train between departments to "sensitize" staff to what students experienced in a 24 hour program. This required that instead of teaching in my regular daytime reading classes, I would work in the dormitories for one week from 4:00pm in the afternoon until midnight. Interact with the women students in a different setting. Eat with them. Be in the role of residential advisor or a counselor. Talk, listen, tutor, whatever was required.

What a world this opened up to me. My exposure to racial and cultural differences had been radically limited, even at age 26. My sense of educational propriety had been ingrained since childhood. I had distinct ideas of how things should be in the classroom and in life. But here in the dormitory, I was the one learning about the personal lives of students as I moved through my 8 hour shifts with 300 women of vastly different backgrounds than mine. It would be presumptious to say I learned a lot in the dormitories about cultural differences as they existed in the 1960's, but I know this with certainty: there wasn't a student there I couldn't love once I'd heard their story.

I began to see the young women I taught from a completely different perspective than I did when the class bell rang and they streamed in to take their seats. Through this extraordinary opportunity to work in an environment with them outside my classroom bubble, I began to understand with compassion the personal sacrifices and changes these young women were going through being away from their children and families. I could observe first hand dorm relationships and how students navigated the dramas of homesickness, angst and depression that unfolded in their late afternoon and evening program. I gained confidence in how to react to socially inappropriate or aggressive behavior, and not ignore it or fear it. Back in the classroom, a personal interview with each student set a new tone for the individualized lessons. I shifted from dispensing information in traditional ways to facilitating individual student lessons in precisely identified areas of remediation.

Of course, Bernard asked many questions during this flood of career memories. I answered each question, telling about expansion of the Job Corps program over its subsequent 45 years of operation, about national curriculum development, about the program now serving over 60,000 students each year, and decade after decade, the marked statistical increase in success rates of students attaining both a high school diploma and placement into jobs matched to their vocational training.

"Did you ever think when you began teaching Reading in Job Corps 45 years ago that you would stay with the program until retirement?" Bernard asked. I thought long and hard about his question. "Actually,

I'm glad I stayed with the program, for I never wavered once in strong support. I saw many, many thousands of student success stories as program operators grew increasingly efficient in their task as enablers of human renewal, and in their abilities to retool the program according to economic and technological changes occurring throughout society. We didn't succeed with every student by any means. Once in the program, they were not coerced to stay, and dropping out as well as other dramas occurred regularly. But statistics are good, and the government provides strong oversight to this very day. Funding support is solid from both the Republicans and the Democrats in congress. I know, for I worked 17 years in program management for Department of Labor with contract compliance issues and on-site monitoring.

But more to the point of why I worked with Job Corps for 40 years—I personally loved the work. I was doing something for my country. I held many challenging and creative jobs in the program, worked and visited Centers all over the nation. I knew that teaching students, consulting, training teachers, managing and monitoring was not about the job, not about a paycheck, but was always in service to students who were willing to work hard at this second chance to gain a diploma and a job. It all goes back, really, to my mother Irene's love and delight in people, especially students, her encouragement to me to be a teacher, to give everything to whatever job I'd have in life. I saw this in everything she did, especially in her dogged determination to go back to work at age 55 to put me through St. Louis University. And that Jesuit school and its wonderful professors modeled scholarship and social justice. I was molded and transformed by those disciplined six years I spent with them, readied really, to be receptive and to burn with a jet-like flame. Here is a great memory of my days at a Jesuit University. There was a wonderful elderly Jesuit who walked around the St. Louis campus and each time he saw me he said: "Mary, do you burn with a jet like flame?" That kind of embarrassed me in the 1960's, but I've come to know what he meant—is one's soul, life force, energy and generosity coming fully alive?—is the extraordinary experience of extended study igniting a jet like flame in one's heart that hopefully will burn in creative service to mankind?

I have realized that jet like flame over and over in the major life decisions I've had to make, especially in maintaining a social and ethical philosophy by which to live. I think that's the way I lived my career with Job Corps. Bernard commented: "Thank God for the Jesuits." And we had a good laugh. As each of us admired the other's youth directed programs, we both knew with gratefulness that we had been gifted with worthy life work, and taken the surer path dedicated to a greater cause.

I changed the subject. "Bernard, what you tell me of Virlanie reminds me of a program in Pune, India which in some ways is similar to your program serving desperate children, but with some distinct variations. It is called Maher. Do you know of it?" Bernard shook his head and encouraged me to share both similarities and differences between Virlanie and Maher.

I told him what I remembered. The word Maher means Mother's Home. Maher was started by an Indian Catholic nun named Sr. Lucy Kurian. Living apart from her order, she has created a network of more than 20 rehabilitative homes that take in the most desperate and difficult cases of abused Indian women (and often their children) and literally saves their lives. These women and children taken in by Sr. Lucy come to Maher under the most startling circumstances growing out of deep societal problems, including mental disorders, suicide attempt, abandonment, homelessness, domestic violence, prostitution, female infanticide, wife burning, dowry disputes, starvation and child marriages.

Love, respect and wholistic care and safety for body and soul of each woman and child is Maher's first principle of operation. No preference for a particular religion, caste or cultural background is exercised. The strong influence of interfaith spirituality is evident as abused individuals are assimilated into the homes without regard to the dualities of caste distinctions so prevalent in India. All the houses are operated with a categorical rejection of the idea that people are inherently inferior or superior by virtue of the particular caste, race or indigenous tribe into which they were born.

Like Virlanie, safety and love permeate the philosophy of the program. Medical care and therapy is begun, if needed, to stabilize each individual. Women receive professional, legal and personal counseling to sort through family difficulties, to approach reconciliation with their families if possible, and unique to this project, the women begin vocational training to support themselves if return to the family is not feasible. To the degree possible, women are kept with their children, enabling healing and normalcy for the mothers and children to occur. Housemothers and assistants in the homes are women who have successfully completed the program.

To me, there are two completely unique structural aspects of Maher that undergird the success of Sr. Lucy's programs. The first occurs as traumatized women and children are integrated into the various Maher homes. Meditation (with complete tolerance for all religions,) is introduced as part of each day's schedule, and all staff, women and children partake daily in two periods of group meditative silence. This integral meditative component is considered crucial to the overall healing of the women and the children, creating conditions supportive of tolerance, equality, unity and peacefulness in the homes. No common practice or method is taught. They simply sit in respectful silence together.

The second unique perspective of Maher's programmatic aspects is the wholistic approach to children's education. Each child is immersed in basic education, play, daily periods of silence, chores and leadership training. But in addition to this, each enters an intensive and disciplined music, drama, painting and classical Indian dance program which promotes healing, self-confidence and self-sufficiency. The program has had well-known Indian dancers, musicians and artists as unpaid teachers and the students give frequent performances throughout Pune.

Bernard and I discussed Verlanie, Job Corps and Maher, the possibilities and impossibilities of adapting or replicating strengths of each. These three programs were not like factories, where raw materials come through one door and are fabricated into products that go out the other. There is no assembly line in human renewal programs, no guaranteed outcomes. We touched on the timeless philosophy of Meng Zi, (c. 300 BCE) "All the children who are held and loved and cherished will know how to love others. Spread these virtues in the world. Nothing more need be done." "How does Sr. Lucy continue, day after day," asked

Bernard, "involved as she is in taking in troubled women, involved in the always critical funding arena, dealing with government officials, angry husbands and families, and all the other dramas of running a program?"

"Bernard, there is a wonderful book available through www.satyana.org that is a scholarly but highly readable research study about Maher written by two American authors William Keepin and Cynthia Brix. It's called Women Healing Women—A Model of Hope for Oppressed Women Everywhere. Their book is well worth a read—engaging, at times shocking, practical, thought provoking and visionary. You'll get a lot of insight into Maher as a Model of Hope as the dramatic stories of Sr. Lucy, the women and children unfold. And you will see what makes Sr. Lucy tick. The entire Maher model and the disciplined energies required to bring the Mother's Homes to life, grow out of Sr.Lucy's deeply meditative and personal prayer life—her experience of Ultimate Reality—or whatever you want to call it—God, Great Spirit, Brahman, Allah, or the Absolute. It's Sr. Lucy's love and groundedness and spirituality that catapults her into action. Like Mother Teresa, she has a pipeline to God in prayer. But in public, she's a fearless and shrewd business woman and a tough negotiator." Again, Bernard and I just had to laugh at our evening's discussion, its intensity as we relived our programs and the unique ways they operate to help people regain stability.

"Well, Bernard, thank you for our conversation tonight. I am happy to learn about Virlanie, and don't forget to read Maher's story: Women Healing Women. You know, it's hard to believe that we are only a couple days away from our destination of Santiago. Buen Camino . . . now I must go navigate that dormitory of high school students. I hope they are asleep." We shook hands and headed into our separate dormitories. It was nearly 11:30pm as I finished brushing my teeth and slipped into bed. All was quiet, except for some gentle snores. As I adjusted my covers, a voice in the darkness called out: "Good night, Maria. Sweet Dreams. I'll see you in Santiago." Several muffled giggles erupted. I was tickled with joy. "Good night. Sweet Dreams," I answered. And not another sound was heard.

CAMINO—DAY 47

Santiago Within Grasp

Postcard # 47—June 9, 2010 written at Monte del Gozo, Espana

Elena: I am staying tonight in an enormous Albergue housing 500 Pilgrims & guess what!!!! I walked 24km or14.5mi. Hard slog in the rain & mud. But I am only 3 mi from Santiago & I could see the city at a distance as I checked in. Today walked extensively in eucalyptus forests. The smell so fresh in the rain. Was detoured 3km due to road work. Tried to notice the smallest things: frogs croaking; cuckoos in fence rows; cats licking their paws; corn growing, figs fattening on trees; sheep gently grazing; the clicking poles and the beat of my feet the last few miles—and big things as well—walked by end of Santiago Airport's runway and powerful planes taking off just over my head . . . oh my! I'm back in civilization & soon will be home to you. Love and big juicy kisses from Grandma

Journal—Day 47 (Wednesday) June 9, 2010—written at Monte del Gozo

I could sense today as I walked both in me & in other pilgrims that we draw near to Santiago. Last night in Santa Irene I slept well & after the noisy 16 year olds left at 6:00am, I slept on until 8:15. Oh my. A good breakfast & out into the rain but not unpleasant walk through beautiful eucalyptus groves, villages & mud & detours. Stopped 3 times & found the 24.1km or14.5mi long on the uphill. But I'm here at Albergue Monte del Gozo, enormous complex holding 500—of course exhausted Pilgrims. Cannot get menu until 8:00pm. The hardest part of this has not been the walking (although taxing) but in understanding that I've been doing this in earnest for 47 days & that poof!! tomorrow I'm there—Day 48—I'm there . . . relief, gratefulness, thankfulness, joy—Monte del Gozo—means Mountain of Joy. Santiago is within grasp, mentally and physically.

Reflection on Day 47, written back home in San Francisco

"Sometimes we're not where we are . . . And sometimes we are where we're not."

A line from a poem by Allan King, a contemplative friend

Almost every book I've read about the Camino has the author referencing arrival at the Monte del Gozo, a hilly area above the city of Santiago and from where, if the weather cooperates, the pilgrim may first glimpse the spires of the Santiago Cathedral, some 3½ miles away. If one has strength and a tight schedule, one presses on to Santiago. But my last full day of walking was in rain and mud, and after 14.5 miles, I was fully content to stay at the Monte del Gozo albergue. I recall in my exhaustion that I walked to a crest and strained at the foggy view of Santiago in the distance. I also stopped in at the historic little chapel where I tried to say a prayer of thanksgiving, but found that I was progressing from numb to a condition beyond numb. I stumbled on to locate the albergue to register for the night, queuing with pilgrims on a bench while solicitous attendants copied down personal information, stamped credentials, answered interminable pilgrim questions about food and laundry and distances into the city.

The enormous Monte del Gozo complex, composed of many smaller buildings each housing dozens of Camino pilgrims, had been built as inexpensive accommodations for the crowds attending a papal visit to Spain, and pilgrim reviews I'd read pictured it as grim and forbidding. In retrospect, I liked the place for four reasons: 1) I couldn't have walked 3.5 miles more in the rain on Day 47; 2) the hospitaleros were friendly and accommodating and assigned me to a comfortable lower bunk near the entrance; 3) good food and wine was available in the cavernous dining hall and 4) I needed one more evening to collect my thoughts and feelings before arrival at the pilgrimage destination.

I showered immediately and lay down in the dormitory to rest. Exhaustion had overtaken body, mind and spirit. Drifting off to sleep, I recall thinking "The walk is over. I've seen Santiago from the hilltop. Where's the excitement? I should be feeling exuberant." But I drifted off to sleep, finally admitting that I just wanted the whole walk to be over with. When I awakened two hours later, hunger coaxed me back out in the rain to explore Monte del Gozo complex. I gravitated towards the hub of the place—shops, bar and restaurant.

I was happy to sip a glass of wine and attend to the postcard and journal routine while waiting for the dinner hour. In writing on my last full night on the Camino before arriving in Santiago, I shifted from an attitude of exhaustion to one of renewed curiosity about the journey I was just completing. I no longer needed to look forward—I was virtually at Santiago. I had made the pilgrimage on the Camino. And so instead of looking forward, I gave myself the luxury of thinking backwards through the 47 days it took me to reach the outskirts of my destination.

I examined my tiny calendar in which I had so carefully plotted in each little square the progression of days from 1-47, plus where I stayed each night and exactly how far I walked each day, both in kilometers and miles. I paged through my well-worn Brierley guide book that had allowed me to better understand the Camino with the practical information about towns and albergues, sites of interest, elevation and distances. That guidebook had been a key factor in my safely navigating the pilgrimage. And my trusty little journal which I somehow or other never lost—every page filled with whatever impressions came from brain through pen each evening or noted in the daytime about special things I observed. I'd been completely faithful to daily tending the calendar, the guidebook and the journal. As Edgar Allan Poe said about his short mystery stories: "To observe attentively is to remember distinctly." Maybe so for Poe, but at my age I needed one more step in the equation: "to observe attentively and then write it down." The unknown in the evening's formula at Monte del Gozo was whether or not the postcards to Elena—numbered each of 47 days—would all arrive in San Francisco. Not to worry about the postcards. Surely most of them would arrive and my granddaughter and I could take an afternoon putting those postcards into a little book for her.

It was close to dinnertime when I finished and I sat quietly observing how normal the end of this last evening before Santiago was for me—all the elements were there—solitude in the midst of pilgrim activity, a very sore and still swollen right foot, a glass of wine, completed postcard and journal entry, guidebook studied, the pictures of my family perched up where I wrote, and very calm and steady emotions despite near completion of my quest. I was safe. My body was not yet there in Santiago, but in my head, I was there. I pulled back into the present moment. I was not really in Santiago—I had one more night to spend on the road . . . Spend it now. This is one step in a practice of gratefulness that I exercise. Live this moment now. As Cynthia Bourgeault, an Episcopal priest says: "Live in the present. It's practice for living in the infinite."

So I acknowledged the now of my sore foot, my exhausted body, especially my shoulders from the weight of the backpack, my bedraggled clothes worn for so many weeks, my straggly haircut, lack of makeup and jewelry. I was fine just the way I was walking over to eat dinner. I was a pilgrim, and not a tourist out for an evening on the town. I was hungry, and there was a meal waiting to be purchased. I was weary, and there was a bed on which I would sleep. And the next morning, there was a spiritual destination which I would reach, God Willing. Inshallah.

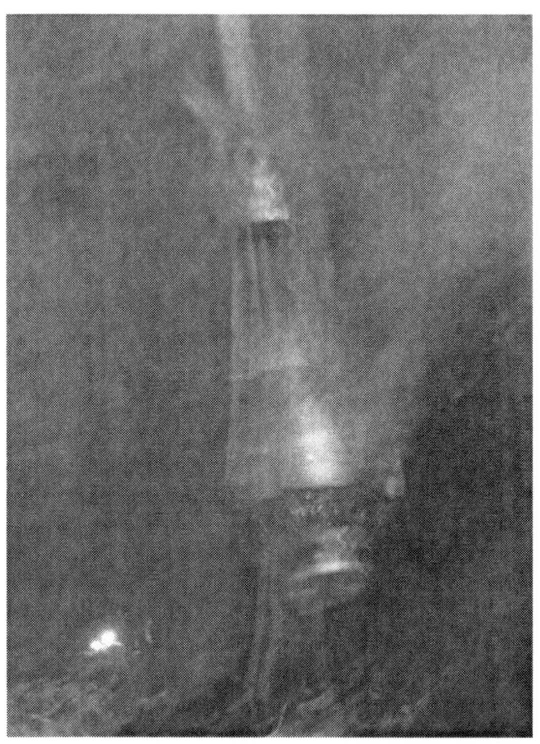

CAMINO—DAY 48

My Fair Estimate—About 3,000,000 Steps

Postcard # 48—June 10, 2010 sent from Santiago de Compostela, Espana

Elena: I arrived today after walking 500 miles from St. Jean Pied de Port in France. Perhaps I am stronger now physically, certainly my feet have healed some. Walking mostly without pain. Loved coming into the Cathedral Square, even in the rain—I'm not overly excited, but I'm filled with awe and love. Not just another church, another Cathedral, but the Church of St. James the Apostle—the goal of the walk. You will come here someday, I hope, and if you do, you will see the Botafumeiro smoking and flying through the air in the Cathedral. Love from Grandma-at-Santiago

Journal # 48 (Thursday) June 10, 2010—written at Santiago de Compostela

What a day in my life! Contrary to some other Pilgrim experiences on the last day, I started slowly & loved every step of the way into Santiago—walking only 5.9km or 3.5mi. Strolled into the medieval section of Santiago—was bowled over by the Cathedral. Walked completely around its 4 huge Plazas. Bought an umbrella (with scallop shells on it, of course.) It started pouring & I luckily was steered straight into a private Pension (33 Euros per night for 4th Floor skylight room.) Delightful & small. Straight over to Mass & that boomerang-ing Botafumeiro. Met Mickus—Greek from Germany, Jill & Sarah, couple from Australia, Takada from Japan. Agreed to meet for dinner. Walked to Renfe Spanish train station—had ticket written for Madrid for Sat am, and with my 20% Pilgrims Discount. Long letter gratefully emailed home. Nice nap. Champagne at Parador. Group dinner. After, spent 1 hour alone in beautifully lit Plaza before midnight. Birds flying over Cathedral, attracted by classical music playing on speakers throughout the Plazas.

Reflection on Day 48, written back home in San Francisco

"Don't boast when you set out, but when you get there."
Old Russian saying

Email sent from Santiago to my family the day I arrived:

"Dear Larry, Nathan, Amelia, Elena, Francisco and family:

Today is Thursday, June 10, 2010 and indeed I arrived in Santiago this morning in time to take a room in a little Pension—the Barbantes Libredon (amazingly only about 50 feet from the Cathedral), drop my backpack and get into the Cathedral for the Pilgrim Mass at noon. The place was packed—I imagine about 1500 people, most of them looking road and path weary. There was a long sermon by a bishop decked out in a tall hat and huge groups of old people who came by bus from all over Spain looking ever so pious with their scapulars front and back, and special scarfs. They certainly got preferencial seating . . .

There is a famous practice after a Pilgrim noon Mass in the Santiago Cathedral whereby 8 Capuchin Brothers, using ropes attached to a pulley on the ceiling, lower a giant botafumeiro which is what you know as the censor that priests swing out to bless folks with smellsome stuff that kind of smokes and perfumes the air.

The giant censor here at the Santiago Cathedral is the size of a cauldron about four feet across and three feet high, and the original purpose was to fumigate Pilgrims who had made the long journey. Well . . . anyhows, the priests dump in a shoebox full of whatever, it is lit with a whoosh, the Brothers each take a rope, and by means of the pulley, lift the botafumeiro up about 5 feet into the air, and a man ceremoniously steps forward and gives that pot a giant push to start its back and forth momentum. The Brothers go to town to control it and with their pulley teamwork—the pot picks up steam and raises up fast about 20 feet and begins swinging back and forth, rising higher and higher to the ceiling, letting off the most incredible clouds of incense. This goes on for five minutes in which I thought if anything happened to that rope, the result would be to take out about 250 Pilgrims at one fell swoop as the botafumeiro swings completely from one side of the Cathedral to the other high over the attendees, practically touching the ceiling.

The organ is playing with all stops out—the congregation goes into shock—I must admit my own pure unmitigated awe—I thought Circus—Cirque du Soleil has nothing on this Church Theatre.

I tended to business right away after Mass, securing my Santiago "Compostela", a kind of completion diploma with my name scrolled out in Latin. I trudged 15 blocks to the train station and I have a reservation for Saturday morning arriving in Madrid about 7:30pm. Best of all, because I have the diploma, I got 20% discount, so I took business class and got it for the same price as tourist. The man assured me I would be "very comfortable" in my window seat that stretches way back, and that someone would bring me coffee as soon as we rolled out of the station. Upon arrival in Madrid, Larry, I get off at the Atocha Station where we picked up the car for our driving trip, and have booked a small pension close by El Prado for Saturday and Sunday. I'll move Monday early afternoon out to the Kris Airport Hotel where you have arranged my last night's stay. And yes, I have the paperwork for the flight home at hand—it's looking a little dilapidated from being carried 500 miles—but be assured that I'm set for my return on June 15. I know that these four days are pure luxury before returning, but I am so grateful to have had the cushion of time and not be rushed on the Camino as so many people were.

And how do I feel? Very good, actually. It's pretty overwhelming to finally arrive. None of that has sunk in yet except that I am here—I have actually made it to Santiago. My feet allow me to walk the past few days with little pain after my Ibuprofhen 600 kick in. I am grateful for the doctor's appointment you have made for me, Larry, and will be happy to have someone give that toe a medical blessing. The nail is bulging so that I'm sure a new nail is now forming underneath. It happened 47 days ago and the big toe is still a sickening shade of purple and very tender to the touch, plus little rivers of pain.

Oh yes, I forgot to say today is the 48th day of walking . . . and it is a bit over 500 miles, and I walked every step of the Camino to Santiago de Compostela. Perhaps it was about 2 ½ million steps, perhaps 3 million steps. A half million steps one way or the other at this point—it's all o'k. I will write more about this, but really, right now I must go to that little attic pension room with a skylight and take a snooze. A great weariness has come over me. A nap is in order.

I am filled with love for all of you.

Mary"

POST CAMINO—DAY 49

The Deepest Silence of All

Postcard # 49—June 11, 2010 sent from Santiago de Compostela, Espana

Elena: Arrival yesterday was wonderful, even in the rain. I am staying in Pension Residencia, the Barbantes Libredon right by the Cathedral. Let me try to explain what I saw last night in the rain!! I walked in front of the Cathedral at 11:00pm & stayed on the Plaza for an hour. Classical music was playing on a loud speaker. The Cathedral was lit & appeared mossy green. The sky was blue-black & that late at night 3-4 doz huge white sea-gull like birds swooped & dived only over the Cathedral—moving to the music—no bird cries, only silent flying. I had never seen birds fly at night. It was the single most mystical nature experience I have ever had. Back in my little 4th Floor room with the giant skylight, I discovered that in the floodlit city at night, I could see 1 spire of the Cathedral, 1 enormous tower of another building with flags flying, the spire of the Museum (shaped like a pogoda) & on top of another building, a statue of a man on a horse—perhaps St James???? I slept like a baby with her "doo-doo" blanket. Love from Grandma Mary

Journal—Day 49 (Friday) June 11, 2010—written at Santiago de Compostela

Raining again today, but because I am staying right at the Cathedral & because the old medieval Centro Ciudad of Santiago is laced w. porticos, all was comfortable & convenient to sit outside and have morning coffee. Saw the high school students this morning—a very friendly little reunion. Many said: "Hello, Maria. I will see you in Santiago." Stood in line for "hugging St. James". Spent 2 hours from 10:00 to noon in Chapel of Silence, tending to prayer requests from people I'd met on the Camino . . . Bernard arrived in the Cathedral on his way to the airport & we watched the spectacle of the Botafumeiro together. Ate alone a fine seafood stew & oxtails for lunch. Then walked for maybe 3 hours, looking in Churches & shops &at people & Pilgrims. A lot of activity. Attended an evening concert of Camerata. 26 beautiful Japanese women from Kyoto with classically trained voices performed in the sanctuary of the Santiago Cathedral. Attended evening Mass & was front-row for another blow-out of the Botafumeiro performance. Very, very lucky to see the censor swinging 3 different times. At 11:30pm sky was clear & Pilgrims & tourists were out walking, eating, drinking, visiting—what an atmosphere. I came to the room, repacked, read & went to bed very, very happy. I have walked the Camino to Santiago.

Reflection on Day 49, written back home in San Francisco

"It is work to learn how to pray, largely the work of emptying the mind and filling the heart—that is prayer in one concise and truthful phrase. Or, as some say, 'pulling the mind down into the heart' until they both operate as one."

Richard Rohr—Breathing Under Water

I awakened at dawn in my little hotel room to the lovely sound of rain on the skylight. Where was I on the map? Somewhere on the Camino? Days of walking still to go? I stepped from my bed to the skylight and there was the Cathedral tower in plain view. It was beginning to sink in—I had arrived safely at Santiago de Compostela after 48 days of walking 500 miles from St. Jean Pied de Port in France. A celebration was in order. I would sleep another hour. As I settled in and closed my eyes, an alertness came over me, pushing sleep aside . . . something was struggling to be recognized. A clear picture came unbidden into my mind of the man I'd met weeks earlier on a bridge whose wife was in a coma. I'd tried to tamp that memory down as I walked, not knowing what I'd do with his request for me to pray to St. James about his wife. But there was the man, full-blown and insistent.

Sleep was no longer possible. As I dressed, I decided I didn't have to do this special "prayer request" thing for the man. It had been a chance encounter with a distraught person grasping at any straw, and I just happened to be the pilgrim at the bridge over the canal where he was working when he had a tearful breakdown. I had no obligation to tell St. James about this, and besides, it was embarrassing to even think that I could believe prayer for the man would do any good. That was that, I would just forget this whole business of praying for the man and his wife. It was too impossible—and way too improbable.

I went for café con leche which a sleepy waiter served me at an outdoor table under a lovely portico looking out on the wet and slippery Cathedral Plaza. Despite light rain showers, individual pilgrims were arriving early from every direction. Touring groups under seas of umbrellas were huddling around leaders who held up flags to guide their members. Busses clearly marked with signs indicating church organizations from all over Spain were disgorging onto the plaza older men and women who wore little matching scarfs. There was much tourist activity around the entrance to the pricey and fancy Parador hotel facing the Cathedral. I was beginning to relax into the scene when full-blown in my mind appeared the woman from St. Jean Pied de Port who had followed me down the street, insisting I not start up into the Pyranees in the fog and rain. "God go with you and pray for me," she'd said. I took out my journal reluctantly. There were others, too, who had requested prayers and I scanned page after page collecting these requests and listing them . . . the janitor to whom I'd given my old backpack; the woman cook and her waiter son who had been so gracious to me at their restaurant in Leon; the doctor and her assistant who worked so solicitously on my painful feet in Astorga; the couple from Denver I'd met in a bar one morning and told them about St. James the Apostle. And all the others.

From my vantage point at the outdoor café, I observed guards cordoning a line at a side entrance to the Santiago Cathedral, for pilgrims to enter the Church for the practice of "hugging the Saint." This is an ancient well-known part of a pilgrim's experience upon reaching Santiago. An enormous, gilded and garishly painted statue of St. James is on the high altar facing the congregation. But for the pilgrim to approach the saint—to touch or hug him, one needed to go behind the high altar and climb some wobbly little steps leading to the back of St. James. "It's now or never," I thought, so joined one long, single line of pilgrims in the rainy plaza. We finally entered the side door of the cathedral in single file, happy to be out of the rain, and began snaking forward around pillars and posts towards the rear of the altar.

I was not an eager participant, nor necessarily a reluctant one—certainly I was not filled with religious sentimentality, but I admit I was propelled forward by some interior push, perhaps a kind of spiritual curiosity. The line moved slowly, as one person at a time, pilgrims wobbled up the little steps to a narrow platform and awkwardly hugged or kissed the back of the Saint, laid their heads on his shoulder, probably praying, sometimes sobbing. Lingering at the top of the steps was not an option. Anyone whose private time with the saint exceeded the guard's notion of appropriateness was helped down from the steps, and the next pilgrim pressed forward.

The slow line presented an opportunity for me to examine this part of the Cathedral. Most noteworthy were the pillars over which hovered enormous, gilded and gorgeous angels, maybe 18 feet high, breathtaking, mind-boggling, out of control angels and cherubs. Something about my neck bent upwards fiercely at an angle looking at all this golden plaster of paris and concrete replicas of angels on clouds—something about the smell of incense and candles burning, and the sound of soothing organ music—something about the rose windows and stained glass colors illumined by rainclouds instead of sun, caused me to feel quite faint . . . and I left the line and promptly sat down on the cold, marble floor, leaning against a nearby pillar and feeling quite pale and wan.

What to do? One good option was to go back to my little room for a rest. But I reconsidered. Here I was, in line and close to St. James and the chance to dispense my obligation to pray for the people who had asked for prayers. What better chance than to stand back up and seize the opportunity to tell St. James about these people, then be free of this burden? I made it to my feet with the help of two male pilgrims who graciously ushered me back into line. Only a few more pilgrims in front of me before my turn—then soon, too soon, I stood at the bottom of the steps. I felt the tension and emotion rising. The man in front of me came down from St. James, sniffing and wiping his eyes red from crying. I couldn't think straight. Why was I here, climbing these rickety little steps? I was now one foot from St. James. He was bigger than life. What was it I was supposed to do? Whatever should have or might have happened was lost on me, and I didn't do anything properly. I dissolved in tears and put my arms around this dear, germy, carved wooden statue of St. James. Vision blurred. Time stopped. The guard touched my elbow. I too left St. James in tears, and had attended to none of my obligations to pray for people.

I made the circuit around the interior of the Cathedral. It seemed like hundreds of people were lining up at the many confessionals waiting their turns to tell their sins to the priest and to receive Holy Year absolutions. In the main part of the church, groups of men and women were seated, gawking and awed by the sheer size of the interior, and straining to hear the subdued voices of their guides telling the story of the Cathedral. Dazed looking pilgrims slowly wandered from chapel to chapel, exhausted from way too much to take in on an initial visit. There was the usual conversational hum that penetrates the silence of all major European cathedrals. But there over to one side, was a Chapel of Silence. I stepped in and took a seat.

Quiet . . . Just sit . . . Just be . . . Breathe deeply. "My intent is to be with You. Available to You in my heart, within my being." Just be . . . Breathe deeply. Don't think, but let the inevitable thoughts come. There's a thought, forming into an idea. That's o'k. Repeat the sacred word, and let the thought go, whether it's important or unimportant. Let the thought go. Exercise a gentle intent again to sit quietly and be fully available. Over and over. A full blown thought occurs—then a gentle return to my intent to be available—and let the thought go. Once again, intend to be in union and fully available to God. To drop my thinking agenda. To be fully available to God. Over and over. Some time later—20 minutes? A half hour? I left the chapel and returned to my room a block away to consider how to spend the rest of my last day in Santiago.

I sat at my desk in my little skylight room to gather my thoughts. A list of things to do emerged. I would attend the noon Pilgrims' Mass. I would have a leisurely lunch. I would shop for souvenirs. I would maybe take a nap. I might be able to get a haircut. But something far more important insistently pressed itself onto my to-do list, and only I could take care of it. I dug out the list of prayer requests.

My reluctance to deal with the prayer requests had lessened considerably in the past hour since Centering Prayer. What in me had shifted? While before the requests had seemed an imposition to me, now it seemed important that something had been asked of me—prayer for another, and I needed to plan how to willingly do this—how to "pray for" people who had asked for my prayers. Who would they want me to pray to now that I was in Santiago? St. James? Jesus? God? Should I just list the requests on a piece of paper and leave it at the altar, maybe at communion? Could a Hail Mary, an Our Father, even the Rosary be my avenue of request? As I scanned the list again—the request from the man with the wife in a coma was definitely the most specific and urgent. I realized that during the short time I was with him, my heart had been wounded in listening to his story. The scab was still there and aching as I recalled his tears and despair. For the others, their requests seemed more general, almost casual. And yet, I was overcome with love as I thought of each of these souls whose paths my soul had crossed on the Camino. Each had reached out to me or helped me in some way.

The light across my desk shifted. I looked through the skylight and smiled at the view. Fluffy clouds were now playing with the sun's rays. The drizzle of rain had stopped. I was startled when I thought how close I had come to refusing my privileged task to pray for these folks. It was no longer an obligation I'd incurred, but was, I now believed, essential to the integrity of my pilgrimage. Encountering and interacting with these people had been an active part of being alone on the Camino. Praying fervently for them here in Santiago would be part of the essential completion of my pilgrimage. I thought of a quote by Edwin Land, an American inventor whose writings and speeches had always inspired me: "Do not undertake a project unless it is manifestly important and nearly impossible." Praying for others fit his assessment to a tee. But I was not responsible for the unknown results. Merely a messenger, I, a beloved daughter of God, would lay these manifestly important prayer requests in the womb of the universe . . . and into the Trinitarian arms of God the Father, the Daughter/Son and the Holy Spirit.

The Cathedral bells solemnly rang ten times. I walked to the Cathedral for the second time that day, my little list of names and requests in hand. "Do not hurry. Do not wait."—my favorite quote from Goethe rippled through my mind. But another reassuring quote reared its head from Saint Clare of Assisi: "What you hold, may you always hold. What you do, may you always do and never abandon. But with swift pace, light step, unswerving feet, so that even your steps stir up no dust, may you go forward securely, joyfully and swiftly, on the path of prudent happiness."

For the second time that day, I entered the cavernous church with its swirl of activity and made my way through the throngs of pilgrims to the Chapel of Silence. I took a seat on a bench alone and quieted. There arose the distinct impression that my mother Irene was by my side. That faith-filled woman certainly appeared in my mind as smiling, encouraging, confident that I would stay on task and offer these petitionary prayers with which she felt so comfortable her whole life. "O'k, mama, help me out here. You know I'm not so good at this."

And I started tentatively. "Dear God, here I am in Santiago. Thank you for the gift of your grace and strength that has kept me going on this pilgrimage day after day. And you watched over me and brought me here safely, without serious injury, illness or harm. Thank you for all that I saw along the Camino—your creation, your evolution 'writ large'. Thank you for the people—all the people. Perhaps I will never understand what any of this means, but I hope that I followed your will in walking the Camino."

I quieted, breathing slowly and deeply, feeling an engagement with Spirit, a quickening of energy. The distant hum of noise in the Cathedral disappeared. I recall with certainty that faith emerged, along with a conviction that I should continue with these prayer requests. My heart was praying instead of my mind.

I began now in earnest. "Dear God, let me surrender to You these petitions for the several people I name on this list. Let me shift my thinking in these prayers from a petitionary stance for them to one of thankfulness for your mercy and acceptance of right outcome, whether or not the results are to their liking, their pleasure, or their happiness. Let me offer instead a passionate and fully conscious acceptance and gratefulness for your Divine Will to be fully realized, case by case. Thy will be done on earth for each person I mention, as it is in heaven. It is not my will, not their will, but Your Will. Out of tranquility and silence, I offer my gratefulness for your intervention or answer that they (and certainly not I) can never know in detail, but only in faith. Thank you. Amen."

And almost as soon as the prayer began, it was over. With this petition laced with thankfulness, I realized that I just let go of all confusion, all pride, all investment in Camino outcome. Happiness—glimmers of joy and hope replaced my earlier dread of being responsible for the prayer requests. I stood and placed the little list of names at the base of a statue of the Blessed Virgin Mary. I remembered with a smile the encounter with the man named Vincent the first week I walked: "Your heart knows the answers, but you don't trust your heart yet. Ask Mary to open your heart." I looked intently at Mary and felt an indescribable peace descend to which I consented fully. My eyes seemed clearer. I seemed to wake up spontaneously and intimately in my heart. I left the Chapel of Silence feeling hopeful. A change had occurred in me on the Camino.

POST CAMINO—DAY 50

I Left My Heart in Santiago

Postcard # 50—June 12, 2010 sent from Madrid, Espana

Elena: I was excited to find this card because it shows the tower I saw out my 4th Floor Pension skylight in Santiago. As I write, this is my hope for you: "Elena will travel so easily with her French & Spanish even as fluent as her English. She will see things deeply; appreciate the gifts of life; feel deep gratitude for sunsets & birdsong & flowers profuse; & delicious food & restorative wine & sleep; & all the lovely & unlovable souls along her Camino. (Be kind to the unkind. They need it the most.) She will always use her head to understand & operate, but she will also be guided by the heart. She will have a philosophy be it from Jesus the Christ or the Buddha, or Mohammed, which will guide her relationships . . . she will develop her passions in life; she will do unto others as she would have them do unto her & her dear ones; she will know in her mind & heart that we are not two, not separate from each other, not this or that, not we/them, nor black or white or brown people, but one universe bound in unity, equality . . . Love forever from Grandma Mary

Journal—Day 50 (Saturday), June 12, 2010—written in Madrid

This am up to a misty day, took a slow exit from the pension & walked to Santiago train station, taking the 9:45am Talgo to Madrid. It tickled me to have a 20% discounted Pilgrim seat, even though it did not represent a lot of money. Preferente seating—but Spanish Renfe trains are not luxurious. Scenery all the way gorgeous, varied. Semi-mountainous, then flat plains with ripening grain. Saw dozens of those ravine bridges (very high), beautiful distant villages, vegetable gardens, farms, vineyards—the whole range of gorgeous Spanish countryside. Passed through & by Avila—a memorable medieval city. Met Pilgrim Takuda on train & spent an hour with him having a drink & deciphering his English. Really nice man from Japan who walked the Camino after his newspaper job vaporized, as he put it. Arrived in Madrid in late afternoon and I walked across the huge plaza & boulevard in front of the train station Atocha & straight into very satisfactory hostel @ 33.5 Euros per night. Took a long walk. Dinner. Going to bed very early. Very peaceful & happy. Great email from Larry—home seems only hours away, although it's still 3 days and thousands of flying miles. I'm grateful to have this upcoming time in Madrid to transition from Spain to California.

POST CAMINO—DAY 51

Revisiting Madrid

Postcard # 51—June 13, 2010 sent from Madrid, Espana

Dear Elena: I have finished walking through dozens and dozens of villages & cities from St. Jean Pied de Port to Santiago . . . will I remember them individually, collectively? What will I remember of the Camino? Whatever it is, will be remembered from my heart & from the tremendous love I felt for you each day I walked. You are my 1st grandchild, & as precious to me as the lives of Grandpa Larry & myself. A venture as extravagant & elegant as the Camino must come from the heart & be shared with people closest to one's heart. Tonight in Madrid, I am tired, having spent the whole day on my feet walking to and through the El Prado Museum, then several miles revisiting the old center of Madrid, retracing happy steps made with Larry back in March & April. Love from Grandma Mary

Journal—Day 51 (Sunday) June 13, 2010—written in Madrid—day 2

Surprised to have slept 12 hours last night so up & dressed to a gorgeous cool day outside. Arrived at El Prado Musee shortly after opening for breakfast & truly amazing time in the Museum. The Cloisters upstairs and the extraordinary Mercury & Herse tapestries engaged me for 2 hours. Actually methodically walked through entire museum again (1st time April 1 with Larry) Total infusion of El Greco, Fra Angelico, Rafael, Caravaggio, Velasquez, Goya, Bruegal, Tiziano, Tintoretto, Rembrandt, Rubens, Murillo, Durer—& many more I forget. I'm fully awestruck & seemed today to see these pictures with their incredible themes & styles in a far different way than I did before the Camino walk. Divine lunch in Museum & out for a 6 hour walk up Atocha Blvd to Puerto del Sol & Calle Mayor & Plaza de Mayor. Ate at a vegetarian restaurant, delicious composed salad. There were 1000's of people out at 9:00pm promenading, dozens of street musicians, clowns, jugglers, mimes . . . I also visited several Madrid Churches. Slow walk—everything seemed so familiar from when I was here with Larry. Began to feel very fatigued. Big toe hurts again . . . nail is definitely almost off now, lifting/moving as I walk. Came home, cleaned & wrapped that toe like a mummy.

POST CAMINO—DAY 52

Back to the Future

Postcard # 52—June 14, 2010 sent from Madrid, Espana

Dearest Elena: My last postcard to you is a picture of a woman pilgrim and a little girl. I like to think this is Grandma and Elena on the Camino. Don't we have nice hats and walking poles? My extraordinary 52 days alone in Spain is about to end. I'm really entering the swing of being off the Camino, having started this am in downtown Madrid sitting in a Starbucks with a Coffee Grande & a muffin surprisingly like the ones I get at my local Starbucks in San Francisco. Fortified with that caffeine and sugar hit, I left the hotel & was very pleased that I could maneuver my way to the airport by underground with my backpack & poles, get the lay of the airport for tomorrow's flight, then find my way on a shuttle for my last night's stay in Spain—luxury at the Aeroporto Hotel Kris arranged by Grandpa Larry. Settled into the Kris, then spent several hours walking in an enormous mall nearby, got haircut, spiffing up for my trip home. Today was a big transition from the typical Camino walking day to a return to my normal city based, traffic filled life. I've just finished my last evening in Spain steeped in the Now of a delicious Spanish multi-course meal and a fine Rioja wine—finally realizing that the Now of Spain is shifting to an incredible longing for the family and home to which I return tomorrow. Love, love, love from Grandma Mary

Journal—Day 52 (Monday) June 14, 2010—written in Madrid last night in Spain

"Even Socrates, who lived a very frugal and simple life, loved to go to the market. When his students asked about this, he replied, I love to go and see all the things I am happy without."

Jack Kornfield in After the Ecstasy, the Laundry

Today was transition day from downtown Madrid to the Kris Hotel Aeropuerto preparatory to going home to San Francisco. Starbucks Coffee started me out, then so easily I went to Atocha Train Station—train to Nuevos Ministerios, then metro to Airport & I emerged from the train directly into United Airlines Terminal for a trial run for tomorrow am. Kris Hotel picked me up with no wait, short drive & soon ensconced in Kris Suites—pure luxury after Camino accommodations—washed something to wear on the plane tomorrow, showered and rested & out (ten minute walk) to a gigantic mall. Had my hair cut (razored) by a nice man. I was grateful, but found the result choppy. He was thrilled with it, so I figure I must look very 'au courant.' Looked at many things in the mall, but bought nothing. Terribly interesting to me to see a large Spanish Mall & compare the similarities to American Malls. Far more similarities than differences, as this one seemed a mirror image to any efficient and glitzy American mall with multiple levels connected by moving stairs, shops of every ilk and appealing to every pocketbook, clothing, electronics, books, children's toyshops, candy, bakeries, a fast food mall, some good restaurants. Suddenly, all this commercialism and consumerism gave me a bad headache. There wasn't a souvenir or gift there that any member of my family would need, want or use. The Sufi poet Hafiz nailed it when he said: "Learn to recognize the counterfeit coins that may buy you just a moment of pleasure, but then drag you for days like a broken man behind a farting camel." Back to the Kris Hotel. Completed work on repacking & went downstairs to watch an international soccer match on TV, then have an excellent dinner—plate of fresh grilled vegetables; salad & beef stew. The best ever creamy rice pudding!!!! Note: Best wine tonight of the trip—Crianza from Rioja—vintner Marques de Caceres. I'm sure to find it back home. Probably at Costco or Trader Joe's. Concerning Soccer: it can be beautiful in motion, brilliant in maneuvers, but it's also brutal on the body, soul, spirit of the players. Why did I watch television & all this activity before dinner? Of course!!!! Dinner in Madrid is not available until 9:00pm. I am no longer a weary pilgrim accommodated with a 7:00pm seating, but a well-coifed tourist dining alone in an expensive, paneled restaurant.

Post Camino—Day 53

Leaving Madrid

Journal—(Tuesday) June 15, 2010—written enroute from Spain to America

"My obligation is this: to be transparent."
Pablo Neruda

Really only slept a bit last night & was up & ready for a hearty & elegant Kris Hotel breakfast buffet. Airport transport & then just trusted that my dilemna (desire to take my hiking poles through security and back to SF) could in some way be accommodated. Man on my shuttle bus shortened the poles. I had not been able to do this. Then at airport the idea came to have the backpack & shortened poles shrink wrapped as a unit which I did for 6 Euros. And through security the transparent cocoon of belongings went, clearing customs easily in Madrid, Washington DC and St. Louis. The route from Madrid to Washington DC (8 ½ hours). Then from DC to St. Louis, where in transit called Genny, my sister—great fun. She announced that now I'm back safely, her breathing will return to normal. Now I'm on the last leg home to San Francisco.

I certainly feel a mix of emotions here on the airplane as I hurtle through space from Spain to the United States—traveling farther in one hour than I walked in 48 days on the Camino. But what now, Mary? What next? I'm only somewhat calm about matters of past, present and future. How will it be to reconnect to my husband, my family and neighbors and dearest friends? To my Centering Prayer group? And especially to myself? How will I ever make sense of the Camino and the efforts it took to walk it, day after day, rain after rain, blister after blister? Will I eventually come to understand how such a fire ignited my passion to walk that particular trail? And for what reason? What result?

I am startled by an idea that has come to me full-blown as I scribble these words in my journal. I will come to understand the Camino by recording it all for granddaughter Elena, my husband and children and son in law—I'll have the postcards and the journal entries of the day, and in addition I will reflect in brief essays about the daily experiences I had and how they resonated with who I am, and am becoming, what I have read, and am reading, shifts in personal philosophy and worldview. If I have changed on the Camino, writing about it will help identify how and why. There is a great distance between said and done, but how hard could it be to write a Camino memoir for my family? I'll let my feet heal and my body rest for awhile. Then I'll pick at Camino memories, tease them, make them bleed, and write about it. Perhaps I'll even heal into enough wholeness for another Camino somewhere else on Planet Earth. I close today's journal now, for the pilot has announced descent into San Francisco.

Post Camino—Day 54

Back Where I Began—San Francisco

Last Journal Entry—Wednesday, June 16, 2010

"Rule for Happiness—Something to do, Someone to Love. Something to hope for."
Immanuel Kant

How lovely to sit this morning at my desk back home, coffee cup at hand, classical music drifting through the house . . . my only immediate task to bring this journal to a close.

I was surprised last night at how excited I grew as the pilot announced descent into San Francisco. Couldn't stop smiling. High spirits. Gratefulness. Joy. So fast the dreamlike deplaning, and once at the luggage carousels, the great reunion with my beloved children Amelia and Nathan . . . a little competitive jockeying for hugs & kisses, (no changes there), and then there was my husband Larry driving up with the car and the concrete assurance that we were indeed back to each other, that body and soul sustained in the long separation.

As I walked through the front door of the house, I smiled at the scallop shell hanging on the door. Indeed, I was home safely from the Camino. Flowers on the coffee table. A pot of soup on the back of the stove. How beautiful everything looked as I went from room to room. I sat at my desk, but thought: 'that pile of mail can wait until tomorrow.' Larry went to the refrigerator and poured two glasses of wine. Stepping out onto the deck, we let the fog and chilly air of a San Francisco June evening envelop us. We only smiled at each other. Gratefulness in the homecoming was palpable. A glass of wine and a bowl of soup triggered the jetlag and I was off to sleep in my own bed.

And now, Elena, here's what happened this morning. Your mama let you come across the street early before school, creep up to my room and awaken me. It was a sweet and very gentle reunion, short and almost shy, and you reminded me right away that I had suggested we make a little book from the 50 postcards I had sent you. "Thank you for the postcards. I got one everyday, but Grandma, what's the Camino?" We blinked at each other. "Oh," I said smiling at my granddaughter, "the Camino is a hike, a long walk that takes many days, and it will take me a long time to tell you about it." Satisfied, you jumped off the bed, blowing me a kiss and running off to school. I was as happy as I ever remember being.

Today I am home, and finishing my journal entries, having safely walked the pilgrimage route to Santiago. I know that I will tell Elena parts of the story, but I now feel deeply committed to also write a book about the Camino for her. Perhaps Elena's question at age five is the most prescient of all: "But Grandma, what's the Camino?" It's similar to the question posed to me over and over: "Mary, why do you walk the Camino?" I continue to struggle with that answer. And it's somewhat like Ti-ts'ang's question: "What is the purpose of pilgrimage?" And Fa-Yen's answer "I don't know," to which Ti-ts'ang observed: "Not knowing is nearest."

I think, Elena, that for me not knowing is nearest! Not really knowing reality as I think I know it. Not really knowing spirituality as I feel I know it. Not knowing the answers with certitude of mind is nearest the truth. And yet I know many things with absolute certitude, Elena, that are anchored in my heart—things seen and unseen, finite and infinite. I will venture only this: the Camino pilgrimage to Santiago de Compostela pried open my heart for a new kind of seeing, and a new kind of knowing.

As my life has unfolded, Elena, so too shall your life unfold. My greatest wish is for you to operate from a deeply grounded life of specialized study and service. May your education and work in life not be motivated by power, control or greed, but by commitment to dedicated and loving service to others. I wish you great capacity for committed love, abiding good humor, generosity of spirit and boundless energy for serving others. May these wishes develop in you and spring from your mind and heart operating in union. Here are two lines from a favorite poem of mine.

Tell me, what is it you plan to do
With your one wild and precious life?"

Mary Oliver from The Summer Day

And now I bring this to a close. I remember hearing Deepak Chopra say in a lecture: "When I'm finished with my work and gone, I'll have done what I came to do, and that's enough."

Permissions and Acknowledgements of Origin and Rights

Postcard Images

Mary O'Hara Wyman gratefully acknowledges the following individuals and companies granting her permission to print their postcard images in *Grandma's on the Camino*

Christian Brandstetter—Days 31, 36, 45, and 51; camino_at@yahoo.de

Marika—Days 1, 2, 3, 4, 5, 6, 7, 8, 9, 10, 11, 12 29; chemin.marika@yahoo.fr Marie Touron and Catherine Ka

Jill Day—Days 14, 15, 21, 22, 33, 38, 40, 41, 43, 44, and 48; Katoomba, Australia

Sarah Dillane—Day 35; Katoomba, Australia

Colon Artes Graficas, S.L.—Day 28; colonag@gmail.com

EDICIONES A.M. and Studio Editores S.L.—Days 13, 17, 18, 20, 23, 24, 25, 26, 30, 34, 37; info@edicionesam.com

Editorial FISA Escudo de Oro, S.A.—Days 27, 49, 50; info@eoro.com

FAMAVIGO S.L.—Days 39, 42, 46, 47; info@famavigo.com

Catedral de Burgos—Patrimonio de la Humanidad—Day 19; info@catedraldeburgos.es

Prayer Card picked up in Church in La Rioja—Day 52; no identification of Publisher

Postcard given by attendant in Ponferrada Church—Day 32; no identification of Publisher

Postcard: Camino de Santiago—Redecilla del Camino (Burgos)—Day 16; no identification of Publisher

Quotes

During my teen and adult life, I have habitually copied down quotes or sayings from prayers and readings, or poetry that amused me, or touched and inspired me deeply. I drew on these quotes as memories were triggered about the Camino pilgrimage. To the best of my ability, I cited the author's name, if available, and/or included the actual title of poem or treatise, if available.

I offer these quotes, both anonymous and cited by name and author, in the spirit of "fair use", that is, using short quotations that do not usurp the "entire value" of the original work. It is my hope that these quotes inspire my grand daughter, Elena Varela and my readers. It is also my hope that any of the living authors feel the reverence and honor I extend to them by quoting from their work(s).

CPSIA information can be obtained at www.ICGtesting.com
Printed in the USA
BVOW071536210513

321290BV00002B/4/P

9 781477 289235